HEALTHY ENVIRONMENTS,
HEALING SPACES

HEALTHY ENVIRONMENTS, HEALING SPACES

Practices and Directions in Health, Planning, and Design

Edited by

TIMOTHY BEATLEY, CARLA JONES,
AND REUBEN RAINEY

University of Virginia Press

CHARLOTTESVILLE AND LONDON

University of Virginia Press
© 2018 by the Rector and Visitors of the University of Virginia
All rights reserved
Printed in the United States of America on acid-free paper

First published 2018

1 3 5 7 9 8 6 4 2

Library of Congress Cataloging-in-Publication Data
Names: Beatley, Timothy, 1957– editor.
Title: Healthy environments, healing spaces : practices and directions in health, planning,
    and design / edited by Timothy Beatley, Carla Jones, and Reuben Rainey.
Description: Charlottesville : University of Virginia Press, 2018. | Includes bibliographical
    references and index.
Identifiers: LCCN 2017057647| ISBN 9780813941134 (cloth : alk. paper) | ISBN
    9780813941141 (pbk. : alk. paper) | ISBN 9780813941158 (ebook)
Subjects: LCSH: Health facilities—Design and construction. | Architectural design—
    Health aspects.
Classification: LCC RA967 .H46 2018 | DDC 725/.51—dc23
LC record available at https://lccn.loc.gov/2017057647

Unless otherwise specified, illustrations are by the essay authors.

Cover photograph: Credit Valley Hospital near Toronto, Ontario, Canada.
(Tom Arban Photography)

CONTENTS

HEALTHY ENVIRONMENTS, HEALING SPACES

INTRODUCTION

Health and wellness provide an unusually potent and powerful lens through which to understand the design of the built environment. Few frameworks have the potential to bring together so many different voices, professions, and disciplines on behalf of good design and placemaking: from physicians and nurses to public health officials, to grassroots health advocacy organizations, and to architects, landscape architects, and urban planners.

And it is about time, as the world is faced with a remarkable set of health and wellness challenges:

— Accelerating health effects of climate change, including growing numbers and extent of heat waves, drought, infectious diseases;

— Much of the world's population experiences unhealthy and dangerous levels of air pollution, as seen in many cities, especially in the Global South, such as New Delhi and Beijing;

— Growing food insecurity and worries about how a global world population that will likely reach ten billion will be able to feed itself;

— Rising rates of global depression, with women experiencing much higher levels;

— Major inequalities in health and longevity between developing and developed nations, and inequality between rich and poor within nations;

— Designed and planned environments that actually damage health rather than promote it;

— A limited understanding of health as the absence of disease, which fails to grasp its social and psychological dimensions.

It is a paradox and a tragedy of modern life that in many parts of the world there is a growing awareness about health and active efforts to pursue and support healthier lifestyles, while in other parts of the world it is a struggle to provide even the basic conditions for survival (clean water, air, adequate shelter). In the industrialized North, the growth of wearable health-tracking devices is one form of evidence of the former (Fitbit, for example, has sold some twenty-one million of these devices), though with questionable results. In the Global South, availability of adequate drinking water, safe and secure housing, and breathable air are the concerns that dominate (though these are concerns in more affluent nations as well). We are at a global moment where progress can and must be made in improving health for all.

There is a growing recognition of the many ways that design and planning of the built environment can both exacerbate and help solve these global health challenges. While not the only answer, it has an important contribution to make. We increasingly understand that the design and planning of the built environment has profound and lasting impacts on health. It creates the essential context for living a healthy, happy and meaningful life. There are many factors that influence health and well-being, and the causal pathways are complex, varied, and interconnected. Health, wellness, longevity, and quality of life are all intimately intermeshed, a complex function of the interplay of social, economic, and environmental conditions. This book seeks to examine and better understand these pathways and influences, but importantly, it also seeks to sketch out a vision for healthy, flourishing communities. The essays to follow reflect on balance a profound optimism that despite the seriousness of the global health challenges there is much that can be done, and many deeply impacting ways in which design and planning interventions can make a remarkable difference.

Buildings, landscapes, and communities are often overlooked for their potential to both harm and hinder health, but also for their tremendous potential to enhance healing and wellness. Opportunities to enhance health and wellness exist to better design the everyday spaces and places of the homes, schools, and offices where we spend much of our day, the medical and health facilities where we find ourselves in times of sickness, and the neighborhoods, cities, and suburbs that constitute the larger environments and physical settings that either facilitate or impede well-being.

The good news is that there is growing recognition of the need for designers and planners to think more carefully and systematically about health. This can be seen in the growing importance given to walking, bicycling, and physical activity in the planning of communities and the generous funding of planning researchers by health-committed foundations such as Robert Wood Johnson Foundation (which has done much over several decades to advance and support scholarship around active community design). Equally true, the medical, nursing, and public health communities have awakened to the health-enhancing power and potential of design. Howard Frumkin's afterword to this book reflects this new emphasis. His work, and the work of the many others, such as Dr. Mindy Fullilove, a professor of psychiatry at Columbia University, who writes eloquently about the mental health benefits of socially integrated, physically connected neighborhoods, is encouraging. And it is not new, of course, for community designers and planners to be concerned with health. We are reminded of Frederick Law Olmsted, designer of Central Park, and his belief in the recuperative powers of gardens and nature, and more recently of Ian McHarg, whose personal history included a bout of tuberculosis and an influential stay in a Swiss hospital. McHarg, author of the important book *Design with Nature,* was an early proselytizer of the value that nature holds and its importance in community design. We dare not compare our book to his, but we do note that the essays to follow build on a history and heritage, and a kind of logical trajectory that has gradually embraced and increasingly understood the essential role of community, place, design, and nature.

These essays grew directly out a conference organized by the Center for Design and Health at the University of Virginia (UVA) in the spring of 2013. The conference, "Healthy Environments, Healing Spaces," brought together a distinguished group of leading scholars to address the essential question: How can we design, plan, and sustain built environments that will foster health and healing? Most of the essays to follow were commissioned for, and presented at, this cross-disciplinary conference.

The authors of these essays reflect the important reality that there are different dimensions and points of intervention in this agenda: the design for health care and healthcare facilities (hospitals, clinics, centers), improving the conditions for healthy, meaningful, and happy aging, the importance of daily access to and contact with nature, the power of food and the importance of a healthy, sustainable food system, and the design and planning to foster walking and physical mobility. Each of these topics represents a critical dimension and a key opportunity to enhance health and well-being, and taken together they suggest the essential elements of a healthy city or place.

The agenda of healing spaces is multidisciplinary, but also multiscaled: we must think at once about the role of indoor environments, and the design of the interior spaces of homes and offices, but also about the outer world in which we live, play and interact, including the parks and schoolyards and urban streets we visit.

In many fundamental ways, design of the built environment shapes our decisions and choices: Whether we choose to walk to work is determined to considerable extent by whether there exist in our communities safe, interesting, pedestrian environments and infrastructures, as much as by the weather, our own inclinations (do we feel like walking?), or the surrounding culture (do we live in Spain where walking is embedded in the life of the culture and society?).

Knowing this means that while we know that the design of built environments influences health and wellness, we may not fully understand the range of design and planning interventions available, or which are likely to be most effective and deliver the greatest health benefits (as well as which are most cost-efficient, legally defensible, and politically acceptable).

Our conference, and resulting book, reflect the need for designers, planners, and health professionals to join together in a common mission. And to do this we begin to overcome the various disciplinary barriers (and physical ones as well) and the differing languages, acronyms, methods, and methodologies. The value of forging and working on a unified agenda of a healthy built environment is great indeed, and one that we have begun to work on in earnest here at UVA.

This goal is in many ways at the heart of the mission of our Center for Design and Health (CDH), which was created in 2010. Reuben Rainey and Tim Beatley have had the pleasure and honor to be co-executive directors (and cofounders along with David Kamp) of the center and Carla Jones to serve as its first program director. The center has cosponsored lectures and symposia, funded research in the School of Architecture, and created a CDH Fellows program to invite faculty outside the School of Architecture to join with us in studying and designing healthy places while also encouraging faculty members in the school to explore these issues. Mostly we have fostered new connections and relationships and started many new conversations across the university. Much has already been accomplished, and even more is anticipated under the new directorship of accomplished environmental psychologist Jenny Roe.

We are optimistic about the future of our center and hope this symposium and resulting book help shape and steer this future in some important ways. There are a number of key open questions we explored in the conference and in the resulting essays of this book:

— What is working (and what isn't) in the areas of design and planning, and what then are the most promising design interventions that will have a powerful positive impact in improving health?
— We know there are significant inequalities in living conditions across the United States (and the world), and major disparities in access to positive health-enhancing elements in the built environment (e.g., parks and trees, pedestrian infrastructure). How can our design and planning interventions help address these inequities and inequalities?
— How do we define and measure healthy environments, healing spaces, flourishing communities? And what metrics or measures do we use in determining whether our interventions have been successful? How will we know we've succeeded (eradicating polio might be an achievable

goal in medicine, but in design and planning such goals are difficult to measure)?

—If we had the political will and the economic resources, what kinds of places—neighborhoods, health facilities, communities, cities, and regions—would we create, and can these visions serve to motivate and inspire us as we move forward?

—How do the potential dimensions of healthy, sustainable places—day-lit buildings, trees and nature, food and nutrition, physical activity and patterns of social interaction and contact, and streets and other built infrastructures that make these possible—interact to amplify health and well-being (or conversely to dampen their positive effect)?

—On the other hand, there are valuable synergies to be noted and utilized. For example, if we grow food in hospitals, for instance, can we at once provide new sources for healthy nutritious food, cultivate (literally) new connections to nature and the natural world, and provide the conditions for socializing and forming new and meaningful friendships? In this way, a simple garden creates a win-win-win-win scenario, and how many other steps of this kind are possible in cities and communities?

—What are the obstacles to these interventions? Are they regulatory, political, simply a lack of knowledge and imagination?

—To what extent do new and emerging environmental and other global threats—climate change, global loss of biodiversity, growing scarcity of water, food, and oil—represent special challenges (and opportunities) for the design of healthy cities and living environments? Are there ways we can design and plan that will at once enhance resilience and health?

There are several different audiences for this book, and they may be interested in different questions. We seek with our book to influence, first, the professions likely to be engaged in design and planning. Through the discussions and examples to follow, an architect, landscape architect, or urban planner will have a strong and new sense of the importance of health as an essential for what they can do, for what they can accomplish in their practices and in their careers. But equally important we seek to reach a larger set of professions—medicine and nursing, especially—which ought to (indeed must) increasingly concern itself with community design and planning. Significant progress toward health and well-being will be difficult, as the essays demonstrate, without addressing these. And we seek through our book the chance to bring these professions together and to begin to nurture and cultivate a larger joint mission—a common healthy built environments vision and a joint set of ideas, concepts, terms and terminology, and emerging practice experience that will help create the glue and connections to carry this agenda forward.

In these ways we see our book as appealing especially to an audience of designers, planners, and public health and medical professionals, and as (we hope) essential reading in classes and curricula for all of these fields. There will be much here for graduate students to glean, students who are, say, taking a Healthy Cities or a Healing Spaces class (two of the courses we, in fact, offer through the UVA School of Architecture). But there will also be much that practicing planners (and doctors) can learn from these essays. While there are points in the book where technical language prevails, this is a book that we have sought to keep readable and accessible to the general public, and we are hopeful that individuals in the community (nonprofessionals), who might be active in promoting health through community design, say, through a community organization or NGO, or by serving on a local planning commission, will also find this book valuable. In short, we see the book appealing to multiple audiences, each important to moving the health and design agenda forward, and we hope in this way the book will have a wide and lasting impact.

The essays to follow address to varying degrees these key questions, yet they are but opening discussions moving forward. The book is organized into four main sections, preceded by this introduction and followed by an afterword written by Howard Frumkin, of the University of Washington's School of Public Health. Frumkin's afterword is a comprehensive overview of many of the current challenges we face and the new and emerging directions in health. And the various authors of this book address many of the points he discusses in their individual essays.

Part I includes essays organized around "The Design and Planning of Healthy Cities." Essays here discuss the critical importance of designing communities for walking and evaluating their transportation systems (Andrew Mondschein), strategies for achieving health equity (Jason Corburn), the limits and potential of evidence-based design and the promise of tools such as health impact assessments (Ann Forsyth), and the power of public spaces to help build health-enhancing social capital (Ellen Bassett).

Part II addresses "The Healing Power of Biophilic Design." Essays here explore the role of nature and biophilia at several scales, including in the design and planning of flourishing cities (Timothy Beatley), design at the building scale (Judith H. Heerwagen), and the special role of gardens in healthcare facilities (Reuben Rainey).

Part III explores aspects of "Art and Architecture for Health." Essays address a wide range of important design strategies, including creative health-care facility design (Tye Farrow), the use of architecture and the graphic and performing arts to foster health in healthcare settings (Reuben Rainey and Christina Mullin), and design for healthy aging (Emily Chmielewski and J. David Hoglund).

Part IV addresses the challenges of "Creating a Healthy Community Food System." Essays explore how cities might develop and strengthen community food infrastructure (Samina Raja and Jennifer Whittaker) and how we might begin to understand food system interventions as community healer through two case studies, initiated at the grassroots level by community members themselves (Tanya Denckla Cobb and Carla Jones).

Finally, in the book's concluding essay, the editors (Beatley, Jones, and Rainey) speculate about future directions for healthy design and planning, offer some suggestions about future models for designing healthy buildings, neighborhoods, and cities, and pose some important and as-yet largely unan-swered research questions especially worthy of future scholarship.

There are many individuals to whom we owe thanks, too many to mention individually. These include our many colleagues here in the School of Archi-tecture who have helped advance the cause of the center and who participated in our conference and other programs. Funding from the School of Architec-ture Harry W. Porter Jr. fund helped immensely and made it possible to cover the travel and other costs associated with the conference. Former dean of the University of Virginia School of Architecture, Kim Tanzer, was incredibly sup-portive of the conference and more generally the work of the center.

PART I

THE DESIGN AND PLANNING
OF HEALTHY CITIES

HEALTHY TRANSPORTATION

A Question of Mobility or Accessibility

ANDREW MONDSCHEIN

Introduction

Dreaming of Walking in New Delhi

Billboards punctuate the verge of the Grand Trunk Road in New Delhi. Perched above an incomplete sidewalk along a highway choked with noxious traffic, wedged between a former landfill and the dying Yamuna River, signs advertise all kinds of needs and wants. One offering stands out in particular contrast with its surroundings, selling travel to Reims, France (see figure 1). The image depicts a pedestrian promenade lined with cafes, people sitting and socializing while others stroll casually in the middle of the road. The billboard image alongside the roadway mixes two urban extremes. In the France of the billboard, walking is safe and wholesome, physically beneficial and emotionally restorative. In the "real" Delhi, walking is poisonous and stressful, and being in a car at least filters the air and provides protection from noise and other vehicles.[1]

Certainly, the juxtaposition oversimplifies the complex environmental realities of both locales. Delhi's inward-facing urban villages continue to facilitate walkability, and French cities are currently facing some of the worst air pollution in decades.[2] Equity and access cloud the picture further, as who typically walks and drives in each locale varies significantly (see figure 2). The rest of the world's streets likely lie somewhere between the Delhi and Reims exemplars. How do we balance among the sometimes contradictory solutions to our healthy mobility objectives, particularly when it comes to walking and biking, and what are those objectives anyway?

Rethinking Healthy Transportation Planning

In this essay, I review the state of research and practice in health-oriented transportation planning and design. The current approach to healthy transportation significantly emphasizes quantity of travel over the "qualitative" or

Figure 1. Billboards, like this one in New Delhi, India, demonstrate the desire of people to prefer environments where walking is easy. This billboard is advertising a vacation to Reims, France, where the streets are pedestrian friendly, which contradicts what pedestrians in this part of New Delhi face every day.

experiential component of travel. Because of this emphasis, transportation planners, along with designers and engineers, are less able to effectively address key dimensions of the relationship between human health and everyday travel. To understand what may be missing, and what steps we can take to improve the situation, I examine the objectives of health-oriented transportation planning as they exist today. To a great degree, healthy transportation planning today is a matter of increasing quantities of nonmotorized trips—an emphasis on mobility. Even when the local built environment is taken into account, such as in the design of walkable communities, the primary objective remains increased walking and biking.

Then I explore how the experiential components of travel, not captured by standard transportation metrics, may also affect healthy travel. Some factors, such as collisions and environmental hazards, have been acknowledged for decades but have arguably not been successfully integrated into recent mobility planning trends. Other aspects of the travel experience, such as mental health and well-being, have only recently and tentatively come onto plan-

Figure 2. Crossing Grand Trunk Road in New Delhi, India, provides an example of the equity and access concerns of pedestrians.

ners' radar screens. Overall, I argue that as with travel as a whole, healthy transportation should prioritize access—to positive experiences and useful destinations—over undifferentiated nonmotorized mobility. Finally, the essay concludes with a discussion of how planners, as well as public health specialists, urban designers, and others, might take a more comprehensive and effectual approach to mobility and health, emphasizing three objectives for healthy mobility planning: (1) enhanced measurement of currently unmeasured human-environment variables, (2) better coordination of health with equity and social capital objectives, and (3) increased openness to a multiplicity of transportation–land use solutions that foster health.

Current Transportation Planning Practice
The Quantitative Metrics of Travel

As a systems-focused discipline, transportation planners primarily measure *how much* and *how far*. Regardless of travel mode—whether it be on foot, by bike, by transit, or in a private car—transportation planning is heavily driven by metrics of system usage and travel behavior. For decades, transportation planners have assiduously monitored the number and length of driving trips through surveys, observation, and modeling, and increasingly have done the same for transit, biking, and walking.[3] Not surprisingly, then, transportation planning goals are almost always characterized in relation to these types of quantitative travel metrics. Environmentally sustainable travel is character-ized as lower vehicle miles traveled (VMT), and a successful transit system may be characterized as increased ridership by both existing and "choice" riders.[4] It follows that the typical way to characterize public health in trans-portation terms has been in terms of less driving and more walking and bik-ing. One of the most cited papers in the *Journal of the American Planning As-sociation,* "Travel and the Built Environment," among many others, shows the centrality of this approach to analyzing and measuring the success of walking and biking interventions.[5]

Why is counting trips and trip lengths, by any mode, so important? Caus-ing travel behavior change is central to transportation planning. Planners and allied disciplines seek to change people's lifestyles and travel choices to en-courage more active, nonmotorized travel and less driving.[6] Most models of behavior change come down to increasing the relative utility of active travel over driving. As conceptualized within a behavioral economic framework, the dominant approaches seek to change travel behavior by changing an individ-ual's or household's utilitarian decision making, raising the cost or inconve-nience of driving or incentivizing walking and biking.[7] These approaches un-derstand travel as a "derived demand," only useful inasmuch as it gets people to the activities and destinations at the end of the trip.[8] While travel demand models take into account trip lengths or times, very little else about the trip itself is accounted for directly, though experiential factors that may have a direct impact on travel choices, such as wait times at bus stops and perceived safety, may be included as travel cost modifiers.[9]

Increased Active Travel, the Central Objective of Healthy Mobility

Within this derived-demand framework privileged in transportation plan-ning, encouraging travel by one mode over another depends on making des-tinations relatively more accessible by one mode than another. So when ac-tivities, whether jobs, shopping, or otherwise, are easier to access on foot than by car, people will walk more and drive less, all else being equal. This access-based way of thinking about travel behavior is powerful and does a good job explaining the travel we actually observe in American cities.[10] Encouraging more active travel for health, whether on foot or by bike, is conceptually the same. In fact, access to destinations has been found to be the most significant explanatory factor of increased *utilitarian* walking across numerous travel be-havior studies. Walk Score, a web-based service that provides a 0 to 100 score for any location across the United States ranking that location's "walkability," as well as metrics for bikeability and transit-friendliness, bases its scores solely on the spatial proximity of a mix of destinations to each location.[11] Walk Score's metric, in turn, has been found to very strongly explain actual walking behavior in urban areas, similar to other metrics that emphasize the density or accessibility of destinations within a walkable area.[12]

Based on Walk Score and similar findings, planners have established a role for land use and urban design in healthy transportation. They argue that neighborhoods and cities that improve access to a range of destinations for walkers and bicyclists will facilitate the objective of increased active travel and reduced driving.[13] Walkable, bikeable, and transit-oriented communities are all predicated on this basic behavioral principle, that these modes are more competitive with driving for accomplishing everyday activities when destina-tions are more mixed, densely packed, and linked by enhanced nonmotor-ized infrastructure. Importantly however, not all travel is destination-focused. Better access to destinations is associated with increased *utilitarian* walking, those everyday trips to work, errands, socializing, or other activities. However, *recreational* walking is more associated with access to nature and aesthetically appealing places.[14] Regardless of whether walking or biking is for utilitarian or recreational purposes, however, the research has held to the idea that more is better than less.

Increasing nonmotorized travel with investments in infrastructure and walkable, bikeable urban form has a clear relationship to physical activity.[15] Thus, the surge in obesity rates across the United States from the 1980s to the 2000s was and remains a major public health crisis, and insofar as physi-cal activity is one component of a healthy BMI (body mass index), increased driving and overall sedentary lifestyles were identified as at least one possible cause of the obesity crisis.[16] Ultimately, the linkage among the increases in automobility, reduced active travel, and obesity has been shown to be com-plex and tenuous in some cases.[17] Americans started driving for most of their trips decades before the obesity crisis, and some of the most obese groups in the country, particularly poor and minority populations, also drive the least. The increase in unhealthy diets among populations worldwide, particularly low-income populations, is likely a more significant causal factor.[18] Still, the hypothesized connection between reliance on cars and poor physical health outcomes in the early 2000s was galvanizing for transportation planners and public health officials across the country, as the prevalence of public health and active transportation studies suggests. In addition, even if trading driving

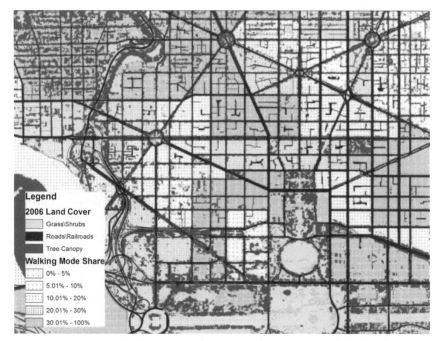

Figure 3. Map of central Washington, DC, with tree cover and walking rates overlapped to determine if higher tree cover leads to greater walking rates.

for nonmotorized modes wasn't the source of the epidemic, increased walking and biking continue to be understood as part of the treatment, not just for obesity and associated ailments, but mental health through exercise as well.

Measuring Trips: The Effect of Nature in DC

How does an emphasis on quantitative travel metrics skew healthy mobility research and practice? An analysis comparing walking rates to natural features in Washington, DC, shows the ease with which it may be possible to miss the forest for the trees, when considering health outcomes solely in terms of *how much* active travel. Figure 3 juxtaposes two datasets across central DC: green land cover and walking rates, as a percentage of travel by any mode.[19] The satellite-based land cover data show that for a major city, DC is fairly well treed and parked, but significant variability exists across neighborhoods, from the National Mall and verdant Northwest DC to the dense business district in Downtown. Walking is also far more frequent in central DC than most American cities, with trips on foot accounting for more than 30 percent of all trips in some neighborhoods, shown using data from a 2008 regional travel survey. These two datasets, analyzed at the neighborhood scale, can illustrate

Table 1. Correlations between walking trip rates, destination density, and nature[1]

	Walking mode share[2]					
	All trips	Work	Shop	Social	Meal	Exercise
Destinations/acre[2]	**0.330**	**0.309**	**0.274**	**0.185**	**0.255**	**0.165**
% Tree cover[3]	–0.043	*–0.092*	*–0.102*	–0.005	*–0.069*	**0.071**
% Green cover[3]	0.017	0.001	*–0.103*	**0.097**	*–0.146*	*–0.060*

1. Correlations shown for 192 Washington, DC, transportation analysis zones in center of DC. Positive correlations over r=0.05 shown in **bold**, negative correlations below r=–0.05 shown in *italics*.

2. Source: Metropolitan Washington Council of Governments (2008).

3. Source: U.S. Department of Agriculture (2006).

the association, if any, between walking rates and presence of nature in terms of trees and green open space.

Table 1 presents simple correlations between walking for different types of trips, utilitarian and recreational, and land use measures including destination density and green land cover, for the central portion of DC, comprising 192 transportation analysis zones (TAZs), which are substantially analogous to census tracts. The "destinations per acre" measure is derived from the Metropolitan Washington Council of Governments (MWCOG) survey that also supplies the walking data. It measures accessibility in terms of generalized destination density, much like the proprietary Walk Score measure. Two measures of green land cover are included, the percentage of land covered in trees and the percentage covered by trees, shrubs, or grass.

Relationships in the table include a strong association between destination density and walking rates, even for exercise trips. The tree and green cover measures have a far more mixed, and often negative, association with walking rates. Walk rates for social trips have a mildly positive relationship with green cover, possibly because more of these trips remain within residential areas with open space. Walk rates for exercise are positively associated with tree cover, consistent with other findings, but weakly negative for overall green cover. On the face of these correlational results, nature has little relationship to actual walking behavior in cities. At a minimum, destination density has a much clearer connection to walking frequency.

Building on the correlation results, figure 4 illustrates results from a logistic regression analysis, modeling the likelihood that a trip for a variety of purposes will be taken on foot. The chart shows the effects of tree cover on the odds of walking, while controlling for destination density, as well as income, age, gender, housing type, and vehicle availability. Here, nature in urban Washington, DC, measured as tree cover, does not have a negative relationship to walking rates for trip purposes other than going out for a meal. The positive

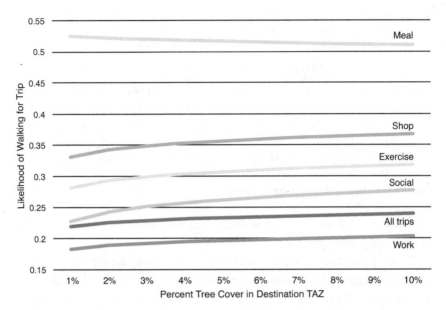

Figure 4. Effects of tree cover on walking likelihood in Washington, DC

effect of nature on walking, however, is relatively slight. The sharpest increases in the likelihood of walking are observed when tree cover increases from a low base, leveling off gradually as tree cover approaches 10 percent. Notably, tree cover does appear to have a stronger effect on social and exercise trips, both trips that are less likely to require commercial areas. Still, DC residents in the sample are more likely to walk, overall, for shopping or going out for a meal. For those trip purposes, the odds of walking are weakly related to the presence of nature, whether positive or negative.

Of course, these travel behavior analyses shed no light on the actual health outcomes of more walking. Rather, the analysis is framed in terms of a particular—possibly insufficient—perspective on transportation, where the question of interest remains the quantity of travel by nonmotorized modes. As I explore more below, exposure to nature while walking may have salutary effects on human health, and the fact that, all else being equal, people walk somewhat more than they otherwise would in the presence of nature is not unremarkable or unimportant. Making urban neighborhoods compatible with both dense activity and nature is a challenge for planners and designers that has by no means been solved. However, the focus on the travel metric itself, rather than the experiential component of the travel, is fundamental to almost all travel behavior research today but limits us to a narrow set of findings. That limited focus may cause planners to miss some of the most important interactions between transportation systems and health and ultimately diminish the potential for transportation planning to make the most effective contributions to public health overall.

The Other Side of Active Travel: Experiences and Exposures

If the vast majority of transportation planning practice and research hinges on the quantity of travel people take by driving, transit, walking, bike, or otherwise, what lies beyond these metrics? The experience of travel—how mobility shapes daily life—goes beyond distance traveled or number of trips. Intuitively, we understand that trips of the same distance, for the same purpose, even of the same mode, provide wholly different experiences for the traveler. Framed as "exposures," the experiences that travelers face when they move through the city may shape public health outcomes just as much, if not more, than the distance traveled by any mode. With some notable exceptions, planners and others charged with shaping transportation have been less engaged with travel exposures' implications for nonmotorized travel than the benefits ascribed to increased physical activity described above. In the next section I review how exposures have been treated traditionally in transportation planning and then introduce an expanded set of exposures and experiences that may impact human health while travelling.

Physical Exposures: Collisions and Emissions

"Exposure" often takes on a negative connotation, and exposure in travel has primarily been framed in terms of negative health outcomes, the most well-recognized outcome being the effects of vehicle collisions and emissions. Collisions have been understood as a threat to well-being since the advent of the horsecart, if not even before.[20] Without a vehicular envelope, nonmotorized travelers are particularly endangered by collisions. From a purely quantitative point of view, nonmotorized travel safety generally increases as trips, and thus exposure to risky incidents, goes down.[21] Only recently has a new framework been proposed, that increasing numbers of nonmotorized travelers conditions vehicle drivers to be more cognizant of walkers and cyclists, thus reducing accident rates.[22] Regardless of these trends in road safety, exposures to collisions vary significantly across locations and circumstances on a road, city, or beyond.[23]

Emissions—from tailpipes, from the vehicle manufacturing process, and now even from power plants powering electric vehicles—also negatively impact human health. In the case of emissions, recent evidence demonstrates that pollution does not just have regional impacts, but some of the most serious effects are highly localized around highways and other congested roads, due largely to microscopic particulate matter from the combustion of diesel fuels.[24] Importantly, these localized emissions impacts fall particularly hard on those on the road but outside of vehicles.[25] The combination of deep breathing from exertion and a lack of air filtering means that walkers and cyclists bear the brunt of local emissions. Because, so often, locations with dirty air are associated with marginalized populations, exposures to emissions become an issue of environmental justice, with highly disparate impacts across race, ethnicity, and income.[26]

Certainly planners acknowledge the health effects of collisions and emissions and continue to advocate for advances in vehicle engineering and road design to reduce death, injury, and illness from these exposures. However, planners and other advocates for nonmotorized modes have also taken on an intriguing approach to framing these negative exposures. A set of recent studies have analyzed the "trade-offs" between the health benefits of walking and cycling and the health risks from collisions and emissions.[27] For example, a recent report from Active Living Research, a leading advocacy group for active travel, summarizes findings from multiple studies specifically examining these trade-offs.[28] The report cites that "30 health impact modeling studies . . . have consistently demonstrated that health benefits from active travel outweigh risks," while also acknowledging that effects vary by location.[29] Such studies, however, suffer from the false dichotomy of designating on-road walking or biking as the sole alternative to "sedentarism." In addition, the significant variability in exposures within and across urban areas is acknowledged but rarely emphasized. Globally, these differences are particularly significant. While parts of the developed world have indeed curbed the most excessive emissions, deaths from air pollution continue to increase worldwide, largely in the developing world.[30] However, even in the developed world, emissions remain a significant hazard, particularly in the context of localized particulate emissions along busy streets.[31] Far more likely is that active travel is safe and highly rewarding in some situations, dependent on location and personal circumstance, but in other situations quite risky. While still fully acknowledging the value of nonmotorized travel, transportation planners should understand more clearly under what circumstances nonmotorized travel is riskier and unhealthier than other modes.

Beyond Physical Health: Exposures, Nature, and Quality of Life

We are learning that not all exposures on the road are bad. Today, the salutary effects of nature on human health have been established and are being reinforced through extensive research in environmental psychology, urban design and planning, and public health.[32] Integration of nature into daily life not only can improve sense of well-being but also enhance mental health and physical health outcomes tied to psychosomatic processes. The concepts of biophilia, an essential bond between humans and other living things, and biophilic cities that bring people together with nature, are important parts of the conceptual puzzle uniting health with urban planning and design.[33] How does transportation find its way into this relationship? Travel, whether utilitarian or recreational, is an important way that most people are exposed to nature in cities. Flipping the relative effects of collisions and emissions on their heads, walking and biking may provide a stronger health benefit than being in a car. Inside a vehicle, people witness nature whizzing by at high speeds, but on a bike or especially on foot, people can have a fully embodied experience of their surroundings, whether natural or highly constructed.

Even more than collisions and emissions, exposures to nature and the possible benefits are not recorded in standard travel surveys or traffic counts. Further, our understanding of *how much* nature a person needs or *how long* a person needs to be walking or biking to receive a healthy dose are still being studied.[34] This is a promising area of study and practice, and transportation planners should become more engaged in the process of examining how roadside nature—trees, plantings, parklets, water features, and even weeds—contribute to health benefits ascribed to nature elsewhere. It's too soon to say, for example, that street trees on a quick utilitarian walk to the grocery store will have a measurable effect on psychological health outcomes.[35] However, the fact that those trees are also available for an occasional long stroll after work may be essential for coping with urban life. Ultimately, a "more is better" framework for understanding the benefits of nature when walking may be fundamentally correct but largely insufficient overall in capturing the true benefits of nature over a single walk or bike ride, over a season, or a life span.

Quality of life, and healthy living in particular, encompass far more dimensions than simply the old mobility metrics of travel distance or frequency can capture, even when focused on walking and biking. Historically, only some of the experiential facets of travel have been measured and even then only in terms of the network and not an individual's trip making.[36] In addition to safety from collisions, health may be influenced by exposure to emissions, noise, and what we see and feel when we travel, particularly nature. Only recently have new methods appeared that make it possible to measure not just distance traveled, but the environmental qualities of that travel experience. Lightweight sensors, many of which are built into smartphones, can now capture local emissions, noise, comfort factors such as light and humidity, and images of travelers' surroundings as they walk, bike, and drive.[37] As those working on cities and travel learn to collect this diverse set of experiential information during typical travel, coupled with measures of immediate and longer-term health outcomes, we may open a new door to understanding the relationship between travel behavior and human health.

Prospects for a Unified Approach
Redefining Access

In the long run, the exposures and experiences that most contribute to health, positive or negative, may best be understood as a matter of access rather than pure mobility. *Accessibility*, as it is deployed by planners, has generally been reserved for access to specific types of destinations, particularly those meeting economic and social demands such as jobs, shopping, and socializing.[38] This concept of access fits readily with the need for access to healthy places, such as healthcare facilities and open space. However, can we apply an accessibility framework to travel experiences as well as destinations? Even trips with no particular destination, or routes selected because of perceived safety or the number of trees, may be best understood as a function of "access to experiences." Access to experiences may help transportation researchers and professionals theorize, and empirically measure, some of the distinctive health effects that travel supplies to humans.

While access to health-related *destinations* remains essential, we can extend access to include health-related *experiences* as well. Nonmotorized travel is an affordance for healthy experiences: certainly physical exercise, but also access to safety and security, clean air, and stimulating natural and built environments. For all but exercise, the quantity of walking or biking is not a sufficient metric. Going for a jog along an exposed, polluted, naturally decimated roadway may still provide cardiovascular benefits, but so can a treadmill. Between New Delhi and Reims are nearly unlimited configurations of our transportation networks, and we can and should ask more often where and when do those networks actually provide the healthy outcomes that are distinctive to the travel experience.

A More Expansive View of Healthy Transportation Metrics

So far, the interface between health and transportation has been highly constrained. The vast majority of research and practice has emphasized increased walking and biking as the primary objective of healthy transportation. As the review of current practice shows, while more walking and biking could benefit many, the circumstances under which those benefits may manifest are variously unclear, unproven, or unexamined. Being a human in an urban environment, outside of any vehicular shell, can open up either amazing or awful experiences, with possible significant consequences for health. Transportation planning requires an expanded set of objectives and methods that may suggest new solutions, or at least new priorities, as we seek to support improved human health.

For better and for worse, transportation in vast contemporary cities and regions is dependent on vehicles, some public, most private. Taking our current transportation system as a starting point, some planning researchers have cautioned that vehicle-based access still often provides better outcomes than transit-based systems in most of the United States.[39] The relative effectiveness of a car for holding and keeping a job is likely also relevant when considering access to healthy destinations such as healthcare facilities, healthy food, and nature. Importantly, the future need not and likely will not look the same as today. However, as shared vehicle systems such as Uber proliferate and autonomous vehicles threaten to make automobility even more ubiquitous that it is today, vehicle-based access to healthy destinations may remain an important means of providing key services and opportunities to the broadest population.[40]

Nonmotorized travel, for the numerous possible health requisites and benefits that it may provide, should still remain at the heart of health-centered transportation planning and design. The basic model, however, of seeking undifferentiated increases in walking and biking through destination-focused changes to the built environment should be complemented by an expanded concept of travel behavior. Rather than valuing only frequency and distance and portraying walking- and biking-supportive access only in terms of the destinations at the end of the trip, planners and designers should consider access to the en-route experiences that nonmotorized trips provide. We require a better understanding of the value of an everyday or irregular trip beyond its cardiovascular effects. Working with environmental psychologists, biologists, and others concerned with human-environment interactions, planners and designers can begin to better understand what these experiences may mean and how they manifest on the road. Because measurement remains a critical component of planning and allied fields, we also need new tools for measuring travel experiences, both the qualities of the trip that shape experience and the health outcomes that result. Those tools may utilize new technologies for measuring both human health and perception and environmental quality and may entail bringing together information sets so far rarely examined in combination, such as detailed travel patterns and environmental data.

Emphases on Equality, Self-Determination, and Diversity

A focus on the complex determinants of travel generally, and walking and biking in particular, may help shed light on persistent challenges planners have faced in making increased walking and biking a reality for a wide range of diverse communities defined by income, gender, race, and ethnicity. Recent findings demonstrating that walking increases in urban areas have been concentrated among the most–well off communities reinforce the challenge planners face. For example, healthy food access is a critical issue in many low-income communities. Though many low-income communities are dense and therefore relatively walkable, grocery stores are often located outside such communities and only accessible by cars that may be unavailable to many residents.[41] Of course, access to safe, clean open space and natural features is another important health-related destination. Ideally, parks and other natural open space would be accessible on foot or by bike. However, in cities across the United States and globally, those places may be quite far from most homes and workplaces. Thus, from a practical standpoint, optimizing access to many health-related destinations remains a multimodal planning objective, and vehicular access may be most effective at getting many low- and middle-income residents to the healthcare, food, and recreational and natural experiences they need.

Beyond walking rates, exposures and experiences on the street are a matter of environmental justice, and road safety, air quality, and the natural features of the built environment are all highly skewed by race and income, whether in New Delhi or New York. Affordances of high-quality, safe walking infrastructure, along with high-quality natural and built features, are more difficult to supply in places with underinvestment overall and limited tax bases. Even in shared spaces such as major roads, experiences such as filtered car air and dirty tailpipe emissions are skewed inequitably. Public health-oriented transportation policies can go beyond walkability and bikeability and address issues, such as vehicle emissions, that foster inequity on shared streets. Technological solutions, insofar as they reduce and do not increase inequities on the road, may be as critical to health as mode shifts.

To fully realize the potential health benefits of our transportation system, transportation planners and allied disciplines can also shift from an emphasis on passive behaviors to more active capabilities on the part of urban residents: to choose what's best for them as they engage in daily travel.[42] The behavioral economic framework underlying travel behavior theory is powerful, but behavior change is predicated on simple shifts in incentives, focusing on utility maximization without necessarily working to shift what constitutes utility to the traveler. As discussed above, planners have generally sought to increase walking and biking by establishing environments amenable to those behaviors. In general, these theories do not engage individuals' capabilities to make conscious choices for their own benefit. While medical practice now preaches that individuals must consciously take charge of their own care, conscious choice in travel may actually be in decline, especially as information technologies, and someday autonomous vehicles, make ever more travel decisions for the traveler. Thus, as we learn the possible health impacts of travel experiences, some of these benefits will only become accessible once travelers are aware that they exist, or understand what to avoid. While efforts to educate, and even market, the benefits of walking and biking are increasingly prevalent in practice, additional research is needed to show how city dwellers can increase their own capabilities, consciously using daily travel to gain control over their lives and well-being.

Acknowledging Multiple Futures in Healthy Transportation

Focusing not just on travel mode but on access, experience, equity, and capability, the route to healthy transportation becomes far more complex. More travel by foot and by bike may not always be the right answer for all, particularly in the short run as we confront significant, unaddressed environmental challenges in cities around the globe. None of this suggests that vehicular mobility is superior, or that increased transit, biking, and walking do not contribute to health through both benefits to the individual and reduced climate change impacts. However, the realities of an auto-based mobility system that continues to grow and evolve globally, along with a built environment already shaped around the car, suggest that planners and designers should at least engage in visions of healthy transportation that are fundamentally multimodal. In particular, we should work to ensure that the health benefits and positive effects of automobility—access to health care and open space, protection from emissions—are not reserved only for those who can most easily afford these types of access.

Having introduced this essay with the juxtaposition of New Delhi and Reims, I'd like to conclude with another. Barcelona is another European city with remarkable advantages: terrific transit, biking, and walkability, with a built environment that, while highly urban, also integrates natural features through its neighborhoods. The car, while part of the urban fabric, does not dominate. The former chief architect of Barcelona, Vicente Guallart, has stated, "You are either Barcelona, or Bladerunner."[43] Though easy to say for a justly proud Barcelonian, the statement has significant implications. Anything less than the walkable, bikeable, profoundly livable environments of Barcelona and similar places are an unacceptable dystopia. The reality is that most human settlement, then, is unacceptable, yet we must still find a way to live in it. Whether looking globally or within the North American context, some places and people are ready for more active travel, but many locales are not. Increased walking and biking are surely parts of the solution, but in order to make these experiences truly beneficial, we need to understand far more than we do today about providing access to healthy destinations *and* experiences. In cases where we do not yet have the capacity to provide this access to the entire population, we may need to consider how to make Bladerunner, flying cars and all, healthier as well.

Notes

1. Sahu, Beig, and Parkhi, "Emissions Inventory of Anthropogenic Pm 2.5 and Pm 10,"; Narain, Roychowdhury, and Chattopadhyaya, *Delhi Clean-Air Action Plan.*

2. Willsher, "Paris to Stop Traffic."

3. Santos et al., "Summary of Travel Trends"; McCourt, *Parking Generation;* Schrank, Eisele, and Lomax, *TTI's 2012 Urban Mobility Report.*

4. Randall Crane, "On Form versus Function"; Taylor et al., "Nature and/or Nurture?"

5. Ewing and Cervero, "Travel and the Built Environment"; Frank et al., "Many Pathways"; John Pucher et al., "Walking and Cycling."

6. Ewing and Cervero, "Travel and the Built Environment."

7. Boarnet and Crane, *Travel by Design.*

8. Mokhtarian and Salomon, "How Derived Is the Demand."

9. Exel and Rietveld, *Perceptions of Public Transport;* Loukaitou-Sideris, "Is It Safe to Walk?"

10. Levinson and Krizek, *Access to Destinations.*

11. Walk Score, "Walk Score Methodology."

12. Manaugh and El-Geneidy, "Validating Walkability Indices."

13. Ewing and Cervero, "Travel and the Built Environment."; Chatman, "Does TOD Need the T?"

14. Handy, Cao, and Mokhtarian, "Self-Selection in the Relationship."

15. Frank et al., "Many Pathways."

16. Jacobson, King, and Yuan, "Note on the Relationship"; Frank, Andresen, and Schmid, "Obesity Relationships."

17. Swinburn et al., "Global Obesity Pandemic"; Joost et al., "Persistent Spatial Clusters."

18. Swinburn et al., "Global Obesity Pandemic."

19. U.S. Department of Agriculture, "Urban Tree Canopy Assessment"; Metropolitan Washington Council of Governments, "Regional Travel Survey."

20. Norton, *Fighting Traffic.*

21. Runge and Cole, "Crosswalk Markings"; Umesh Shankar, *Pedestrian Roadway Fatalities.*

22. Jacobsen, "Safety in Numbers."

23. Shankar, "Pedestrian Roadway Fatalities"; Beck, Dellinger, and O'Neil, "Motor Vehicle Crash Injury Rates."

24. Fruin, Winer, and Rodes, "Black Carbon Concentrations."

25. Quiros et al., "Ultrafine Particle Exposures."

26. Houston et al., "Structural Disparities"; Schweitzer and Zhou, "Neighborhood Air Quality."

27. De Hartog et al., "Do the Health Benefits."

28. Buehler, Gotschi, and Winters, "Moving toward Active Transportation."

29. Ibid., 3.

30. Hsu, "2016 Environmental Performance Index."

31. Houston et al., "Structural Disparities."

32. Berman, Jonides, and Kaplan, "Cognitive Benefits"; Tang, Sullivan, and Chang, "Perceptual Evaluation"; Barton and Pretty, "What Is the Best Dose."

33. Kellert and Wilson, *Biophilia Hypothesis;* Beatley, *Biophilic Cities.*

34. Van Den Berg, Hartig, and Staats, "Preference for Nature"; Van den Berg, Jorgensen, and Wilson, "Evaluating Restoration."

35. Van den Berg, Jorgensen, and Wilson, "Evaluating Restoration."

36. Frank et al., "Many Pathways."

37. Agapie et al., "Seeing Our Signals"; Hu et al., "Personalising Pollution Exposure Estimates"; Sharples et al., "Sense-It."

38. Levinson and Krizek, *Access to Destinations.*

39. Ong and Miller, "Spatial and Transportation Mismatch"; Blumenberg and Ong, "Cars, Buses, and Jobs."

40. Fagnant and Kockelman, "Preparing a Nation."

41. Walker, Keane, and Burke, "Disparities and Access."

42. Fullilove, *Urban Alchemy.*

43. Guallart, invited talk.

References

Agapie, E., Chen, G., Houston, D., Howard, E., Kim, J., Mun, M. Y., Mondschein, A., et al. (2008). Seeing our signals: Combining location traces and web-based models for personal discovery. *Proceedings of the 9th Workshop on Mobile Computing Systems and Applications,* 6–10.

Barton, J., & Pretty, J. (2010). What is the best dose of nature and green exercise for improving mental health? A multi-study analysis. *Environmental Science & Technology,* 44(10), 3947–55.

Beatley, T. (2011). *Biophilic Cities: Integrating Nature into Urban Design and Planning.* Washington, DC: Island Press.

Beck, L. F., Dellinger, A. M., & O'Neil, M. E. (2007). Motor vehicle crash injury rates by mode of travel, United States: Using exposure-based methods to quantify differences. *American Journal of Epidemiology,* 166(2), 212–18.

Berman, M. G., Jonides, J., & Kaplan, S. (2008). The cognitive benefits of interacting with nature. *Psychological Science,* 19(12), 1207–12.

Blumenberg, E., & Ong, P. (2001). Cars, buses, and jobs: Welfare participants and employment access in Los Angeles. *Transportation Research Record,* 1756, 22–31.

Boarnet, M., & Crane, R. (2001). *Travel by Design: The Influence of Urban Form on Travel.* Oxford: Oxford University Press.

Buehler, R., Gotschi, T., & Winters, M. (2016). Moving toward Active Transportation: How Policies Can Encourage Walking and Bicycling. San Diego: Active Living Research.

Chatman, D. G. (2013). Does TOD need the T? On the importance of factors other than rail access. *Journal of the American Planning Association,* 79(1), 17–31.

Crane, R. (1996 On form versus function: Will the new urbanism reduce traffic, or increase it? *Journal of Planning Education and Research,* 15(2), 117–26.

de Hartog, J. J., Boogaard, H., Nijland, H., & Hoek, G. (2010). Do the health benefits of cycling outweigh the risks? *Environmental Health Perspectives,* 118(8), 1109–16.

Ewing, R., & Cervero, R. (2010). Travel and the built environment. *Journal of the American Planning Association,* 76(3), 265–94.

Exel, N. J. A. van, & Rietveld, P. (2009). Perceptions of public transport travel time and their effect on choice-sets among car drivers. *Journal of Transport and Land Use,* 2(3), 75–86.

Fagnant, D. J., & Kockelman, K. (2015). Preparing a nation for autonomous vehicles: Opportunities, barriers and policy recommendations. *Transportation Research Part A: Policy and Practice,* 77, 167–81.

Frank, L. D., Andresen, M. A., & Schmid, T. L. (2004). Obesity relationships with community design, physical activity, and time spent in cars. *American Journal of Preventive Medicine,* 27(2), 87–96.

Frank, L. D., Sallis, J. F., Conway, T. L., Chapman, J. E., Saelens, B. E., & Bachman, W. (2006). Many pathways from land use to health: Associations between neighborhood walkability and active transportation, body mass index, and air quality. *Journal of the American Planning Association,* 72(1), 75–87.

Fruin, S. A., Winer, A. M., & Rodes, C. E. (2004). Black carbon concentrations in California vehicles and estimation of in-vehicle diesel exhaust particulate matter exposures. *Atmospheric Environment,* 38(25), 4123–33.

Fullilove, M. T. *Urban Alchemy: Restoring Joy in America's Sorted-Out Cities.* New York: New Village Press, 2013.

Guallart, V. Invited talk, University of Virginia School of Architecture, Charlottesville, August 31, 2015.

Handy, S., Cao, X., & Mokhtarian, P. L. (2006). Self-selection in the relationship between the built environment and walking: Empirical evidence from Northern California. *Journal of the American Planning Association,* 72(1), 55–74.

Houston, D., Wu, J., Ong, P., & Winer, A. (2004). Structural disparities of urban traffic in Southern California: Implications for vehicle-related air pollution exposure in minority and high-poverty neighborhoods. *Journal of Urban Affairs,* 26(5), 565–92.

Hsu, A. (2016). 2016 environmental performance index. New Haven, CT: Yale University.

Hu, K., Wang, Y., Rahman, A., & Sivaraman, V. (2014). Personalising pollution exposure estimates using wearable activity sensors. Paper presented at the 2014 IEEE Ninth International Conference on Intelligent Sensors, Sensor Networks and Information Processing (ISSNIP), April 21–24, Singapore.

Jacobsen, P. L. (2003). Safety in numbers: More walkers and bicyclists, safer walking and bicycling. *Injury Prevention,* 9(3), 205–9.

Jacobson, S. H., King, D. M., & Yuan, R. (2011). A note on the relationship between obesity and driving. *Transport Policy,* 18(5), 772–76.

Joost, S., Duruz, S., Marques-Vidal, P., Bochud, M. Stringhini, S., Paccaud, F., Gaspoz, J.-M., et al. (2016). Persistent spatial clusters of high body mass index in a Swiss urban population as revealed by the 5-year Geocolaus Longitudinal Study. *BMJ Open, 6*(1).

Kellert, S. R., & Wilson, E. O. (1995). *The Biophilia Hypothesis.* Washington, DC: Island Press.

Levinson, D., & Krizek, K. (Eds.). (2005). *Access to Destinations.* Amsterdam: Elsevier.

Loukaitou-Sideris, A. (2006). Is it safe to walk? 1 neighborhood safety and security considerations and their effects on walking. *Journal of Planning Literature, 20*(3), 219–32.

Manaugh, K., & El-Geneidy, A. (2011). Validating walkability indices: How do different households respond to the walkability of their neighborhood? *Transportation Research Part D: Transport and Environment, 16*(4), 309–15.

McCourt, R. S. (2004). *Parking Generation.* Washington, DC: Institute of Transportation Engineers.

Metropolitan Washington Council of Governments. (2008). Regional Household Travel Survey. https://www.mwcog.org/transportation/data-and-tools/household-travel-survey/.

Mokhtarian, P., & Salomon, I. (2001). How derived is the demand for travel? Some conceptual and measurement considerations. *Transportation Research Part A: Policy and Practice, 35*(8), 695–719.

Narain, S., Roychowdhury, A., & Chattopadhyaya, V. (2014). *Delhi Clean-Air Action Plan: The Agenda to Reduce Air Pollution and Protect Public Health.* New Delhi: Centre for Science and Environment.

Norton, P. D. (2011). *Fighting Traffic: The Dawn of the Motor Age in the American City.* Cambridge, MA: MIT Press.

Ong, P. M., & Miller, D. (2005). Spatial and transportation mismatch in Los Angeles. *Journal of Planning Education and Research, 25*(1), 43–56.

Pucher, J., Buehler, R., Merom, D., & Bauman, A. (2011). Walking and cycling in the United States, 2001–2009: Evidence from the National Household Travel Surveys. *American Journal of Public Health, 101*(S1), S310–S317.

Quiros, D. C., Lee, E. S., Wang, R., & Zhu, Y. (2013). Ultrafine particle exposures while walking, cycling, and driving along an urban residential roadway. *Atmospheric Environment, 73*, 185–94.

Runge, J. W., & Cole, T. B. (2002). Crosswalk markings and motor vehicle collisions involving older pedestrians. *Journal of the American Medical Association, 288*(17), 2172–74.

Sahu, S. K., Beig, G., & Parkhi, N. S. (2011). Emissions inventory of anthropogenic Pm 2.5 and Pm 10 in Delhi during Commonwealth Games 2010. *Atmospheric Environment, 45*(34), 6180–90.

Santos, A., McGuckin, N., Nakamoto, H. Y., Gray, D., and Liss, S. (2011). *Summary of Travel Trends: 2009 National Household Travel Survey.* Washington, DC: U.S. Department of Transportation.

Schrank, D., Eisele, B., & Lomax, T. (2012). *TTI's 2012 Urban Mobility Report.* College Station: Texas A&M Transportation Institute, Texas A&M University System.

Schweitzer, L., and Zhou, J. (2010). Neighborhood air quality, respiratory health, and vulnerable populations in compact and sprawled regions. *Journal of the American Planning Association, 76*(3), 363–71.

Shankar, U. (2003). *Pedestrian Roadway Fatalities.* Washington, DC: U.S. Department of Transportation.

Sharples, M., Aristeidou, M., Villasclaras-Fernández, E., Herodotou, C., & Scanlon, E. (2015). Sense-It: A smartphone toolkit for citizen inquiry learning." In: Brown, H. T., & van der Merwe, J. H. (Eds.), *The Mobile Learning Voyage—from Small Ripples to Massive Open Waters: 14th World Conference on Mobile and Contextual Learning, mLearn 2015, Venice, Italy, October 17–24, 2015, Proceedings,* 366–77. Cham, Switzerland: Springer International.

Swinburn, B. A., Sacks, G., Hall, K. D., McPherson, K., Finegood, D. T., Moodie, M. L., & Gortmaker, S. L. (2011). The global obesity pandemic: Shaped by global drivers and local environments." *Lancet,* 378(9793), 804–14.

Tang, I.-C., Sullivan, W. C., & Chang, C.-Y. (2015). Perceptual evaluation of natural landscapes: The role of the individual connection to nature." *Environment and Behavior,* 47(6), 595–617.

Taylor, B. D., Miller, D., Iseki, H., & Fink, C. (2009). Nature and/or nurture? Analyzing the determinants of transit ridership across US urbanized areas." *Transportation Research Part A: Policy and Practice,* 43(1), 60–77.

U.S. Department of Agriculture, Northern Research Station. (2006). Urban tree canopy assessment. Burlington: University of Vermont, 2006.

Van Den Berg, A. E., Hartig, T., & Staats, H. (2007). Preference for nature in urbanized societies: Stress, restoration, and the pursuit of sustainability." *Journal of Social Issues,* 63(1), 79–96.

Van den Berg, A. E., Jorgensen, A., & Wilson, E. R. (2014). Evaluating restoration in urban green spaces: Does setting type make a difference? *Landscape and Urban Planning* 127, 173–81.

Walk Score. (2017). Walk Score Methodology. https://www.walkscore.com/methodology .shtml.

Walker, R. E., Keane, C. R., & Burke, J. G. (2010). Disparities and access to healthy food in the United States: A review of food deserts literature." *Health & Place,* 16(5), 876–84.

Willsher, Kim. (2015). Paris to stop traffic when air pollution spikes." *Guardian,* November 3. http://www.theguardian.com/environment/2015/nov/03/paris-to-stop-traffic-when -air-pollution-spikes.

PROMOTING HEALTH EQUITY THROUGH COMMUNITY PLANNING

JASON CORBURN

Where you live and how that place is governed can determine when and if you get sick, receive medical treatment, and die prematurely. City living can be beneficial for human health, since urban areas generally offer greater economic and educational opportunities, medical services, political and gender rights, affordable housing, and cultural, political, and religious expression. This holds true in both rich and poor cities of the Global North and South. Yet, not everyone in cities can take advantage of these socially produced resources, and the poor and socially marginalized often experience health inequities, or differences in access to health-promoting resources that are unnecessary, avoidable, and unfair (Braveman and Gruskin 2003). As the UN-Habitat and World Health Organization (WHO) stated in their 2010 report, *Hidden Cities: Unmasking and Overcoming Health Inequities in Urban Settings*:

> Health inequities are the result of the circumstances in which people grow, live, work and age, and the health systems they can access, which in turn are shaped by broader political, social and economic forces. They are not distributed randomly, but rather show a consistent pattern across the population, often by socioeconomic status or geographical location. No city—large or small, rich or poor, east or west, north or south—has been shown to be immune to the problem of health inequity (WHO and UN-Habitat 2010).

An example of the persistence of health inequities is in the San Francisco Bay Area where an African American child born in West Oakland will die, on average, 15 years earlier than a white child living just a few miles away in the Oakland Hills (ACPHD 2008). In the Bay Area, life expectancy for everyone increased between 1960 and 2006, yet the difference in life expectancy between whites and African Americans has persisted and is increasing; in 1960 the difference between white and African-American life expectancy was about 2.3 years, but by 2006 the difference was over 7.8 years (ACPHD 2008). This is what public health researchers call a health inequity: an avoidable difference that is unfair and unjust. Health inequities are increasing in cities and neighborhoods around the world and present one of the greatest equity challenges for urban planners today.

This essay defines health inequities and offers some explanations for why they persist in communities around the world. I explore how urban planning practice might be considered a powerful factor in either perpetuating or reversing health inequities. I close with some examples of planning practices that might promote greater health equity.

What Explains the Persistence of Health Inequities?

The U.S. government, in its Healthy People 2020 strategy, defines a health disparity as

> a particular type of health difference that is closely linked with economic, social, or environmental disadvantage. Health disparities adversely affect groups of people who have systematically experienced greater social or economic obstacles to health based on their racial or ethnic group, religion, socioeconomic status, gender, age, or mental health; cognitive, sensory, or physical disability; sexual orientation or gender identity; geographic location; or other characteristics historically linked to discrimination or exclusion. (U.S. Department of Health and Human Services)

Thus, we can describe health disparities as differences or variation in the incidence, prevalence, mortality, and burden of diseases and other adverse health conditions among specific population groups. But there is a key difference between health disparities and health inequities; health inequities are differences in health that are not only unnecessary and avoidable but, in addition, are considered unfair and unjust (Braveman et al. 2011). Health equity in this context is not equality (sameness) for all, but rather implies societal efforts to ensure that historically marginalized groups have enhanced opportunities to access health-promoting resources and that existing access barriers are removed (WHO 2008). In short, health equity means addressing distributive and procedural justice, or who gets what and how much, and ensuring openness and fairness in the political processes that make these decisions (Corburn 2013).

What explains the persistence of health inequities across population groups and places? A large and compelling body of evidence suggests that social and environmental factors—apart from medical care—shapes health across a wide range of health indicators, settings, and populations (Adler et al. 1999; WHO 2008). Social and environmental factors associated with poor health, disability, and premature mortality range from poverty and low educational attainment to dangerous and insecure housing to exposure to toxins and violence in one's neighborhood. This evidence does not deny that medical care influences health; rather, it indicates that medical care is not the only influence on health and suggests that whether one has access to medical care does not determine who becomes sick or injured in the first place. Particularly striking in the United States is the persistence of health inequities across different racial and ethnic groups. Recent research suggests that even when African Americans have higher incomes, more years of education, do not smoke tobacco, and have regular access to primary health care providers (all frequently addressed "risk factors" in public health), their health outcomes are worse than low-income, poorly educated whites who smoke and do not visit a primary care physician (Mathews and MacDorman, 2012).

Thus, health equity must be attentive to the forces beyond health care and class that might be perpetuating the distribution of disease and premature death among racial and ethnic groups, particularly in wealthy nations in North America and Europe.

Embodiment and Toxic Stress: A Framework for Understanding Health Inequities

Nancy Krieger, a social epidemiologist at Harvard University, suggests that health inequities can only be understood by acknowledging the "multiple exposures" that the poor and people of color experience in their everyday lives, noting that

> a person is not one day African American, another day born low birth weight, another day raised in a home bearing remnants of lead paint, another day subjected to racial discrimination at work (and in a job that does not provide health insurance), and still another day living in a racially segregated neighborhood without a supermarket but with many fast food restaurants. The body does not neatly partition these experiences—all of which may serve to increase risk of uncontrolled hypertension, and some of which may likewise lead to comorbidity, for example, diabetes, thereby further worsening health status. (Krieger 2005, 353)

These multiple social inequalities link to health inequities because they act as "toxic stressors" on the body that over time (and as one stressor adds to the others) and damage the body's immune and neurologic systems (Shonkoff et al. 2012). While stress can be life saving in some conditions—think of the fight-or-flight mechanism—constant adversity is toxic, meaning that the prolonged activation of the stress response systems can disrupt the development of the brain architecture and greatly compromise other biologic systems. Under toxic stress circumstances, the oversecretion of cortisol and adrenaline trigger

other biologic responses like poor glucose regulation and constant feelings of
hunger that can contribute to chronic diseases such as obesity, diabetes, hy-
pertension, cardiovascular disease, stroke, asthma, and other immune-related
illnesses (Shonkoff et al. 2012). Some known toxic stressors include chronic
poverty, racial, gender and other forms of discrimination and marginalization, physical and emotional abuse, exposure to violence and housing insta-
bility—and these stressors start influencing health in utero and have cumulative impacts over a lifetime (Velasquez-Manoff 2012). For example, reports of
discrimination by African Americans and Asian Americans have been linked
with visceral fat accumulation, which increases the risk of metabolic syndrome (and thus the risk of heart disease and diabetes) (Gee, Walsemann, and
Brondolo 2012).[1] Toxic social stressors over one's life course are also suspected
in influencing epigenetic processes that regulate whether genes are expressed
or suppressed. Allostaic load—or the "wear and tear" on the body when one
is exposed to chronic stressors and the inefficient turning off of stress-induced
biologic responses—has been linked with changes in the length of telomeres,
which are DNA-protein complexes capping the ends of chromosomes that
protect them against damage. Telomere shortening is considered a marker
of cellular aging (Price et al. 2013). Since many "toxic stressors" can be linked
to one's neighborhood, the U.S. Centers for Disease Control and Prevention
stated that longevity and health are more determined by your zip code than
they are by your genetic code (Yoon et al. 2012).

The implication is that planning focused on one social stressor, risk in the
built environment, or altering one behavior, such as enhancing physical activity, is unlikely to reduce the burden of cumulative toxic stressors that are
contributing to the persistence of health inequities. Instead, planners need
to work with others outside the discipline to develop integrated responses to
mitigate the chronic neighborhood and community stressors experienced by
some populations in some places.

City and Community Planning as a Determinant of Health

City planning is a discipline and professional practice that includes political
processes, institutions, and discourses that generate policies, rules, and physical plans that shape where we live, learn, work, and play in cities and towns.
Yet city planning is much more than rules and regulations concerning land
use and the built environment; planners regularly make discretionary decisions that shape the implementation of formal rules, can provide greater
public access to (or stymie) forums for democratic decision making, and interpret national and even global ideologies about urbanization and develop-

ment. In these ways, city planning helps structure the distribution of social, physical, and economic "goods and bads" that influence human health and explain persistent urban health inequities. In other words, city planning acts as a structural determinant of health through its formal and informal institutions, its micro and macro politics, and how these intersect with our day-to-day activities, from access to employment and food to the qualities of our neighborhoods and housing to the allocation and distribution of social services (Corburn 2013).

Planning for Greater Equity

In the following section, I review three approaches for planners to promote greater health equity. First, I suggest planners and others ought to take a more relational view of health and place, rather than focusing on individual neighborhood variables that might correlate with health. I suggest that a relational view of place and health is necessary to begin to address place-based cumulative toxic stressors. Second, I suggest that Health in All Policies (HiAP), now widely endorsed by the World Health Organization and European Union, among others, is a practical approach for integrating health equity into urban planning and policy decisions. Third, I suggest that emphasizing the planning and enhancement of community health centers, as the U.S. Affordable Care Act requires, is a strategy where planners and the medical care sectors can come together to prevent illness and promote wellness, not just treat disease and send people back into the living conditions that are making them sick in the first place.

A Relational View of Place and Health

A relational view of place and health integrates work from interpretive policy analysis, relational geography, and institutional analyses, as well as practices such as adaptive environmental management (Healey 2006). The relational approach avoids weaknesses in "neighborhood-effects and health" and "built-environment and health" research that tend to focus on static variables of people or places (Ellaway et al. 2012; Kimbro and Denney 2013). These studies aim to explore for significant "neighborhood effects" on well-being using a subset of quantitative variables such as the amount of green space, land use mix, residential density, and width of sidewalks, and when little or no statistical influence is found, they often conclude that individual biology, behaviors, or genes must be responsible for health status, not "neighborhood characteristics." A relational approach explores an alternative to this work, namely that there are mutually reinforcing relationships between places and people and the position of places relative to each other. A relational approach to place and health asks planners to consider the endogenous and exogenous processes that influence the social determinants of health and operate at a variety of spatial scales, not just the neighborhood scale (Cummins et al 2007).

A relational view of place and health demands research and analysis that combines multiple ways of characterizing and understanding places, including resident narratives, systematic observation, spatial mapping, and quantitative and qualitative measures of the location and accessibility of resources. For health equity planning this means documenting not just if a health-promoting resource exists, but also the opportunities and barriers different population groups might face in utilizing that resource. In the relational view, geographic scales must explore the interactions between local and global decisions, not just static administrative boundaries (Corburn 2013). Distance under the relational view ought to include physical and social relations and view populations and places embedded within networks. This concept of distance is important for health equity planning because community members might not use a resource, such as a service or health care, that is physically close to them, especially if they perceive that service as not being culturally appropriate or affordable and if traveling far away from one's home might reduce the chances of being stigmatized for being treated for a disease in one's community.

Importantly, in a relational view of place, population groups are not treated as static, with fixed characteristics, but rather as dynamic and heterogeneous so that they are understood as having multiple and constantly evolving features. Thus, intersectionality is a central feature of the relational view of health equity planning. Importantly, governance and political power are essential features that are investigated, analyzed, and incorporated in the relational approach, not "controlled for" as confounding or ignored in urban health research and practice. What all this means is that health equity planning cannot simply focus on physical resources in space but must also be attentive to how distributive decisions are made and by whom. Thus, participation in place-based governance should be understood as a positive social determinant of health (Burris et al. 2007; U.S. Department of Health and Human Services 2017).[2]

Health in All Policies

Health in All Policies (HiAP) is an approach to decision making that aims to put a relational view of health equity into practice. HiAP recognizes most public policies have the potential to influence health and health equity, either positively or negatively, but policy makers outside of the health sector may not be routinely considering the health consequences of their choices and thereby may be missing opportunities to advance health. HiAP emerged, in part, from the World Health Organization's Declaration of Alma-Ata in 1978 and reflects numerous international calls for policy action to address the social determinants of health (Kickbusch, McCann, and Sherbon 2008). The European Union endorsed HiAP in 2006, and the governments of Finland, Norway, Sweden, United Kingdom, Canada, South Australia, Malaysia, Sri Lanka, Iran, and Brazil have all adopted some form of HiAP within governmental practice. The Dutch government actively supports municipalities to draft and implement HiAP strategies, but very few have managed to complete and implement these strategies, noting the difficulty in getting government actors and institutions outside the health sector to consider health impacts in their work (Storm et al. 2014). While the United States has not formally adopted HiAP at the federal level, many national and state health promotion activities reflect the core tenants of HiAP. One of the most clearly defined HiAP programs at the state scale in the United States is in California, whose Strategic Growth Council formally adopted HiAP in May 2012 and integrated the practice into a newly created Office of Health Equity within the California Health and Safety Code in 2013 (California Strategic Growth Council 2013). Some cities are actively working to integrate HiAP into their land use and planning decision making. For example, Washington, DC, passed the Sustainable DC Transformation Order in 2013, creating a HiAP Task Force, and the Chicago Department of Public Health created the Healthy Chicago Interagency Council to integrate health across all city departments.

The City of Richmond, California, in the San Francisco Bay Area, became the first U.S. city to pass a HiAP ordinance in 2014 (City of Richmond 2014). Richmond's HiAP Ordinance is aligned with their General Plan and Budget and includes intervention areas focused on how city policy, management, and service decisions can reduce the multiple toxic stressors residents and planners identified in Richmond. The HiAP Ordinance address six planning areas: (1) Governance and Leadership, (2) Economic Development and Education, (3) Full Service and Safe Communities, (4) Neighborhood Built Environments, (5) Environmental Health and Justice, and (6) Quality and Accessible Health Homes and Social Services. In addition, HiAP includes a racial equity evaluation for all city projects, policies, and plans, which was modeled after the Seattle/King County, Washington, Race and Social Justice Initiative (City of Seattle n.d.).

Community Health Centers

Community health centers (CHCs) are the third integral part of a place-based strategy planners can pursue to address health inequities. CHCs in the United States and around the world act as primary point of medical care for the poor and reach populations that formal institutions often cannot. Entire health systems around the world have been organized around community-based health centers that go beyond care to address living conditions and social inequalities in disadvantaged neighborhoods. For example, Brazil's national health system, Sistema Único de Saúde (SUS), delivers most of its services through neighborhood-based family health clinics (Programa de Saúde da Família), where nurses and lay health workers address community-specific health needs. The widely hailed program is administered by municipal governments and prioritizes social programs in urban favelas, or slums, such as violence reduction, transportation and food access, housing rights, and youth employment (Paim et al. 2011). In India, a new National Urban Health Mission (NUHM), which will also be administered by municipal, not national government, agencies will provide health care to slum dwellers and also focus on improving place-based determinants of health, such as drinking water, sanitation, education, gender rights, poverty alleviation, and other social issues (NUHM 2015).

In the United States, neighborhood health centers emerged during the late nineteenth century as a one-stop location in poor, often immigrant, urban areas, where ambulatory health services were combined with community participation in development and planning decisions (Rosen 1971). A federal policy, the Sheppard-Towner Maternity and Infancy Protection Act of 1921, funded a network of community health centers in urban and rural areas. A central feature of the early twentieth-century health center was the creation of block committees with community representatives. These committees met regularly and provided an opportunity for residents to participate directly in community affairs, while also using the professional skills of the health center's physicians and nurses. Block workers represented residents and visited families, keeping them in touch with the center and raising their concerns at meetings. Another committee run by the health center, the occupational council, organized local business and professional groups and gathered their input and support for the work of the center. Neighborhood health centers declined rapidly after the American Medical Association accused the centers of practicing "socialized medicine," and federal financial support ended when the Sheppard-Towner Act expired in 1929 (Rosen 1971).

Neighborhood health centers would return as a key strategy of the 1960s

War on Poverty and were funded through the Office of Equal Opportunity (OEO) (Lefkowitz 2007). The OEO health centers "were designed to reduce or eliminate health disparities that affected racial and ethnic minority groups, the poor, and the uninsured. The CHCs were to constitute a key component of the national public safety net, focused simultaneously on the care of individual patients and on the health status of their overall target populations. With their host communities involved in their governance, the centers were to be 'of the people, by the people, for the people'" (Adashi, Geiger, and Fine 2010, 2047). Despite some success in addressing broad social determinants of health, federal funding for community health centers declined in the 1970s. Financing was increasingly tied to clinical services and specific disease outcomes, and the ability of health centers to work on the social and economic drivers of health inequities was constrained (Lefkowitz 2007).

In the 2010s, community health centers again gained attention through the Patient Protection and Affordable Care Act (ACA), which provided $11 billion to expand CHCs across the United States and created a new School-Based Health Center Program (Krisberg 2014). According to the Health Resources and Services Administration, twenty-five million adult Americans (62 percent of whom are members of racial or ethnic minorities) rely on a CHC for primary care, disease prevention, and accessing social services, and over 30 percent of all children rely on CHCs (HRSA 2014). In addition to primary care and mental and dental health services, CHCs also offer what are called "supportive services" that include food access, translation services, and legal aid especially concerning housing, transportation subsidies, and shuttle services; all include a community planning board that aims to prioritize locally defined health promotion needs.

CHCs also contribute to community economic development, directly by employing local people, such as lay community health workers and center-related jobs, but also by purchasing goods and service from local businesses and nonprofits. The economic benefits of CHCs also indirectly support the local economy and wealth of families by reducing the costs of health care and increasing local spending (Kotelchuck, Lowenstein, and Tobin 2011). Planners can help link community development processes with federal and state resources targeted for building new and expanding existing community health centers, such as accessing New Markets Tax Credits and private capital. Planners can also take a more active role with CHCs ensuring that the three-year "community health needs assessments" that are now required by the ACA and the IRS for all tax-exempt hospitals address priority needs of the local community (CHNA 2014). The city of Hartford, Connecticut, is one of only a few cities where planners aligned community development, healthcare service delivery and land use planning into an integrated plan that included extensive public participation (City of Hartford 2013). These strategies offer concrete ways place and population-based community development plans can be combined with essential service delivery needs to address health equity.

Conclusions: Planning for Greater Health Equity

Planners ought to focus on promoting health equity rather than just reducing disparities. Yet, reorienting urban design, planning, and policy making will require moving toward integrated, multisector partnerships that target equity. Planners can promote health equity by expanding the narrow framing of the "built environment and health" to include social and political determinants of health, such as an attention to how racial discrimination contributes to place-based toxic stressors. This also demands that planners work with epidemiologists and others to break down issue and sector fragmentation and the tendency in medicine and public health to focus only on one disease, risk factor or behavioral change at a time. Health equity planning demands a more relational approach that grapples with the multiple and cumulative effects of toxic stressors. As discussed here, planners cannot wait until the science of health equity is definitive, but instead can rely on over a century of evidence that relational approaches that address context-specific social, environmental, and economic inequalities can promote greater health equity. I have offered some concrete strategies for planners, but more work is needed to track and monitor the impacts of these interventions on community health equity.

Notes

1. While race is an unscientific, societally constructed taxonomy that is based on an ideology that views some human population groups as inherently superior to others on the basis of external physical characteristics or geographic origin, the concept of race is still socially meaningful. A preponderance of research suggests that racial and ethnic variations in health status result primarily from variations among races in exposure or vulnerability to behavioral, psychosocial material and to environmental risk factors and resources. Racism encompasses prejudice, negative attitudes and beliefs about other groups, and discrimination, which is the differential treatment of people based on their race or ethnicity. The toxic stress concept suggests that racism, not race, affects health status by, among other hazards, diminishing social status, increasing exposure to risk factors and resources, and directly affecting health through increasing stress and the biologic response.

2. The World Health Organization(WHO) has described the importance of the relationships between urban governance, public participation, and addressing the social determinants of health in the following way:

Taking a social determinants approach requires governments to coordinate and align different sectors and different types of organizations in the pursuit of health and development—for all countries, rich and poor—as a collective goal. Building governance, whereby all sectors take responsibility for reducing health inequities, is essential to achieve this goal. Intersectoral action—that is, effectively implementing integrated work between different sectors—is a key component of this process.

The governance required to act on social determinants is not possible without a new culture of participation that ensures accountability and equity. Facilitating participation can help safeguard equity as a principle and ensure its inclusion in public policies.

Besides participation in governance, other aspects of participation, such as individual participation in taking up services or participation of communities in service delivery, are also important for reducing health inequities. However, the participation of communities and civil society groups in the design of public policies, in the monitoring of their implementation, and in their evaluation is essential to action on social determinants. (WHO 2012)

References

Adashi, E. Y., Geiger, J. & Fine, M. D. (2010). Health care reform and primary care: The growing importance of the community health center. *New England Journal of Medicine,* 362(22), 2047–50.

Adler, N. E., Marmot, M., McEwen, B. S., & Stewart, J. (Eds.). (1999). *Socioeconomic Status and Health in Industrial Nations: Social, Psychological, and Biological Pathways.* New York: New York Academy of Sciences.

Alameda County Public Health Department (ACPHD) (2008). *Life and Death from Unnatural Causes: Health and Social Inequality in Alameda County, California.* Oakland, CA: Alameda County Pubic Health Department. www.acphd.org/media/53628/unnatcs2008.pdf.

Braveman, B., & Gruskin, S. (2003). Defining equity in health. *Journal of Epidemiology and Community Health,* 57(4), 254–58.

Braveman, P. A., Kumanyika, S., Fielding, J, Laveist, T., Borrell, L. N., Manderscheid, R., et al. (2011). Health disparities and health equity: The issue is justice. *American Journal of Public Health,* 101(S1), S149–S155.

Burris, S., Hancock, T., Lin, V., & Herzog, A. (2007). Emerging strategies for healthy urban governance. *Journal of Urban Health,* 84(1), 154–63.

California Strategic Growth Council. (2013). Health in All Policies Task Force Implementation Plan: Health and Health Equity in State Guidance. http://sgc.ca.gov/hiap/docs/publications/Endorsed_HiAP_Implementation_plan_Health_and_Health_Equity_in_State_Guidance.pdf.

City of Hartford, Connecticut, Department of Health and Human Services. (2013). Strategic Plan 2013–2018. http://www.influentiald.com/hhs.html.

City of Richmond, California. (2014). Richmond Adopts a Health in All Policies (HiAP) Strategy and Ordinance. http://www.ci.richmond.ca.us/index.aspx?NID=2575.

City of Seattle, Washington, Race and Social Justice Initiative (RSJI). (N.d.). http://www.seattle.gov/rsji.

Community Health Needs Assessment (CHNA). (2014). http://assessment.community commons.org/CHNA/.

Corburn, J. (2013). *Healthy City Planning: From Neighbourhood to National Health Equity.* London: Routledge.

Cummins, S., Curtis, S., Diez-Roux, A., & Macintyre, S. (2007). Understanding and representing "place" in health research: A relational approach. *Social Science & Medicine,* 65(9), 1825–38.

Ellaway, A., Benzeval, M., Green, M., Leyland, A., & Macintyre, S. (2012). "Getting sicker quicker": Does living in a more deprived neighbourhood mean your health deteriorates faster? *Health and Place,* 8(2), 132–37.

Freiler A., Muntaner, C., Shankardass, K., Mah, C. L., Molnar, A., Renahy, E., & O'Campo, P. (2013). Glossary for the implementation of Health in All Policies (HiAP). *Journal of Epidemiology and Community Health,* 67(12), 1068–72. doi: 10.1136/jech-2013-202731.

Gee, G., Walsemann, K., & Brondolo, E. (2012). A life course perspective on how racism may be related to health inequities. *American Journal of Public Health,* 102(5), 967–74.

Healey, P. (2006). *Urban Complexity and Spatial Strategies: A Relational Planning for Our Times.* London: Routledge.

Healthy People, Office of Disease Prevention an Health Promotion. (N.d.). Disparities. http://www.healthypeople.gov/2020/about/disparitiesAbout.aspx.

Kickbusch, I., McCann, W., & Sherbon, T. (2008). Adelaide revisited: From healthy public policy to health in all policies. *Health Promotion International,* 23, 1–4.

Kimbro, R. T., & Denney, J. T. (2013). Neighborhood context and racial/ethnic differences in young children's obesity: Structural barriers to interventions. *Social Science and Medicine,* 95, 97–105.

Kotelchuck, R., Lowenstein, D., & Tobin, J. N. (2011). Community health centers and community development financial institutions: Joining forces to address determinants of health. *Health Affairs,* 30(11), 2090–97.

Krieger, N. (2005). Embodiment: A conceptual glossary for epidemiology. *Journal of Epidemiology and Community Health* 59(5), 350–55. doi: 10.1136/jech.2004.024562.

Krisberg, K. (2014). Community health centers lead health insurance enrollment: Implementing the Affordable Care Act. *Nation's Health,* 47(6). http://thenationshealth.apha publications.org/content/44/1/1.1.full.

Lefkowitz, B. 2007. *Community Health Centers: The People Who Made it Happen.* New Brunswick, NJ: Rutgers University Press.

Mathews, T. J., & MacDorman, M. F. (2012). Infant mortality statistics from the 2008 period linked birth/infant death data set. *National Vital Statistics Reports,* 60(5). Hyattsville, MD: National Center for Health Statistics, http://www.cdc.gov/nchs/data/nvsr/nvsr60/nvsr60_05.pdf.

National Urban Health Mission (NUHM). (2015). https://www.nhp.gov.in/national-urban-health-mission_pg?—jmc%7D%7D.

Paim, J., Travassos, C., Almeida, C., Bahia, L., & Macinko, J. (2011). The Brazilian health system: History, advances, and challenges. *Lancet,* 377(9779), 1778–97.

Price, L. H., Kao, H. T., Burgers, D. E., Carpenter, L. L. & Tyrka, A. R. (2013). Telomeres and early-life stress: An overview. *Biologic Psychiatry,* 73(1), 15–23.

Rosen, G. (1971). The first neighborhood health center movement—Its rise and fall. *American Journal of Public Health,* 61(8), 1620–36.

Shonkoff, J. P., Garner, A. S., Committee on Psychosocial Aspects of Child and Family Health, & Committee on Early Childhood, Adoption, and Dependent Care (2012). The lifelong effects of early childhood adversity and toxic stress. *Pediatrics,* 129(1), e232–e238.

Storm, I., Harting, J., Stronks, K., & Schuit, A. J. (2014). Measuring stages of health in all policies on a local level: The applicability of a maturity model. *Health Policy,* 114(2–3), 183–91.

Velasquez-Manoff, M. (2012). *An Epidemic of Absence: A New Way of Understanding Allergies and Autoimmune Diseases.* New York: Scribner.

World Health Organization (WHO), Commission on Social Determinants of Health. (2008). *Closing the Gap in a Generation: Health Equity through Action on the Social Determinants of Health.* Final report. Geneva: World Health Organization.

World Health Organization (WHO), Commission on Social Determinants of Health. (2012). Taking action to improve health equity. http://www.who.int/social_determinants/action_sdh/en/.

World Health Organization (WHO) and UN-Habitat. (2010). Hidden cities: Unmasking and overcoming health inequities in urban settings. http://www.who.int/kobe_centre/publications/hidden_cities2010/en/.

Yoon, P. W., Bastian, B., Anderson, R. N., et al. (2012). Potentially preventable deaths from the five leading causes of death—United States, 2008–2010. *Morbidity and Mortality Weekly Report,* 63(17), 369–74.

EVIDENCE-BASED PRACTICE

Challenges in a Changing World

ANN FORSYTH

The Obvious and the Evidence-Based

It seems obvious today that the built environment affects people's health. If that is the case, urban planners, urban designers, landscape architects, and architects can potentially play an important role in making lives better. They can be heroes in an epic and nonpartisan battle against death and disease. They can draw on the body of research connecting health and place to inform better practice, create new allies, and generally improve the world.

My argument is that this idea of evidence-based practice has a lot of potential but is difficult to pull off. First are practical concerns of using research in practice. This is in part to do with mismatches between the scope and character of problems practitioners seek to solve and the forms of research conducted in universities and similar institutions. There is also a mismatch between the kind of evidence that practitioners are accustomed to using— their training honed by personal experience, for example—and the findings of research that may come from different settings and populations, beyond their immediate experience. Such research can be very useful, but practitioners may have difficulty locating the full range of studies, not be sure how to apply the research, and may have difficulty seeing the big picture given the multitude of highly specific findings.

Theoretically too it can be difficult to figure out what are the key points of intervention—many current conceptual frameworks focus on highlighting the wide range of issues relevant to health, even if some of them have a very modest role. However, a practitioner cannot work on everything at once and needs guidance about where best to intervene. The urban world is changing relatively rapidly—environmentally, demographically, in terms of the location of growth. Applying research from the current period to future problems in a shifting context requires skill and judgment. Examples from projects connecting health and place illustrate some of the opportunities and constraints faced when making such connections. Overall connecting health and place in practice is both important and complex.

Diverse Connections between Health and Place

Evidence-based practice—using research evidence to inform what we do—is an area of some growth across a variety of fields (Krizek, Forsyth, and Shively Slotterback 2009). In urban planning and design, relevant research cuts across a great many fields and areas of expertise. While this is perhaps common enough in professional fields, planning in particular operates at a variety of scales from the site to the region and aims to coordinate across domains— physical, social, economic, ecological, and institutional. This can mean that relevant research comes from a wide range of disciplines. The following list, drawn from the Health and Place Initiative, outlines some of the topics where health and place are connected, illustrating the broad array of environmental features and health-related behaviors at this intersection.

Exposures
1. Air quality
2. Disasters
3. Noise
4. Toxics
5. Water quality
6. Climate change
7. Housing

Connections
8. Geographical accessibility to community resources
9. Geographic healthcare access
10. Social capital
11. Mobility and universal design

Behavior supports
12. Physical activity options
13. Mental health effects
14. Food options
15. Safety (accidents, crime)

It is both an exciting opportunity and a daunting challenge.

In some of these topical areas there is a great deal of research on how health-related exposures, behaviors, and outcomes relate to places, and in

others there is very little. For example, the major health research database
PubMed has literally hundreds of thousands of articles mentioning "urban,"
"rural," or "city" in their abstract. It has only hundreds that mention "urban
planning." There are many projects to make such research more accessible—
from professional associations and universities—with exemplary projects like
InformeDesign (2015) initially funded by the American Society of Interior
Designers (ASID). However, the task of engaging with findings across many
domains can be daunting.

Theoretical Complexities

These multiple intersections mean that a broad array of determinants or
causes of health and health-related behaviors are important to consider—
from biology and behavior to policies and pricing. To explain how all these
influences interact much recent work has used what has been called the "social ecological model." This is a generalized model drawing on the work of
Bronfenbrenner (1979) on ecological systems theory and others on the social
ecology of health promotion (McLeroy et al. 1988; Stokols 1992). It has much
in common with work on social epidemiology and determinants of health
(Kawachi 2002; House 2002). Certainly other models are available to those
interested in intervening to improve public health. Baranowski et al. (2003)
provide a useful review of major theories used to guide behavior change including the knowledge-attitude-behavior model, behavioral learning theory,
health belief model, social cognitive theory, theory of planned behavior, trans-
theoretical model/stages of change, social marketing, and social ecological
models. However, the social ecological model has been much used in part
because it easily incorporates the larger context (including the built environment and social inequalities). Intervening at the level of context is attractive
in cases such as obesity prevention where public health proponents have been
frequently unsuccessful getting individuals to change behaviors.

The social-ecological model is often represented by a diagram that is
shaped like a rainbow or a set of concentric circles (Sallis et al. 2006, 2012;
Dahlgren and Whitehead 1991, 2007; Rao et al. 2011). In typical representa-
tions the individual is in the center (including such factors as age, sex, health,
or biology), enclosed by radiating bands of perceptions, behaviors, social
networks (family, peers, school, neighborhood, work, etc.), the environment
(built, social, policy), and general conditions (e.g., wider culture, economy).
While the number of bands and their exact content varies, versions have in
common the basic idea that individuals are surrounded by numerous influences at varying scales.

The importance of context is hardly a surprise in the field of urban planning. However, in the area of health, which had been dominated by biological or psychosocial theories, social ecological models have provided a way of incorporating environments, organizational contexts, and policies. This framework has supported a number of productive collaborations between health and environmental researchers particularly in the area of energy balance (physical activity and food environments).

This social ecological model's strength is its comprehensiveness. This is very useful in terms of raising awareness about the wide range of influences on health. By being broad, the social ecological model has allowed researchers to design research that looks at many variables in, for example, the wicked problem of reducing obesity (Pothukuchi 2005; Rittell &Webber 1973, 161; Rao et al. 2011). Such research doesn't too quickly focus in on a single answer, narrowing options too soon. Its weakness, in the rainbow or nested circle form, is that it says little about relative strengths of various determinants, their interactions, and causal pathways. Even if research is modified to deal with one health issue such as obesity, or in a form that includes some causal pathways (e.g., Schulz and Northridge 2004), it can be difficult to clearly identify which factors mediate (i.e., explain how two variables are linked) and which moderate (i.e., affect the direction or strength of a relation between variables). Visually, it provides a great deal of space to most distant contextual factors that may not accurately represent their (perhaps modest) importance. However, those who use the model are surely aware of such problems, and the model has been very useful as an inspiration for many new research collaborations.

Others have attempted to develop midlevel models that more explicitly show these links for various health outcomes distinguishing major and minor causal paths as well as moderating or interacting effects.[1] These midlevel models can be relatively easy to develop in some areas where there is a direct relation between an exposure and a health outcome (e.g., pollutants leading to respiratory problems). With obesity the relation between environments and health-related outcomes is much more complex. For example, a key aspect of energy balance is the intake of food that in recent decades has increased in availability globally (Swinburn et al. 2011; Rao et al. 2011). While there has been substantial angst about food deserts in the United States, food is typically ubiquitous spatially, particularly in metropolitan areas. Thus factors beyond whether particular foods are available nearby may be crucial in affecting consumption. Healthier options can be more expensive, harder to store, seasonally unavailable, less palatable or culturally relevant to some groups, and less well marketed (Forsyth, Lytle, and Van Riper 2010; Wells et al. 2007). Some relevant aspects of the food environment are quite microscaled, such as how

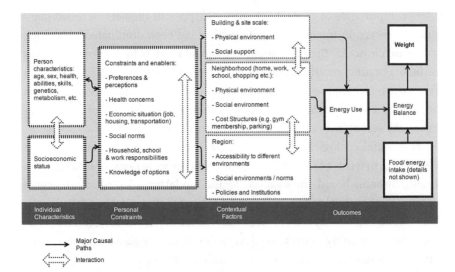

Figure 1. Relationships between physical activity, environment, and weight

food is served on the plate (Wansink and Sobal 2007; Sobal and Wansink 2007). All these affect consumption.

On the other side of the energy balance equation is the topic of physical energy expenditure. Figure 1 is a very simplified attempt to create a midlevel model of how environments moderate such expenditures, as an example of a kind of midlevel theory. Energy expenditure may happen in many locations— at work, at home, in neighborhoods, while traveling from place to place, and in facilities designed for exercise. People typically inhabit several such environments over a day, week, or month, and they may operate as barriers or supports to physical activity (Wells et al. 2007; Leslie et al. 2007). These in turn operate at scales from the micro (e.g., stair signage) to the very large (regional opportunities for active transportation). They may be quite subtle; for example, a home without heating requires more energy to be expended to maintain body temperature.

However, this kind of diagram, like the rainbow or nested circle models, gives a great deal of visual space to contextual factors. It could well be that food intake is key and that individual characteristics and personal constraints on energy expenditure are also quite important (e.g., Stafford et al. 2007; Christian et al. 2011). I have tried to indicate this visually in figure 1 with heavier lines for these variables.

In part because of this complexity, findings about the association between neighborhood physical activity environments and obesity have been mixed. Feng et al. (2010) reviewed 63 papers on the association between objectively measured neighborhood factors and BMI and found great heterogeneity in methods and findings. They proposed it was difficult to draw conclusions from this literature. However, Leal and Chaix (2011) conducted a systematic review of 131 articles that examined the relationship between local environments and cardiometabolic risk factors, including obesity. They found environments with higher residential densities, more street intersections, more services, and higher levels of social cohesion were associated with lower BMIs in a number of studies (also Black and Macinko 2008). However, Lovasi et al. (2009), in a review of 45 studies dealing with the built environment and obesity in disadvantaged U.S. populations, found the strongest associations between higher obesity levels and lack of food store access, lack of local exercise facilities, and (to some extent) safety issues. The problems of using such studies to understand the causes of obesity are, however, substantial (e.g., self-selection, unmeasured variables, lack of neighborhood variation, etc.) (Oakes 2004).

Challenges Using Planning and Design
Research as Evidence for Practice

Carrying off evidence-based practice is difficult enough in any field—its problems are well documented (Krizek, Forsyth, and Shively Slotterback et al. 2009). Practitioners are already busy dealing with multiple issues from logistics and political considerations. Researchers are contributing to bodies of research work that may not cleanly map onto immediate practice concerns.

Finding ways to use research in practice is all the more complex when considering the varying manners in which research itself is conducted. There are a number of ways of thinking about this, for example, empirical versus theoretical/critical (Forsyth and Crewe 2006). But another way is to consider the cultures of research related to the "scope, form, intended audience, and perceived value of research products" (Forsyth 2012). I have previously identified five such cultures in planning. All are used to provide evidence for practice though they vary in terms of the kinds of evidence they can supply.

Those working on the scientific frontier tend to work on projects where many researchers look at small parts of the picture, and knowledge is accumulated from multiple studies (table 1). Methods are precisely defined, funding is typically available, papers are short, and large collaborations are the norm. Those concerned with practical applications conduct research that is likely to have influence, in part because governments and foundations interested in impact have sponsored it. Such research often grapples with multiple dimensions of an issue, trying to assess what can be done. Those assessing practice come in two camps. A smaller number reflect on their own work in practice in a way that is systematic enough to be called research. A larger number

Table 1. Cultures of research in planning compared with practical design

	Example question	Typical scope	How knowledge of an issue is created
Scientific frontiers	Do low-income children who live near fast food eat more of it?	One narrow question per paper (for scientific journals); many papers from one project	Incremental accumulation of knowledge of highly targeted studies over time, systematically synthesized
Practical applications	Do bicycle lanes reduce accident rates?	Multiple issues, e.g., current knowledge + research evidence + implications for practice	From studies that are policy relevant; that provide good enough, timely evidence
Assessing practice	Institutional barriers to HIA?	Raises question + uses experience/ extended case as evidence and illustration; relates to theory	Learning from history and practice about what's possible
Enduring questions	Is a healthy city a just city?	Poses a large question and/or object of criticism; relates to theory; and proposes ways forward	By systematic, theoretically and empirically informed reflection

Source: Adapted and expanded from Forsyth (2012).

look at practice historically. Both provide a great deal of contextual detail. Finally, others ask enduring questions about what is good, right, and just— a set of theoretical issues that may, however, be placed in practical and empirical context.

Obviously work on the scientific frontier is closest to the model of evidence used in the health fields where evidence-based practice initially emerged (Krizek, Forsyth, and Shively Slotterback 2009). However, each paper tends to answer one highly specific question, and finding implications for practice typically means sifting through multiple studies. Work on practical applications is most easily translated into practice but is not always available. Studies that assess practice tend to look comprehensively at the big picture, providing nuance but requiring work to apply to a new context; something similar can be said for those answering enduring questions. All research cultures can provide evidence for evidence-based practice, though the kinds of questions to which they are best suited will vary.

More General Dilemmas of Evidence-Based Practice

A number of additional issues, common to many fields, make it tricky to use an evidence-based approach in planning and design as well. There may be very few studies on a specific topic, such as whether specific kinds of vegetation improve air quality. There may be hundreds or even thousands on topics such as the relation between environments and recreational walking but in a plethora of different contexts and using a great variety of methods. This makes it all too easy to cherry-pick the research articles that seem to gel with one's intuition. While public health provides "systematic reviews" that sift through evidence with great rigor, they are not always available for relevant topics. Many of these reviews may not be sufficiently clear about the character of the finding—for example, they may declare that certain kinds of environments increase physical activity when they find this to be the case for adolescent boys in central cities but not for other populations (Krizek, Forsyth, and Shively Slotterback 2009).

A related issue is that of publication and outcome reporting bias where those studies that find effects are more likely to be published than those that do not, and those outcomes of a study that are statistically significant are more likely to be published than those that are not (Dwan et al. 2008). They are perceived as more interesting by authors, reviewers, and editors. For example, a study of the relationship between neighborhood food access and obesity will have a harder time getting published if it finds that proximity has little effect on consumption but socioeconomic factors are key. The author will feel less like publishing this finding of no environmental effect, and editors will also question it. When systematic reviews are done, they often count the number of studies finding positive, negative, and no effects and make conclusions based on the balance of the studies. But publications and reporting bias means that the body of published evidence is biased toward those studies finding that the environment is important, meaning results need to be carefully considered.

Some of the gap is filled with practice-oriented summaries (including some for my own projects, the earlier Design for Health and more recent Health and Places Initiative [2015], InformeDesign [2015], and the like). However, even these require additional work on the part of users to incorporate into a project that may seem onerous given the many other demands on their time.

Changing Context of Health in the Transition Century

This all happens in the context of major changes in the urban world. According to many projections world population will level off or even fall starting in the middle of the century. By then a vast majority of the population will live in urban areas—though some areas will already be shrinking and others continuing to grow (Forsyth 2014). These challenges are in many ways unprecedented. For millennia a relatively small number of people led mostly short lives limited by disease, famine, conflicts, and the stresses of childbirth. But during the twentieth century the global population increased from 1.6 billion to over 6 billion, largely due to increased life expectancy. Life expectancy in 1900 was 31 years globally (rising to 50 in affluent places such as the United States) (Cohen 2006; Prentice 2006). By 2000 it was 62 years for men and 67 for women, with much higher numbers in very urbanized locations like Japan, Singapore, and Australia (UN 2004; CIA 2011).

Metropolitan areas turned from being sites of ill-health in the nineteenth century to being places where, in countries with sufficient infrastructure and substantial educational opportunities, life expectancies are longest (Montgomery et al. 2003; Satterthwaite 2007, 3; CDC 1999). In a world where most people died young, the social, economic, and health context was quite different. Only the most privileged could expect to beat the odds. Instead in coming years many more people will live longer lives, meaning an aging population will grapple with health-relevant environmental issues in a situation of continuing poverty for many (Forsyth 2014). This makes it even trickier to understand the relationships between health and place as the places, and people who inhabit them, evolve.

One example is the 4:2:1 issue in China where the one-child policy commenced in 1979 and has only recently been loosened. Due to the reduction in birth rates, succeeding generations are smaller with, prototypically, four grandparents and two adult children for one grandchild (Flaherty et al. 2007, 1295; Riley 2004) (see figures 2 and 3). China's population will likely peak in the mid-2020s through mid-2030s even with the new policy The population over 60 will continue to rise, however, reaching 30 percent of the population by 2050 (United Nations 2002). While this is an extreme case of fast demographic change, around the world rising life expectancies and decreasing birth rates are leading to similar situations, with implications for what it means to create a healthy environment.

How Planning and Environmental Design Can Make a Difference

Of course, even with this complexity and change, it is certainly possible to intervene to make environments healthier. Five main strategies frame the tools that are used:

Figures 2 and 3. China's aging population, evident in these photographs, is at the leading edge of a global demographic change, and planning practice and research will need to adapt as this change occurs.

- Assessing environments, policies, programs, and plans in terms of health using either comprehensive systems like health impact assessments or more specific tools such as safety audits and food security assessments.
- Creating regulations, policies, and plans to shape new developments and also frame how the environment is maintained, used, and redeveloped.
- Developing new models for places from master-planned new towns to new types of street design.
- Facilitating targeted programs that help people use places in a healthier way or that reduce harmful exposures. Community gardens that let people connect with nature and each other or cyclovia that reroute traffic on certain days to give over streets to cyclists are examples.
- Fostering collaborations between different parts of government, the private sector, education and research, civic groups, interior designers, and residents. From the WHO's Healthy Cities program to various task forces, these can help target interventions (Forsyth 2015).

Developed in the 1920s by members of the Regional Planning Association of America's members Clarence Stein and Henry Wright, but drawing on British garden city practice, the Radburn planning approach aimed to separate people from cars (UK 1963). Using a superblock pattern, cars reached housing units through culs-de-sac while people circulated through interior park spaces maintained by a resident association. The original Radburn development in New Jersey (figure 4a) and other classic Radburn developments (including Houten, The Netherlands, shown in figure 4b) also reversed the houses to face onto the paths. Such designs were replicated around the world. Cumbernauld (figure 4c), developed outside Glasgow in Scotland from the 1950s, had almost complete separation of cars and people and in its early years had an accident rate less than a quarter of the British average (Sykes, Livingstone, and Green 1967, 10; Forsyth and Crewe 2009). At the same time a survey found 87 percent of the residents felt favorably toward Cumbernauld, citing quiet, open space, a sense of "going places," and health (Sykes, Livingstone, and Green 1967, 31–32). Vallingby (figure 4d), laid out upon similar lines in the suburbs of Stockholm, Sweden, in the 1950s, was a site of pilgrimage for planners from around the world, and there were many more.

However, the story was not the same at all times and places. Over the years Cumbernauld faced challenges. Some were to do with experimental aspects of its modern architecture and difficulties with maintenance following public

Figure 4. The Radburn principles of planning, such as the separation of pedestrians, cy-clists, and cars, have inspired developments across the world. Radburn, U.S. (a), Houten, the Netherlands (b), Cumbernauld, Scotland (c), and Vallingby, Sweden (d), are just a few examples of the Radburn principles.

housing privatization. But over time people also became less enamored of total separation of cars and people, with lack of lighting and poor sight lines con-tributing (interviews with residents in 2006; Forsyth and Crewe 2009). Simi-larly in Sydney, Australia, where Radburn planning was also used extensively in public housing of the 1960s and 1970s, a process of "de-Radburnization" oc-curred in the 1980s and 1990s to reroute pedestrian paths, enclose uncared-for open spaces, and undo the house reversal, in part responding to complaints by residents (Freestone 2004, 198). Some complaints were related to the so-cioeconomic conditions of residents and poor location, but others were to do with the problems of layout (Murray 2007).

These examples show a similar design strategy, in a similar context (outer suburban social housing) working better at some times than others in the same development, and in some places better than others. The implication is not to give up on trying new models but to realize that creating healthy communities is a multifaceted issue.

Example: Design for Health and Health and Places Initiative

Health assessments, feeding into the planning process, are a quite different kind of intervention. The Design for Health project, operating most substantially from about 2004 to 2009, was a collaboration aiming to examine the links between public health and municipal planning and to translate research into tools for practice. Key questions included:

- What are the key relationships between the environment and human health?
- What are some important thresholds at which human health is affected?
- How can planning and design improve human health and ameliorate problems?
- Can we develop tools to more clearly connect health and the work of landscape architects, architects, and planners?

The project developed from work I had been doing with Blue Cross and Blue Shield of Minnesota, investigating new health promotion strategies. Municipalities across the Twin Cities Metropolitan Area in Minnesota are mandated to complete comprehensive plans for the Metropolitan Council, the regional governing body, every ten years, and there was a window in 2008. This opportunity to influence upcoming planning provided the impetus for the Design for Health project. In response, Design for Health created an interdisciplinary project team working with urban planners, urban designers, park planners, public works officials, and public health professionals. The focus of Design for Health was, thus, on a broad range of links between the urban environment and human health.

Design for Health was based on the idea that health research has much to tell us, but it is important to treat it systematically. While it is easy to find one article supporting a position, it is better to look at the balance of evidence. A key aspect of the Design for Health project was clearly identifying how the built environment, including the planted environment, affects health. As I have outlined elsewhere, this project produced many useful health impact assessment materials and collaborated with nineteen local governments to apply them. However, in a world with multiple priorities only those places with champions willing to work to make health a priority used them in any substantial way (Krizek, Forsyth, and Shively Slotterback 2009). Local governments were funded to incorporate health into planning, but a substantial minority did it in the most minimal way possible, feeling overburdened with other issues.

The insight is that while champions are key, they also need tools. More recently the Health and Places Initiative at Harvard that I direct has aimed to expand and internationalize this work to provide an updated version of such tools developing neighborhood design prototypes, planning guidelines, health assessment tools, and research summaries (HAPI 2015).

Reflecting on the Health Turn

The recent health turn in planning started with an interest in obesity and neighborhoods, but the links are obviously much broader in topic and scale. Because of this variety the health turn has taken several forms, and these have different trajectories for the future. Advocates and professionals have found health effects can provide additional justifications for their work and will likely continue to use health in this way. They have found new allies in related fields. Research collaborations with public health have helped academic urban planners and designers learn new methods, refine old ones, and engage questions of public relevance with greater resources.

However, actually managing to do evidence-based practice is tricky at best due to problems of using research to identify where to intervene, gaps in research, and the shifting context of planning. There are ways to intervene, but they require commitment from practitioners and awareness about pitfalls. Overall the link between health planning, urban design, and architecture may not cast our professions as heroes, but it can give our fields relevance to a public absorbed by issues of life and death.

Note

1. There are many other examples of such models for specific health outcomes such as stress (e.g. Rashid and Zimring 2008).

References

Baranowski, T., Cullen, K. W., Nicklas, T., Thompson, D., & Baranowski, J. (2003). Are current health behavioral change models helpful in prevention of weight gain efforts? *Obesity Research,* 11, 23S–43S.

Bauman, A. E., & Bull, F. C. (2007). Environmental Correlates of Physical Activity and

Walking in Adults and Children: A Review of Reviews. Review undertaken for the National Institute of Health and Clinical Excellence. https://pdfs.semanticscholar.org/4977/aeoa5da007fd4021bc0772179183e007b033.pdf.

Black, J., & Macinko, J. (2008). Neighborhoods and obesity. *Nutrition Reviews, 66*(1), 2–20.

Bronfenbrenner, U. (1979). *The Ecology of Human Development.* Cambridge, MA: Harvard University Press.

Brown, A. L., Khattak, A. J., & Rodriguez, D. A. (2008). Neighbourhood types, travel and body mass: A study of new urbanist and suburban neighbourhoods in the US. *Urban Studies, 45*(4): 963–88.

Central Intelligence Agency (CIA). (2011). Country Comparison: Life Expectancy at Birth. World Factbook. https://www.cia.gov/library/publications/the-world-factbook/rankorder/2102rank.html.

Cervero, R., & Kockelman, K. (1997). Travel demand and the 3Ds: Density, diversity, and design. *Transportation Research Part D, 2*(3), 199–219.

Christian, H., Giles-Corti, B., Knuiman, M., Timperio, A,., & Foster, S. (2011). The influence of the built environment, social environment and health behaviors on body mass index. Results from RESIDE. *Preventive Medicine, 53*, 57–60.

Cohen, B. (2006). Urbanization in developing countries: Current trends, future projections, and key challenges for sustainability. *Technology in Society, 28*, 63–80.

Corburn, J. (2005). Urban planning and health disparities: Implications for research and practice. *Planning Practice & Research, 20*(2), 111–26.

Dahlgren, G., & Whitehead, M. (1991). *Policies and Strategies to Promote Social Equity in Health.* Stockholm: Institute of Futures Studies.

Dahlgren, G., & Whitehead, M. (2007). *European Strategies for Tackling Social Inequities in Health: Levelling Up, Part 2.* Copenhagen: WHO Regional Office for Europe.

Dwan, K., Altman, D. G., Amaiz, J. A, Bloom, J., Chan, A.-W., Cronin, E., Deculier, E., et al. (2008). Systematic review of the empirical evidence of study publication bias and outcome reporting bias. *PLOS One, 3*(8), e3081. doi.org/10.1371/journal.pone.0003081.

Feng, J., Glass, T., Curriero, F. C., Stewart, W. F., & Schwartz, B. S. (2010). The built environment and obesity: A systematic review of the epidemiologic evidence. *Health and Place, 16*, 175–90.

Flaherty, J. H., Liu, M. L, Ding, L., Dong, B., Ding, Q., Li, X., & Xiao, S. (2007). China: The aging giant. *Journal of the American Geriatrics Society, 55*(8), 1295–300.

Forsyth, A. (2007). Innovation in urban design: Does research help? *Journal of Urban Design, 12*(3), 461–73.

Forsyth, A. (2012). Alternative cultures in planning research: From extending scientific frontiers to exploring enduring questions. Journal of Planning Education and Research, 32(2), 160–68.

Forsyth A. (2014). Global suburbs and the transition century: Physical suburbs in the long term. *Urban Design International, 19*(4), 259–73.

Forsyth, A. (2015). When public health and planning closely intersect: Five moments; five strategies. In: Mah, D., & Ascencio Villoria, L. (Eds.). *Life-Styled: Health and Places.* Berlin: Jovis.

Forsyth A., and K. Crewe. 2006. Research in environmental design: Definitions and limits. *Journal of Architectural and Planning Research, 23*(2), 160–75.

Forsyth, A., & Crewe, K. (2009). New visions for suburbia: Reassessing aesthetics and place-making in modernism, imageability, and New Urbanism. *Journal of Urban Design,* 14(4), 415–38.

Forsyth, A., Hearst, M., Oakes, J. M., & Schmitz, K. H. (2008). Design and destinations: Factors influencing walking and total physical activity. *Urban Studies,* 45(9), 1973–96.

Forsyth, A., & Krizek, K. (2010). Promoting walking and bicycling: Assessing the evidence to assist planners. *Built Environment,* 36(4), 429–46.

Forsyth, A., Lytle, L., & Van Riper, D. (2010). Finding food: Issues and challenges in using GIS to measure food access. *Journal of Transport and Land Use,* 3(1), 43–65.

Forsyth, A., Oakes, J. M., & Schmitz, K. H. (2009). Test-retest reliability of the Twin Cities walking survey. *Journal of Physical Activity and Health,* 6(1), 119–31.

Forsyth, A., Oakes, J. M., Schmitz, K. H., & Hearst, M. (2007). Does residential density increase walking and other physical activity? *Urban Studies,* 44(4), 679–97.

Freestone, R. (2004). The Americanization of Australian planning. *Journal of Planning History,* 3(3), 187–214.

Health and Places Initiative (HAPI). (2015). Harvard University, Graduate School of Design. http://research.gsd.harvard.edu/hapi/.

InformeDesign. (2015). http://www.informedesign.org/.

House, J. S. (2002). Understanding social factors and inequalities in health: 20th century progress and 21st century prospects. *Journal of Health and Social Behavior,* 43(2), 125–42.

Kawachi, I. (2002). What is social epidemiology? *Social Science and Medicine,* 54, 1739–41.

Krizek, K., Forsyth, A., & Shively Slotterback, C. (2009). Is there a role for evidence-based practice in urban planning and policy? *Journal of Planning Theory and Practice,* 10(4), 455–74.

Leal, C., & Chaix, B. (2011). The influence of geographic life environments on cardiometabolic risk factors: A stystematic review, a methodological assessment and a research agenda. *Obesity Reviews,* 12, 217–30.

Leslie, E., McCrea, R., Cerine, E., & Stimson, R. (2007). Regional variations in walking for different purposes: The South East Queensland Quality of Life Study. *Environment and Behavior,* 39(4), 557–77.

Lovasi, G. S., Hutcon, M. A., Guerra, M., & Neckerman, K. M. (2009). Built environments and obesity in disadvantaged populations. *Epidemiologic Reviews,* 31, 7–20.

McDonald, K., Oakes, J. M., & Forsyth, A. (2011). Effect of street connectivity and density on adult BMI: Results from the Twin Cities Walking Study. *Journal of Environmental and Community Health,* 66, 636–40.

McLeroy, K. R., Bibeau, D., Steckler, A., & Glanz, K. (1988). An ecological perspective on health promotion programs. *Health Education Quarterly,* 15(4): 351–77.

Montgomery, M. R., Stren, R., Cohen, B., & Reed, H. E. (Eds.). (2003). *Cities Transformed: Demographic Change and Its Implications in the Developing World.* Panel on Urban Population Dynamics, National Research Council. Washington, DC: National Academies Press. https://www.nap.edu/read/10693/chapter/1.

Murray, E. (2007). *Remembering Minto: Life and Memories of a Community.* Parramatta, N.S.W.: Information and Cultural Exchange and the Remembering Minto Group.

Oakes, J. M. (2004). The (mis)estimation of neighborhood effects: Causal inference for a practicable social epidemiology. *Social Science and Medicine,* 58(10), 1929–52.

Oakes, J. M., Forsyth, A., Hearst, M., & Schmitz, K. H. (2009). Recruiting a representative sample for neighborhood effects research: Strategies and outcomes of the Twin Cities Walking Study. *Environment and Behavior,* 41(6): 787–805.

Pothukuchi, P. (2005). Building community infrastructure for healthy communities: Evaluating action research components of an urban health research programme. *Planning Practice & Research,* 20(2), 127–46.

Prentice, T. (2006). Health, History, and Hard Choices: Funding Dilemmas in a Fast-Changing World. World Health Organization. Presentation at Health and Philanthropy: Leveraging Change, Indiana University. http://www.who.int/global_health_histories /seminars/presentation07.pdf.

Pucher, J., & Buehler, R. (2008). Making cycling irresistible: Lessons from the Netherlands, Denmark, and Germany. *Transport Reviews,* 28, 495–528.

Rao, M., Barten, F., Blackshaw, N., Lapitan, J., Galea, G., Jacoby, E., Samarth, A., & Buckley, E. (2011). Urban planning, development and noncommunicable diseases. *Planning Practice & Research,* 26(4), 373–91.

Rashid, M., & Zimring, C. (2008). A review of the empirical literature on the relationships between indoor environment and stress in healthcare and office settings: Problems and prospects of sharing evidence. *Environment and Behavior,* 40(2), 151–90.

Riley, N. E. (2004). China's population: New trends and challenges. *Population Bulletin,* 49(2), 1–36.

Rittell, H. W. J., & Webber, M. M. (1973). Dilemmas in a general theory of planning. *Policy Sciences,* 4, 155–69.

Saelens, B., & Handy, S. (2008). Built environment correlates of walking: A review. *Medicine and Science in Sports and Exercise,* 40, S550–S566.

Sallis, J. F., Cervero, R. B., Ascher, W., Henderson, K. A., Kraft, M. K., & Kerr, J. (2006). An ecological approach to creating active living communities. *Annual Review of Public Health,* 27, 297–322.

Sallis, J. F., Floyd, M. F., Rodriguez, D. A., & Saelens, B. E. (2012). Role of built environments in physical activity, obesity, and cardiovascular disease. *Circulation,* 125(5), 729–37.

Satterthwaite, D. (2007). The Transition to a Predominantly Urban World and Its Underpinnings. IIED Human Settlements Discussion Paper. http://pubs.iied.org/pdfs /10550IIED.pdf.

Schulz, A., & Northridge, M. E. 2004. Social determinants of health: Implications for environmental health promotion. *Health Education and Behavior,* 31, 455–71.

Sobal, J., & Wansink, B. (2007). Kitchenscapes, tablescapes, platescapes, and foodscapes: Influences of microscale built environments on food intake. *Environment and Behavior,* 39, 124–42.

Stafford, M., Cummins, S., Ellaway, A., Sacker, A., Wigging, R. D., & Macintyre, S. (2007). Pathways to obesity: Identifying local, modifiable determinants of physical activity and diet. *Social Science and Medicine,* 65, 1882–97.

Stokols, D. (1992). Establishing and maintaining healthy environments: Toward a social ecology of health promotion. *American Psychologist,* 47(1), 6–22.

Swinburn, B. A, Sacks, G., Hall, K. D., McPherson, K., Finegood, D. T., Moodie, M. L., Gortmaker, S. L. (2011). The global obesity pandemic: Shaped by global drivers and local environments. *Lancet,* 378, 804–14.

Sykes, A. J. M., Livingstone, J. M., & Green, M. (1967). Cumbernauld 67: A Household Survey and Report. Occasional paper no. 1. Glasgow: University of Strathclyde, Department of Sociology.

Twin Cities Walking Study. (2005). Twin Cities Walking Survey. http://activelivingresearch .org/twin-cities-walking-survey.

United Kingdom (UK), Ministry of Transport. (1963). *Traffic in Towns: A Study of the Long Term Problems of Traffic in Urban Areas.* London: HMSO.

United Nations (UN). (2002). World Population Ageing 1950–2050: China. http://www.un .org/esa/population/publications/worldageing19502050/pdf/065china.pdf.

United Nations (UN), Department of Economic and Social Affairs. (2004). *World Population to 2300.* New York: United Nations.

Wansink, B., & Sobal, J. (2007). Mindless eating: The 200 daily food decisions we overlook. *Environment and Behavior,* 39(1), 106–23.

Wells, N. M., Ashdown, S. P., Davies, E. H. S., Cowett, F. D., & Yang, Y. (2007). Environment, design, and obesity: Opportunities for interdisciplinary collaborative research. *Environment and Behavior* 39(1), 6–33.

DESIGNING FOR HEALTH

Fostering Social Capital Formation through Public Space

ELLEN BASSETT

Well-planned communities have long sought to integrate open and public spaces into their physical design. The early park planner Frederick Law Olmsted, for instance, was extremely motivated by concerns for human health. When speaking of the purpose of parks, like Central Park and Prospect Park in New York City, he is often credited with saying that parks would function as the "lungs of the city"—providing green open spaces in which urban residents could escape the dirt and pollution of the city and breathe fresh air. But Olmsted's parks also had other articulated goals—among them creating the opportunity for socializing and fostering social cohesion important to health and democracy (Roulier 2010). Olmsted argued that humans had a "gregarious inclination"—a desire to be out among society—and his parks provided settings for "neighborly receptive recreations" that would foster connections (Olmsted 1870, 74, 76). His public parks provided spaces in which one could witness

> an evident glee in the prospect of coming together, all classes largely represented, with a common purpose, . . . each individual adding by his mere presence to the pleasure of all others, all helping to the greater happiness of each. (Olmsted 1870, 75)

Today we increasingly recognize that social isolation and loneliness have a strongly negative impact upon human health, particularly that of older adults and adolescents. Loneliness is an acknowledged risk for a suite of negative physiological and health outcomes, including elevated blood pressure, impaired sleep, obesity, alcoholism, personality disorders, and depression (Cacioppo, Hawkley, and Thisted 2010). While myriad interventions and programs to ameliorate the negative link between social isolation/loneliness and poor health have been tried and evaluated in the literature (e.g., Cattan, et al. 2005), an increasingly important body of research is once again focused on the physical environment—including parks and spaces of recreation and mingling so important to Olmsted—and the role such spaces play and *might* play in fostering social connections and enhancing human health. This essay examines this connection and potential. It begins by presenting an overview of the relationship between social capital and human health as it appears in contemporary literature. Social capital, briefly, can be defined as the features of social organization, such as civic participation, norms of reciprocity, and trust in others, which facilitate cooperation for mutual benefit. The essay then looks at one aspect of the public realm—smaller gathering places like parklets, pocket parks, and informal spaces—and the evidence base to date regarding the role of such places in fostering social capital. Finally, the essay closes with some implications for practice and a few thoughts regarding future research directions.

Social Capital: The Connection to Human Health

Our understanding of what constitutes health and what factors affect human health have become considerably more nuanced in recent decades. Most significantly, the prevailing biomedical model that depicted health as merely the absence of disease and as a product of biologic factors resulting from an individual's genetics and behaviors has yielded to a more robust model often referred to as the social-ecological model. This model of health identifies myriad "upstream" determinants of health, including psychological, social, and environmental determinants (Northridge, Sclar, and Biswas 2003). Social integration and social support are both acknowledged up-stream factors in health in the social-ecological model; in a research environment they are often measured and evaluated as part of the larger concept of social capital.[1]

In his landmark book on social capital and American life, *Bowling Alone*, Putnam (2000) identified two main types of social capital—*bonding* social capital, which can be thought of as ties between similar individuals or groups (e.g., homeowners, Catholics) and *bridging* social capital, which is defined as ties across diverse or different groups (e.g., interracial or interfaith relationships) (Putnam 1995; Pridmore et al. 2007). An important aspect of many studies of social capital is discerning levels of reciprocity—that is, the extent to which a person can rely upon or call upon an unrelated person to help out in a time of need and is willing to help others out as well. Another critical element is trust in others and in social institutions (such as the police). It is thought that trust will influence the development of reciprocal relationships at the individual level; trust is also considered important—potentially a precursor—for participation in civic life at both the neighborhood and citywide levels.

Researchers working on social capital and health differentiate social capital into two types: individual social capital and collective social capital (Bourdieu

Figure 1. Tanner Springs in Portland, Oregon, is a small urban park that provides an opportunity for residents to mingle and enjoy wildlife in the city.

1986; Portes 2000). Individual social capital refers to the ability of persons to secure benefits for themselves due to their membership in social networks. Berkman and Glass (2000) have identified four aspects of social networks that they hypothesize might influence health: (1) social support (e.g., the ability to rely on others, seen as a buffering factor for stress; (2) social influence (e.g., exposure to norms, can be health enhancing if norms are health positive norms like not smoking); (3) social participation (which confers opportunities to learn new skills and builds a sense of community belonging); and (4) material access (e.g., group membership, can give access to resources that can have an impact on health, including information on job opportunities or services). Marmot (2005) has also argued that status is an important aspect of social capital; high status due to group membership is thought to influence health by decreasing stress.[2]

Collective social capital refers to norms and networks that facilitate collective action to benefit an entire community. It might be thought of as higher-level social cohesion. Collective social capital is judged by measures such as strength/density of civic organizations, voter turnout, and levels of volunteerism. The linkage between collective social capital and health is debated and less easily hypothesized than individual social capital. Wilkinson (1996) has hypothesized that collective social capital may be able to mediate between income inequality and health, building on the observation that more equal societies have higher levels of social cohesion. It is also thought that perhaps more social capital could work to address inequities since more cohesive neighborhoods are more effective at lobbying for policies and services (Kawachi, Kennedy, and Glass 1999).

Findings

Greater awareness of social capital and its linkages to societal outcomes, including health, is evidenced through a dramatic rise in number of published studies examining the relationship between social capital and health since the mid-1990s. According to PubMed, the primary library index for medical publications, in 2000 there were 15 articles published with the term *social capital* in the title alone; in 2012 there were 106; cumulatively the search engine yielded 760 articles in total in 2013. Given the physical impossibility of reviewing such a trove, this review highlights a few of the more interesting studies by type of social capital.[3]

Individual Social Capital. The relationship of social capital to positive health outcomes is strongest at the individual level. Writing in *The Lancet* some fourteen years ago, Whitehead and Diderichsen noted:

> It has long been known that at an individual level, networks, social participation, and supportive social relationships are good for a person's health. People with strong social networks, for instance, have mortality half or a third that of people with weak social links. Low control at work and low social support predict coronary heart disease, and in the Whitehall II Study low control in the workplace accounted for about half of the social gradient in cardiovascular disease. (2001, 165)

More recent research has sought to add nuance to this consensus by examining whether the positive effect of social capital holds across individuals differentiated by key characteristics, such as gender, race, age, and income. Relative to gender, for instance, there are a few studies out of Australia that have shown that social capital is particularly important for women's health. A study done by Young, Russell, and Powers honed in on social capital as measured by the feeling of community belonging among Australian women aged seventy-three to seventy-eight. They found that women who had a "better sense of neighbourhood" were associated with better physical and mental health, lower stress, better social support, and being physically active (2004, 2627). Not surprisingly, duration of stay mattered here with women who had lived longer at their present address indicating a stronger sense of belonging. Security of income also influenced feelings of belonging (Young, Russell and Powers 2004). A study by Berry and Welsh (2010) used Australian national data from the WAVE 6 Household, Income and Labour Dynamics Survey to explore social capital and its relation with three forms of health—general health, mental health, and physical functioning. They found that higher participation was (not unexpectedly) related to higher levels of social cohesion, and it was also related to all three forms of (better) health, particularly strongly to mental health. They highlighted the fact that there were notable gender differences here, with women reporting greater community participation and social cohesion than men, but also reporting worse mental health. Their findings of difference by sex and the link of social capital with mental health are reflective of other findings in the literature, namely Baum et al., (2000) and Berry (2008). A 2010 publication by Ball et al. looked at the health status of women in neighborhoods differentiated by their level of socioeconomic disadvantage in Melbourne, Australia. They found that leisure time physical activity was associated with socioeconomic status (e.g., income, educational attainment) as well as social capital measures. Specifically, the most physically active women were university educated; they knew more neighbors, had higher levels of social participation, and reported high levels of interpersonal trust as well as stronger norms of reciprocity and social cohesion.

Researchers have also examined the effect of social capital on just mental health. In a review of extant studies published in 2005, de Silva et al. systematically examined twenty-one papers—fourteen measured social capital at the individual level, and the remainder measured it at the population level. Of the fourteen studies, eleven reported higher levels of social capital to be associated with lower risk of mental illness; in contrast, findings from the studies of "structural social capital" (measured by items like trust, attachment to neighborhood) were inconclusive (only two showing a positive benefit from social capital). They conclude that the "current evidence is inadequate to inform the development of specific social capital interventions to combat mental illness" (de Silva et al. 2005, 619). More recently, Ivory et al. (2011) researched relationships between mental health and social fragmentation (i.e., weak social ties) at the neighborhood level in New Zealand. Their research found that fragmented neighborhoods did affect mental health, but that gender mattered here again, with women, particularly unemployed women, being the most negatively affected.

Collective Social Capital. As noted above, the evidence relating to collective social capital and health is thought to be weaker. We highlight three studies here mainly to give a sense of what this research looks like and the types of conclusions being drawn. A large sample study looking at data from forty U.S. communities by Kim, Subramanian, and Kawachi (2006), for instance, sought to distinguish between the effects of different forms of social capital on human health. It gathered data at both the individual and the community levels and sought to examine differences in effect from bonding versus bridging social capital. They found that higher community bonding was associated with 14 percent lower odds of reporting fair-to-poor health, while higher community bridging social capital was associated with 5 percent lower odds of self-reported fair-to-poor health. They found some interesting effects by race/ethnicity, with the positive effects of higher community-bonding social capital on health being significantly weaker among black persons and among those assigned to the "other" racial/ethnic category. They conclude there may be modest protective effect on health from these two types of social capital. A study by Carpiano, also published in 2006, analyzed data from the U.S. census and the Los Angeles Family and Neighborhood Survey to test a more sophisticated conceptual model of neighborhood conditions and social capital developed by Bourdieu. Carpiano looked at the relationship between neighborhood social capital forms (social support, social leverage, informal social control, and neighborhood organization participation) and select adult health behaviors (namely smoking, binge drinking) and perceived health. He found relationships between social capital and health behaviors—informal social control and higher levels of neighborhood social leverage were associated with lower levels of binge drinking and smoking, but conversely higher levels of social support were associated with higher levels of both behaviors. He notes that this is consistent with social capital theory that points out the negative potentialities of social capital. A final study from 2011 by Kim et al. (2011) drew data from the European and World Values Surveys to estimate the effects of country-level social trust on individual self-rated health for a very large sample of persons living in sixty-four countries. They also looked at whether the relationship varied by gender or individual levels of trust. Their analysis found higher average country-level trust to be associated with better self-rated health in both women and men. Interestingly they also found the effects of country social trust to be stronger for women than men. They argue for the importance of collective social capital, noting that "the estimated health effects of raising the percentage of a country's population that trusts others by 10 percentage points were at least as large as the estimated health effects of an individual developing trust in others" (Kim et al. 2011, 8).

If social capital is potentially good for health, then a clear counterquestion is whether the loss of social capital is bad for health. In a cross sectional study that looked at the relationship between income inequality and social capital using data from thirty-nine states, Kawachi et al. (1997) found just that. Specifically, they found that higher income inequality was negatively correlated with two measures of social capital, namely levels of per capita group membership and social trust. These two negative characteristics, in turn, were positively correlated with total mortality as well as negative health outcomes like higher rates of coronary heart disease and infant mortality. They conclude that their study supports "the notion that income inequality leads to increased mortality via disinvestment in social capital" (Kawachi, et al. 1997, 1491).

Fostering Social Capital through the Built Environment—The Evidence Base

Given the emerging evidence that social capital plays an important role in human health, a critical challenge for urban planners and designers is to create the type of physical places that facilitate social capital formation in our communities. What type of public interventions and public designs best foster the building of connections? Do different types of public places—the street, the plaza, the park—have different impacts upon different populations? What are the key design principles that need to be followed to foster social capital? Research on such questions is really in its infancy—and provides a rich area for potential future investigation. In this section, I briefly present key findings from some exemplary studies focused on smaller-scale public spaces (pocket parks) and informal gathering spaces. The importance of large-scale green spaces (e.g., linear and regional parks) and biophilia to healthy communities and healthcare facilities is covered in other essays.

Findings

The literature on public space is one of the largest in urban design. In addition to Whyte's work referenced above, Clare Cooper Marcus and her students at the University of California–Berkeley conducted research on how people use urban public spaces such as public plazas and how to design them to accommodate an evolving range of social and economic activities (see Marcus and Francis 1998). Likewise, research and design work by Gehl (1987), Wooley (2003), and Shaftoe (2008) show that good public spaces are ones that are well used and accessible to a wide variety of people. Public spaces with those characteristics are optimal settings for the creation of social connections/social capital, which I review as well in this section.[4]

To understand the effect of smaller public spaces, pocket parks, and ad hoc or informal community gathering spaces on health, I examined a handful of recently published studies. These studies were chosen according to their relevance to the topic of social capital and by the characteristics of the sites and populations they examined.[5] While this truncated study is by no means exhaustive, the findings appears consistent with studies of other types of open spaces (e.g., natural or green spaces)—finding, in short, that public spaces contribute positively toward improved human health; in this case a critical pathway is the role they play in fostering community connections.[6]

A recent study from Denmark provides some sense of this literature (Peschardt, Schipperijn, and Stigsdotter 2012). Noting that the use and health benefits of urban green space have received increased attention in recent years, the authors decided to examine whether smaller (and more commonly found) public urban green spaces (SPUGS in their terminology) have similar effects. SPUGS, briefly, are parks that fit the criteria of the city of Copenhagen for "pocket parks," namely they do not exceed five thousand square meters, they have at least some vegetation, and they have their own entrance and some form of distinguishable boundary that separates them from surrounding public space like the street. Peschardt, Schipperijn, and Stigsdotter's (2012) research examined the use of nine SPUGS in the city of Copenhagen and drew on intercept survey responses from 686 park users. They found that Copenhagen's SPUGS were used primarily for "socializing" (by younger users—under forty-nine years of age—on their way home from work) as well as for "rest and restitution" (by older users). The authors suggest that designers should recognize the importance of small parks and take their findings as "inspiration" for the future planning of dense city areas.

In a similar vein, Kaźmierzak (2013) examined small local parks in Manchester, England, to see to what extent they contributed to the development of social ties in three inner-city neighborhoods. Using both a survey of residents and focus group discussions, he gathered data on levels of material deprivation and ethnic diversity for each neighborhood as well as on park utilization and social networks. Associations were found between the quality of the parks, the character of visits (e.g., frequency of visits, duration of stay, engagement in social activities), and the extent of social ties in the neighborhood. He concludes that inner-city parks can play a greater role in supporting social interactions and developing ties, but that their quality and maintenance matters.

A study by Francis et al. (2012) looked at the association between quality of public space and sense of community in new residential communities built in the Perth metropolitan area of Western Australia. The four public spaces were public open space (e.g., parks), community centers, schools, and shops. Sense of community was of interest as it has been associated with improved well-being, increased feelings of safety and security, and greater participation in community affairs. They found a positive and significant association with the perceived quality of neighborhood public open space and shops with measures of sense of community. Interestingly, frequency of use of those assets did not affect the relationship—but having them in proximity was important.

Finally, a study of "mundane public spaces" from the United Kingdom warrants highlighting, particularly given changing demographics in the United States. Cattell et al. (2008) sought to explore the links between public spaces and different conceptualizations of well-being. The research was set in the culturally and racially diverse borough of Newham in East London—a setting that was 60 percent minority and had no large or conspicuous "formal" public spaces. Interestingly, the "public spaces" identified by discussion groups were quite varied—two shopping streets, two public markets, two parks, and a football (soccer) stadium. Not surprisingly the sites played different roles and had different meanings across groups. In terms of social interaction, places of commerce like the market provided a comfortable multiethnic setting through which different groups (e.g., black Africans and Indians) easily interacted, whereas parks were seen as less intense social environments since they did not necessarily involve interaction. The researchers conclude by saying:

> A wide range of everyday public open spaces were perceived as having a positive influence on both individual well-being and community life. Some people derived restorative benefits from the opportunities provided by spaces to be alone, but for many others, it was their social value, their shared and collective use which was instrumental both in alleviating stress and for maintaining health and well-being. (Cattell et al. 2008, 556)

The literature on smaller public spaces, to conclude, indicates that small public spaces do play an important role in supporting the formation of social connections important to human health. All of the studies reviewed indicated that the quality of the public spaces matters and that they necessitate management and maintenance to ensure that they remain attractive to users of diverse genders, ethnic identities, and age groups. While this is an admittedly small number of studies, the uniformity of their conclusions—that smaller public open spaces have beneficial value in terms of social ties—lends support to public efforts to create new spaces at a finer-grain scale (like the individual parcel) or at unexpected locations (like the DIY—do it yourself—approaches

Figure 2. St. James Park in London succeeds in bringing residents and visitors together.

of tactical urbanism). There is clearly a need for more research as well, as is discussed below.

Take Away for Practice

A question for the planning, development, and design communities is what role can design play in cultivating social capital—that is, in facilitating the formation of community connections, creating a sense of community, and building community pride? One evident response is that communities should be designed to provide an enabling environment for social interaction—that is, we should create a high-quality public realm that encourages community members to get out of their private homes and rub shoulders. Luckily for practitioners, ideas of how to best design public spaces like public plazas or urban pocket parks abound—with many of the most fundamental principles harkening back to a foundational study of public spaces, known as the Street Life Project, by William H. Whyte (Whyte 1980). His core design principles still appear to hold today:

(1) Parks must be people-centric. While it may seem self evident—spaces must be designed for people. Successful small public spaces have

abundant and inviting seating options; where possible seats should be moveable so that they can be reconfigured to accommodate individuals as well as groups of different sizes. People-centric parks are not built to deter lingering but to foster it. People draw in other people; the most successful parks are in Olmsted's words "gregarious."

(2) Parks need good, accessible locations: locations that are not marginal, isolated, or hidden. The best small public spaces, while set aside from the hubbub of the city, still maintain a relationship to the street. This enables people watching and instills a sense of safety for park users.

(3) Parks need nature, beauty, and sensory stimuli. Small parks have interior features that draw users in from the street. Attractive features should instill beauty and inspire interest. Among specific design features are tree canopies for shade; water features like fountains to provide auditory background noise facilitative of private conversations; art, particularly sculpture, and accessible food, often provided by small kiosks or food trucks.

But design ideas and examples abound. The Project for Public Spaces (PPS), an advocacy group promoting the renewed embrace of city squares, plazas, and parks, has updated and utilized Whyte's work in their placemaking principles and specific projects in cities across the United States and abroad (PPS n.d.). While we might hope that simply providing appropriately and attractively designed infrastructure and amenities foster positive results, such investment should also be supported by programming (such as street festivals, art fairs, seasonal attractions like ice skating rinks) that keep community members coming back throughout the year. The Project for Public Spaces also has lots of ideas and examples drawn from around the country on innovative programming and events.

An important caveat, however, is the need for planners and designers to think innovatively about just what constitutes a "public space" and formulate creative strategies to better utilize existing land resources, including vacant or underutilized properties, to make them work as community gathering places. While advocacy organizations such as the Project for Public Spaces do provide compelling arguments for public investment in public space, it is often difficult to justify such expenditures in times of fiscal distress. Parks or police officers? Plazas or unleaded pipes? Lower-cost, even informal or temporary, alternatives are needed.

In terms of crafting of such alternatives, open-space advocates and community members are increasingly looking to the most common public space in our cities and towns—the street. Persons familiar with Whyte's 1979 video

The Social Life of Urban Spaces might recall that the documentary begins and ends in the same location, and Whyte confesses that he could have discovered everything uncovered by the research focused on formal places like Seagram Plaza and Bryant Park by simply by observing a lively street in Harlem. In 2005, Rebar, a San Francisco art and design studio, converted one metered parking space in downtown San Francisco into a temporary park as one way to draw attention to and protest the shortage of green space in that part of the city (Rebarn 2005). Since that time, "Park(ing) Day" has taken off globally with 975 parks being "built" in 162 cities in 35 countries in 2011 alone (Park[ing] Day 2016). Inspired by public squares and piazzas, City Repair in Portland, Oregon focuses on creating public gathering places in neighborhoods across the city. During their ten-day "village building convergence," neighbors come together in placemaking exercises like painting intersections, building benches, planting gardens, creating mosaics, and so on. The material cost is low, but the community building effect is reportedly high (City Repair Project n.d.).

Areas for Further Research

The published research looking at the role of the built environment in social capital formation and its subsequent effect on human health outcomes is in its nascent stage. There is clearly a need for more examination of these linkages across different aspects of the built environment (e.g., plazas versus parks), different landscapes and climatic settings, and across different populations. The built environment research reviewed here only looked at smaller public spaces and informal spaces; the settings were in Europe and Australia.

In the American context, given our understanding of the street and streetscapes as ubiquitous public spaces, it would be particularly interesting to examine the changes in neighborhood environments happening in myriad American central cities at present to see the extent to which infill housing and densification, the creation of urban amenities and third spaces, and the development of transit-supportive street environments play a role (or any role) in social capital formation with positive benefits for physical and mental health. Tyson's Corner, an Edge City in the Washington, DC, metropolitan regions, for instance, is a prime example of a car-based, predominantly single-family-home suburb transitioning to a denser, transit-centric, mixed-use community (Garreau, 1991). What will this mean for the health and feelings of social belonging and connection of its residents?

At the same time, we know that American suburbs are also changing—becoming older, more diverse, and less affluent (Cooke 2010; Rosenbloom

2005). As the American suburb is premised on the primacy of private space, it would be important to examine how changing demographics and socioeconomic profiles are affecting community health and investigate the impact of interventions—like shared civic spaces and recreational programming—on different resident populations. Notably, persons over eighty-five years of age—dubbed by demographers as the "oldest old"—are the fastest-growing segment of the total population in the United States (Transgenerational Design Matters n.d.). Their needs (for social support and contact) and preferences (for active lifestyles and places to congregate) will need to be met by local governments, planners, and design professionals. Research should be formulated that can inform such growing areas of practice.

To conduct such research, however, calls for different types of methods and approaches. Much of the research focusing on urban form and health (particularly physical activity as an outcome) is cross-sectional. That is, the studies present statistical comparisons of groups of individuals; the data for these comparisons were collected at one point in time (e.g., Centers for Disease Control and Prevention's *Behavioral Risk Factor Surveillance System,* which provides data on weight and physical activity). These studies are not longitudinal (i.e., they do not examine change over time within a set group of research participants), nor are they experimental (i.e., examining the group at two distinct times, before and then after some form of intervention—preferably with a control group.) Longitudinal and experimental studies can be more challenging and expensive to do, but they are more suitable for investigating the strength of the relationship between health and design. The spatial scale at which we collect health data (county, region), moreover, doesn't accord with the level at which we design and plan our communities (subregions, neighborhoods, parcels). We need a different type of data with more detail on community members, their health and health behaviors, and where they live in order to better understand the relationship between the built environment and health. Finally, much of our research to date is based upon self-reported data. Our understanding of social capital is generally gleaned through survey research; dependent variables measuring health, such as weight, physical activity, and depressive episodes, are also reported by respondents. The use of experimental designs, complete with treatment and nontreatment groups, would raise the rigor of the research. Technology (such as now widely available fitness trackers, GPS, and GIS) and supportive data resources in the realm of "big data" (e.g., crime statistics, consumer shopping data, voter registration and turnout), if properly deployed from a privacy perspective, hold the promise of providing complementary measurements to enhance our understanding of health in all its dimensions.

Notes

1. Social capital has been identified as an important factor in a wide range of outcomes beyond health. Researchers have looked at the role of social capital as a driving agent in poverty alleviation, community development, entrepreneurship, technological innovation, and the management of natural resources, to name a few (e.g., Warren, Thompson and Saegert 2001; Pretty 2003; Dakhli and de Clercq 2004).

2. Marmot's most current research on status, stress, and health outcomes was recently covered by the *New York Times* (Velasquez-Manoff 2013).

3. A relatively recent book by Kawachi, Subramanian, and Kim (2008, 1) warrants review by the very interested reader, and their count is much higher than mine. Search on PubMed for "social capital and health," and one sees over 27,500 articles listed (as of December 2006).

4. While no designers appear to question the importance of good public spaces, there is a lot of discussion in the literature about the privatization of public space (particularly the rise of the mall) and the extent to which this places limitations on use or interferes with social mixing and the democratic functioning of public space. See just about any issue of the *Journal of Urban Design*.

5. This essay focuses on the subject of social capital and is a distillation of part of a much larger literature review prepared in 2012. In this literature review, the research base evaluating the link between different types of public spaces (including regional parks, greenways, and streetscapes) and health was also presented (see Bassett 2014).

6. There is an enormous literature in the fields of community and environmental psychology examining open space, landscape design, and sense of place/place attachment/place identity. A comprehensive review of that was not possible here; however, Manzo (2005) and Manzo and Perkins (2006) provide good overviews.

References

Ball, K., Cleland, V. J., Timperio, A. F., Salmon, J., Giles-Corti, B., & Crawford, D. A. (2010). Love thy neighbour? Associations of social capital and crime with physical activity amongst women. *Social Science & Medicine*, 71(4), 807–14.

Bassett, E. M. (2014). *Designing the Healthy Neighborhood: Deriving Principles from the Evidence Base*. New York: Hart Howerton; Charlottesville: University of Virginia Center for Design and Health. http://www.harthowerton.com/pdf/DesigningtheHealthyNeigborhood.pdf.

Baum, F. E., Bush, R. A., Modra, C. C., Murray, C. J., Cox, E. M., Alexander, K. M., et al. (2000). Epidemiology of participation: An Australian community study. *Journal of Epidemiology & Community Health*, 54(6), 414–23.

Berkman, L. F., & Glass, T. (2000). Social integration, social networks, and health. In: Berkman, L. F., Kawachi, I., & Glymour, M. M. (Eds.). *Social Epidemiology*, 137–73. Oxford: Oxford University Press.

Berry, H. L. (2008). Subjective perceptions about sufficiency and enjoyment of community participation and associations with mental health. *Australasian Epidemiologist*, 15(3), 4–9.

Berry, H. L., & Welsh, J. A. (2010). Social capital and health in Australia: An overview from the household, income and labour dynamics in Australia survey. *Social Science and Medicine, 70*(4), 588–96.

Bourdieu, P. (1986). The forms of capital. In: John G. Richardson (Ed.), *Handbook of Theory and Research for the Sociology of Education,* 241–58. New York: Greenwood Press.

Cacioppo, J. T., Hawkley, L. C., & Thisted, R. A. (2010). Perceived social isolation makes me sad: Five year cross-lagged analyses of loneliness and depressive symptomatology in the Chicago Health, Aging, and Social Relations Study. *Psychology and Aging, 25*(2), 453–63.

Carpiano, R. M. (2006). Neighborhood social capital and adult health: An empirical test of a Bourdieu-based model. *Health & Place* 13(3), 639–55.

Cattan, M., White, M., Bond, J. & Learmouth, A. (2005). Preventing social isolation and loneliness among older people: A systematic review of health promotion interventions. *Ageing and Society, 25*(1), 41–67.

Cattell, V., Dines, N., Gesler, W., & Curtis, S. (2008). Mingling, observing, and lingering: Everyday public spaces and their implications for well-being and social relations. *Health & Place,* 14(3), 544–61.

City Repair Project: Community Development, Permaculture, Urban Design. (N.d.). http://vbc.cityrepair.org.

Cooke, T. J. (2010). Residential mobility of the poor and the growth of poverty in inner-ring suburbs. *Urban Geography,* 31(2), 179–93.

Dakhli, M., & De Clercq, D. (2004). Human capital, social capital, and innovation: A multi-country study. *Entrepreneurship & Regional Development,* 16(2), 107–28.

De Silva, M. J., McKenzie, K., Harpham, T., & Huttly, S. R. (2005). Social capital and mental illness: A systematic review. *Journal of Epidemiology and Community Health,* 59(8), 619–27.

Francis, J., Wood, L. J., Knuiman, M., & Giles-Corti, B. (2012). Quality or quantity? Exploring the relationship between Public Open Space attributes and mental health in Perth, Western Australia. *Social Science & Medicine,* 74(10), 1570–77.

Garreau, J. (1991). *Edge Cities: Life on the New Frontier.* New York: Doubleday.

Gehl, J. (1987). *Life between Buildings: Using Public Space.* Washington, DC: Island Press.

Ivory, V. C., Collings, S. C., Blakely, T., & Dew, K. (2011). When does neighbourhood matter? Multilevel relationships between neighbourhood social fragmentation and mental health. *Social Science & Medicine,* 72(12), 1993–2002.

Kawachi, I., Kennedy, B. P., & Glass, R. (1999). Social capital and self-rated health: A contextual analysis. *American Journal of Public Health,* 89(8), 1187–93.

Kawachi, I., Kennedy, B. P., Lochner, K., & Prothrow-Stith, D. (1997). Social capital, income inequality, and mortality. *American Journal of Public Health,* 87(9), 1491–98.

Kawachi, I., Subramanian, S. V., & Kim, D. (2008). *Social Capital and Health.* New York: Springer.

Kaźmierczak, A. (2013). The contribution of local parks to neighbourhood social ties. *Landscape and Urban Planning,* 109(1), 31–44.

Kim, D., Baum, C. F., Ganz, M. L., Subramanian, S. V., & Kawachi, I. (2011). The contextual effects of social capital on health: A cross-national instrumental variable analysis. *Social Science & Medicine,* 73(12), 1689–97.

Kim, D., Subramanian, S. V., & Kawachi, I. (2006). Bonding versus bridging social capital and their associations with self rated health: A multilevel analysis of 40 US communities. *Journal of Epidemiology and Community Health,* 60(2), 116–22.

Manzo, L. C. (2005). For better or worse: Exploring multiple dimensions of place meaning. *Journal of Environmental Psychology,* 25(1), 67–86.

Manzo, L. C., & Perkins, D. D. (2006). Finding common ground: The importance of place attachment to community participation and planning. *Journal of Planning Literature,* 20(4), 335–50.

Marcus, C. C., and Francis, C. (Eds.). (1998). *People Places: Design Guidelines for Urban Open Space.* 2nd ed. New York: John Wiley & Sons.

Marmot, M. (2005). Social determinants of health inequalities. *Lancet,* 365(9464), 1099–104.

Northridge, M., Sclar, E. D., & Biswas, P. (2003). Sorting out the connections between the built environment and health: A conceptual framework for navigating pathways and planning healthy cities. *Journal of Urban Health,* 80(4), 556–68.

Olmsted, F. L. 1870. Public parks and the enlargement of towns. In: Sutton, S. B. (Ed.), *Civilizing American Cities: A Selection of Frederick Law Olmsted's Writings on City Landscape,* 52–99. Cambridge, MA: MIT Press.

Park(ing) Day. (2016). Park(ing) Day News. http://parkingday.org.

Peschardt, K. K., Schipperijn, J., & Stigsdotter, U. K. (2012). Use of small public urban green spaces (SPUGS). *Urban Forestry & Urban Greening,* 11(3), 235–44.

Portes, A. (2000). The two meanings of social capital. *Sociological Forum,* 15(1), 1–12.

Pretty, J. (2003). Social capital and the collective management of resources. *Science* 302(5652), 1912–14.

Pridmore, P., Thomas, L., Havemann, K., Sapag, J., & Wood, L. (2007). Social capital and healthy urbanization in a globalized world. *Journal of Urban Health,* 84(1), 130–43.

Project for Public Spaces (PPS). (N.d.). http://www.pps.org.

Putnam, R. D. (1995). Bowling alone: America's declining social capital. *Journal of Democracy,* 6(1), 65–78.

Putnam, R. D. (2000). *Bowling Alone: The Collapse and Revival of American Community.* New York: Simon and Schuster.

Rebar. (2005). Portfolio: Park(ing). http://rebargroup.org/parking/.

Rosenbloom, S. (2005). The mobility needs of older Americans: Implications for transportation reauthorization. In: Katz, B., & Puentes, R. (Eds.), *Taking the High Road: A Transportation Agenda of Strengthening Metropolitan Areas,* 312–38. Washington, DC: Brookings Institution..

Roulier, S. (2010). Frederick Law Olmsted: Democracy by design. *New England Journal of Political Science,* 4(2), 312–38.

Shaftoe, H. (2008). *Convivial urban spaces: Creating effective public places.* London: Earthscan.

Transgenerational Design Matters. (N.d.). http://www.transgenerational.org.

Velasquez-Manoff, M. (2013). Status and stress. *New York Times,* 27 July. http://opinionator.blogs.nytimes.com/2013/07/27/status-and-stress/.

Warren, M., Thompson, J. P., & Saegert, S. (2005). The role of social capital in combating poverty. In: Saegert, S., Thompson, J. P., & Warren, M. R. (Eds.), *Social Capital and Poor Communities,* 1–28. New York: Russell Sage Foundation.

Whitehead, M., & Diderichsen, F. (2001). Social capital and health: Tip-toeing through the minefield of evidence. *Lancet,* 358(9277), 165–66.

Whyte, W. H. (1980). *The Social Life of Small Urban Spaces.* Rpt. (2001), New York: Project for Public Spaces.

Wilkinson, R. G. (1996). *Unhealthy Societies: The Afflictions of Inequality.* London: Routledge.

Wooley, H. (2003). *Urban Open Spaces.* London: Spoon Press.

Young, A. F., Russell, A., & Powers, J. R. (2004). The sense of belonging to a neighbourhood: Can it be measured and is it related to health and well being in older women? *Social Science & Medicine,* 59(12), 2627–37.

PART II

THE HEALING POWER
OF BIOPHILIC DESIGN

BIOPHILIC FLOURISHING

The Role of Nature in Creating Healthy Cities

TIMOTHY BEATLEY

Cities around the world face a daunting array of challenges, pressures, and shocks, with significant implications for the long-term health and well-being of their residents—from natural disasters to the severe impacts in many cities of dirty air and water to the exacerbation of many of these health problems as a result of climate change. The design and planning challenge is great indeed, and health planning and healthy cities have understandably reemerged as an important and potent frame for the profession of city planning. Equally evident has been the emergence of new attention to the role of nature in all its forms as at least a partial antidote to many of the health challenges facing cities today. It is the main argument of this essay that enhancing, growing, and integrating new nature into cities and built environments will deliver important (and widespread) health benefits to residents of cities, as well as a host of other benefits, including extensive ecological services. Nature's health *dividend* (to borrow Judith Rodin's words about resilience) is great indeed, and in this essay I attempt to take stock of the many ways that nature in cities can help make urbanites healthier and happier, and the different stages of life and the places and scales where these benefits might manifest.

What is Urban "Nature"?

It is important to recognize that nature itself is open to different meanings and is culturally defined to a certain degree, and this is a key place to start in thinking about how urban health is positively influenced. Table 1 offers a crude effort categorizing the different forms "nature" can take in cities. What "nature" is or means is itself an open question, of course. The agenda of biophilic cities and biophilic urbanism includes both living, growing nature (trees, plants, natural ecosystems, biodiversity) found in cities and the more human-designed forms of nature, including such green buildings elements as skygardens, green rooftops, and green walls, among many others. Nature in cities also includes animals, domestic and wild (from ants to birds to coyotes),

Table 1. The many different forms of nature in cities

Types of urban nature	Examples	Evidence/benefits
Growing, living nature	Trees, flowers, greenery	Donovan et al. 2011; Troy et al. 2011; Haviland-Jones 2005
Designed living nature	Green rooftops, green walls	Lee et al. 2015
Urban ecological systems	Rivers, urban hydrology, typography, and landscapes	Appleton 1975
Water/water bodies	Rivers, oceans, shorelines	Nichols 2014; DePledge
Food-producing nature	Community gardens, community orchards	van den Berg et al. 2010
Animals, wild	Wild birds, insects, coyotes, urban wildlife	Smith 2010
Indoor nature	Aquaria, terraria	Kellert 2002
Animals, domesticated	Cats, dogs, urban livestock	
Sounds/natural soundscapes	Birdsong, katydids, tree frogs	Winterman 2013
Murals and nature-themed art	100 whaling walls	Lankston et al. 2010
Technological nature	Video, virtual windows	Kahn, Severson, & Buckert 2009
Hybrid-designed nature	Singapore Supertrees	
Others		

and a variety of forms of what Peter Kahn calls "technological nature" (digital, mechanical) (Kahn, Severson, and Ruckert 2009). And increasingly there are hybrids, such as the Supertrees of Singapore—metal-framed structures that incorporate large number of actual growing plants (and structures that function very much like real trees). These different elements of nature may vary in their health benefits, but they are all beneficial to some (and usually a considerable) degree. In this essay I am mainly concerned with the more conventional living, growing forms of nature, both remnant and human-designed.

There are many different ways to experience nature in cities, as figure 1 suggests. Nature can be experienced directly by being in and around it—for instance, hiking, picnicking, swimming, fishing, bird watching, among other forms of active engagement. There are more passive forms enjoyment, often with substantial mental and physical health benefits. Enjoying a view of the landscape out of a living room window or from an office window are examples of ocular modes of enjoyment. And a view of nature may be in the form of a panoramic scene of a forested and natural landscape, or of human-designed green rooftops. Often these aspects of enjoying nature occur simultaneously; for instance, visiting a park or hiking will also typically involve enjoying views or enjoying natural sounds. Indeed the experience of nature is multisensory,

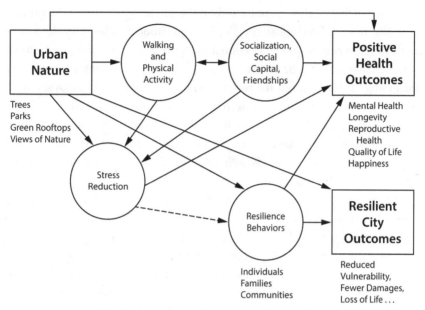

Figure 1. Biophilic cities causal path model

and we increasingly recognize the positive benefits provided by natural sound-scape, such as the positive therapeutic value of birdsong (Winterman 2013).

Proponents of biophilia, such as Stephen Kellert, have sought to categorize these different forms of nature experience in useful ways. Kellert distinguishes between direct, indirect, and vicarious or symbolic nature. A direct nature experience, according to Kellert, is one that "involves actual physical contact with natural settings and nonhuman species," in contrast to an indirect experi-ence that occurs in a more moderated or human-controlled setting such as an aquarium or zoo (Kellert 2002). A third category of nature experience identi-fied by Kellert is what he calls vicarious or symbolic nature. Images of nature in books or on television or, more importantly today, the many ways that nature is depicted and delivered in the digital realm, from computer screen-savers to virtual windows, fall into such a category. While the research is still emergent, there are important ways in which these forms of vicarious nature can deliver positive benefits, such as by reducing the stresses experienced by patients in a hospital or delivering a small but important dose of nature in an otherwise sterile work setting (e.g., DePledge, Stone, and Bird 2011).

What Nature Does for Us in Cities

These different elements of urban nature have the potential to deliver signifi-cant and important health-enhancing benefits. But a second initial question is how we define health. Here I build on the pioneering work of Aaron Antonovsky, an Israeli American sociologist, who famously offered an alternative frame of reference. Antonovsky coined the term "salutogenesis" to refer to an approach that seeks as the primary goal, not the curing of disease (or even the preventing of disease), but the promotion of good health (Antonovsky 1979, 1986). It has been a helpful counterbalance to the prevailing pathogen-based medical (and societal) view of health. In the dominant view we are dichotomous human beings—either healthy or diseased, and if the latter, we are beset by a particular illness or malady, as in the case of cancer or diabetes, requiring a particular medical intervention.

Antonovsky's salutogenic approach, on the other hand, understands human health as profoundly more complex. For him, it was a combination of factors leading to what he called Sense of Coherence: "a generalized orientation toward the world which perceives it, on a continuum, as comprehensible, manageable, and meaningful" (1986, 15). The desire and ability to cope with life's stressors seems a major part of this, and nature helps with this in so many ways. Design and planning of communities offers the chance to incorporate nature, reduce chronic stress, and advance that sense of coherence.

This comes closer to a view of health that strives for conditions of *thriving* and *flourishing*. It is a notion that understands the goal as not just absence of disease or illness, but the achievement of a meaningful, rich life; a life lived in close connection to other people and to the natural world. It is a life of caring for and about others. Nature in cities is uniquely suited to advancing this more holistic view of human health and indeed is essential to it. Flourishing is now advocated by many in the mental health and public health communities as a more appropriate goal. Keyes (2007) has identified thirteen key dimensions of flourishing mental health, including emotional well-being (high satisfaction with one's life), psychological well-being (having purpose in life, personal growth, trusting relationships) and positive social functioning (a sense of belonging, social coherence) (Keyes 2007; see also Keyes and Lopez 2002). This more holistic notion of mental (and physical) health is highly influenced, I argue, by the natural conditions and qualities of nature and by intimate, daily contact and connections with nature.

This expanded notion of health also understands the importance of personal resilience, in a modern urban world where the stresses and pressures are significant and often overwhelming. A healthy urban life, and a life of flourishing, is a life lived in resilient response to, and healthy adaptation to and coping with, the many challenges contemporary life throws at us. Resilience has now been widely embraced at the city level (e.g., the Rockefeller 100 Resilient Cities), and for planners and designers resilience is a desired condition and outcome at individual, family, and larger institutional settings. There is now a voluminous and growing literature on resilience, and many different definitions are offered (e.g., Beatley 2009). Healthy individuals and healthy communities exhibit strong qualities of resilience.

The Power of Nature in Cities

It is a key argument of this essay that design and planning of cities must emphasize the inclusion of abundant nature. Nature, especially the growing, living nature—flora, fauna, fungi found in cities—delivers significant health benefits and lays the foundation for achieving the expanded notion of health envisioned here. Flourishing is influenced by many things, of course, but nature, and the qualities of the natural environment in which cities are situated, have special power to heal, restore, connect, and inspire, and to improve quality of life and healthy living.

The critical importance of access to nature in cities begins, for this author, with the insights of the concept of "biophilia." This term was first coined by social psychologist Erich Fromm, but it is Harvard biologist and entomologist E. O. Wilson who is largely responsible for its contemporary meaning and usage. At the core is the importance of understanding that *Homo sapiens* has evolved over millions of years in, and with, nature, and so understandably we carry it with us in our ancient brains. Wilson defines biophilia as "the innately emotional affiliation of human beings to other living organisms. Innate means hereditary and hence part of ultimate human nature" (Wilson 1984; see also Kellert and Wilson 1995; Kellert, Heerwagen, and Mador 2008). Nature is not optional but absolutely essential to leading a happy, healthy and meaningful life. Every effort at design and planning of the built environment can and must make nature, and contact with nature, a key design priority. More specifically, the biophilia hypothesis holds that we are innately drawn to and prefer elements of nature that are associated with our evolutionary success and survival: flowers, climbable trees, water, natural soundscapes. These are natural elements with which we have coevolved, and to a large degree they have been associated with our thriving and survival as a species. Prospect and Refuge, first postulated by British geographer Jay Appleton, combine to form two biophilic principles that help explain why we prefer panoramic, expansive savanna views (we can see our enemies coming and game to hunt) and places that offer hidden protection (see Appleton 1975).

There is abundant and growing evidence of the power—psychological and emotional especially—of nature, and some conflicting views remain of the

mechanisms at work here. I find compelling the framing of this subject in biophilic terms, but others, notably Stephen and Rachel Kaplan, seek to explain
the power of nature in terms of what has been called Attention Restoration
Theory (ART): that the human brain benefits from nondirected attention, the
kind one obtains from sitting under a tree or watching a cloud; and that such
nature experiences are restorative and deeply beneficial (Kaplan and Kaplan
1989). My view is that these theories need not be seen as conflictual or oppos-
ing, but together help to explain the reasons exposure to nature is so beneficial. My view of biophilic design and planning is a broad and encompassing
one that includes the many ways that viewing or experiencing nature in cities
can indeed be restorative in the senses that the Kaplans identify.

Healthy, Biophilic Cities

We have sought to integrate concepts and theories of biophilia into contemporary urban design and planning through the Biophilic Cities Project at the
University of Virginia, and most recently through the Biophilic Cities Network. We believe that the vision and goal of a biophilic city is a compelling
and powerful one, and one that when fully implemented creates the conditions for a profoundly healthy life (as well as the conditions for sustainability
and resilience).

The emerging evidence and remarkable number of studies in the last decade leave little doubt now about nature's healing power and the value of
greening cities and urban neighborhoods. More than two decades ago Roger
Ulrich's careful study of hospital patients' recovery from gallbladder surgery demonstrated the healing value of a green view from a hospital window
(Ulrich 1984). Fast-forward thirty years, and the mounting evidence is impressive. Kathy Wolf and her colleagues, for instance, have examined some 2,800
articles addressing the relationship between greenspace and health, with the
vast majority published in the last decade (e.g., Wolf and Flora 2010). While
studies that are methodologically rigorous remain few, there has been an immense level of research from a variety of disciplines validating and extending
these findings. Just a sampling of the evidence makes the case clear.

In an era of climate change, cities face a range of serious environmental
problems and challenges, and many now aspire to becoming more resilient in
the face of rising urban heat, drought, storms, and rise in sea level. Cities in the
developing world, from Delhi to Mexico City, moreover, face severe air quality, water quality and sanitation, and water supply challenges, among others.
Natural systems and features in and around cities offer the possibility of sig-

nificantly reducing the severity of these serious health threats. Urban trees and forests, green rooftops, and other urban greening strategies can reduce urban heat and air pollution, for instance (e.g.. Pugh et al. 2012). The ecological services provided by nature are important ingredients in creating healthy communities and cities.

Solving the urban health challenges in cities of the Global South is complex, and there are many culprits, including rapid and largely unregulated industrial and manufacturing growth and the rise in transportation-related pollutants. Nature's solutions here may be harder to envision, though the air pollutant–moderating potential of trees and urban forests has not been lost on planners in these cities. Novak and his colleagues at U.S. Forest Service have undertaken extensive work demonstrating the immense uptake of air pollutants by trees and forests and the resulting improvement of urban air quality; by one estimate urban trees take up some 711,000 metric tons of pollutants, providing nearly $4 billion in benefits (see Novak, Crane, and Stevens 2006).

Better air quality and more resilient environments are clear outcomes of more nature in cities, but the positive health impacts are even more pervasive. The prevalence and abundance of greenery and nature in urban neighborhoods, for instance, have been strongly associated with improved health and with lower rates of disease. In a groundbreaking 2009 Dutch study, for instance, researchers compared the extent of green space within a one-mile radius of home addresses with geo-coded electronic medical records and found the green space highly predictive of better health, controlling for socioeconomic and other factors (Mass et al. 2006). This is consistent with other studies that gauge neighborhood greenness and self-perceived health and well-being. Feda, Seelbinder, and Baek (2015) found a strong inverse relationship between stress in adolescents and proximity to parks.

A number of recent studies demonstrate the specific health benefits of urban trees and the presence of an extensive tree canopy coverage. Donovan et al. (2011) found an inverse relationship between tree canopy coverage and low baby weight, for instance, and Troy, Grove, and O'Neill-Dunne (2011) found inverse correlations between tree cover and crime. The latter received considerable popular attention, with a main conclusion that a 10 percent increase in tree canopy coverage, all else being equal, yielded a nearly 12 percent decrease in crime. In one of the largest studies to date, Karden et al. (2015) analyzed data from thirty thousand residents of Toronto (controlling for variables such as income and education) and found strong association between tree density and perceived health and reported cardio-metabolic illness. As few as ten additional trees on an urban block translate, the authors conclude, to a health profile of a resident seven years younger. The *LA Times* carried the vivid headline: "10 more trees on your street could make you feel 7 years younger" (Netburn 2015). While causality remains a question in much (or most) of this research, the sheer number of studies and the extent of the findings showing positive associations between natural elements and health is compelling and convincing. Selhub and Logan, in their book *Your Brain on Nature* (2012), do an excellent job summarizing much of this work.

The impacts of contact with nature depend on a number of factors. Bratman, Hamilton, and Dailey (2012) identify three: intensity, frequency, and duration. In the context of cities and built environments, the experience of nature may be more or less intense (visiting an immersive park where one is surrounded by sights and sounds of nature), more or less frequent (whether we see or walk by trees and greenery many times during the day, or only once or twice) and fleeting or longer-lasting when encountered. Together these factors often determine the cumulative extent of the nature experienced in urban settings. Nature experiences that are more intense, more frequent, and of longer duration, other things being equal, are likely to deliver greater health benefits, though the research continues to evolve. Recent studies, for instance, suggest that even relatively brief encounters with nature can deliver significant emotional and health benefits. University of Michigan's MaryCarol Hunter concludes that as little as ten minutes in nature, several times a week, deliver considerable reduction in stress levels (Fair 2016). A recent Australian study concludes that even forty-second micro-breaks that involved brief views of an image of a green roof (with a flowering meadow) can deliver significant benefits and restoration (Lee et al. 2015). It remains unclear how long such benefits last, but even small amounts of nature in cities—a brief view, a quick visit to a park, hearing the sound of bird—can add remarkably to quality of life and to enjoyment and health.

Biophilic cities recognize these health-enhancing benefits by investing in living nature throughout a city. The city of Vitoria-Gasteiz, capital of the Basque Country in Spain, has restored wetlands and assembled over a number of years an impressive Green Ring that encircles the city and is within visual and physical access for most residents. Cities like Oslo, Norway, and Wellington, New Zealand, have invested in the infrastructure of urban trails, making it relatively easy, by hiking or bicycling, to quickly visit natural areas. Many of our partner cities have undertaken extensive urban tree planting and urban forestry initiatives. Wellington, for instance, set the goal of planting two million new trees. Cities have set ambitious goals to increase tree canopy coverage—Melbourne has set the goal of doubling canopy coverage there by 2020.

Direct and Indirect Pathways Delivering
the Health Benefits of Nature

There are many different kinds of health benefits that nature in cities can deliver; some are more direct—as when a hike in the woods serves to reduce stress hormone levels. The considerable research in Japan around the practice of "forest bathing" shows the biophysical benefits of such a walk—this research showing that that at the end of such walks, individuals exhibit lowered levels of stress hormones (as measured by cortisol levels) and a boost to immune systems. The Japanese have become so convinced of the value of forest bathing that they have established a network of forest therapy stations in cities around the country (Wang, Tsunetsugn, and Africa 2015).

The following list attempts to show some of the many direct and indirect pathways, or ways in which protecting or integrating nature can serve to positively influence health:

- watching, seeing, listening to actual nature outside
- hiking, camping, spending time out of doors
- feeling the wind, rain, mist on one's body
- purposeful enjoyment of outdoor nature—gardening, tree planting, cleaning up garbage from a stream or beach
- participating in a nature club or organization
- watching nature through a window
- experiencing indoor nature (e.g., looking at a terrarium, aquarium, indoor green wall)
- watching images of nature on a computer screen
- reading about nature
- attending a lecture about nature
- contemplating nature or a memory of a previous experience

Investments in urban nature, for instance, urban tree planting, can deliver direct benefits but also extensive indirect benefits. Evidence suggests that in greener, more forested neighborhoods residents are more likely to engage in walking and spending time outside (e.g., Gong et al. 2014). Nature, while not the only means for doing this, is especially well suited to building social capital in cities. Trees, parks, and green elements help create urban settings in which social contact is greater and where social interaction and formation of friendships is greater. In turn these social connections and capital deliver significant health benefits. There is considerable recent evidence of the curative and health power associated with social contact and connectedness (and inversely the negative health consequences of social isolation). We know increasingly that the social realm—the patterns of social interaction and formation of friendships—strongly influences health, both in terms of holistic health and also periods of time when individuals and families experience acute health challenges. Studies show, for instance, that cancer mortality rates decline for patients who have a more extensive and deeper network of friends. A 2010 meta study (summarizing 148 separate studies, with more than 300,000 participants) concluded that social relationships had a significant effect on life expectancy (Holt-Lunstad, Smith, and Bradley 2010). The study finds a "50% increased likelihood of survival for participants with stronger social relationships," approximately the same benefit one would receive by giving up smoking, and greater than the life-expectancy benefit from exercising! And consistent with our expanded notion of health as flourishing, social connections and connectedness are key goals.

There are now a host of studies that demonstrate this clear connection between measures of health and well-being and social relationships and social capital. A recent study by researchers at the University of Michigan, looking at data from the relatively large Health and Retirement Study, indicate that people who expressed the view that they felt "connected" to their neighbors and indicated through agreement with a set of statements that their neighborhood was high in cohesiveness were less likely to have experienced a stroke (e.g., Goodyear 2013).

How cohesive a neighborhood is or feels, and how connected to neighbors and fellow residents a resident feels, are strongly indicative of positive health outcomes. And nature, and the inclusion of natural features in the design of neighborhoods, can positively influence these. One now-famous example is the neighborhood of Village Homes in Davis, California. Designed and built in the 1970s by Judy and Michael Corbett, the neighborhood is designed around a network of interconnected green spaces, with walking paths and gathering spaces throughout (Corbett and Corbett, 2010). A unique feature is its edible landscaping, with many different varieties of fruit trees found throughout the neighborhood. The neighborhood has been the subject of several studies over the years and at least one that compares the friendship patterns and tendency of residents to know their neighbors. Compared with the surrounding, more conventional suburban-style neighborhoods, residents of Village Homes knew a greater number of their neighbors. One apparent result has been greater social monitoring of activities in the neighborhood by residents and a resulting lower level of crime and break-ins compared to other nearby conventional neighborhoods (see Corbett and Corbett 2010).

So, as the bulleted list above suggests, it is helpful to keep in mind that in design and planning interventions involving nature these benefits accrue through many different potential pathways of influence. There are a host of recent studies demonstrating that the presence of trees and other forms of nature is associated with positive health benefits. We are more likely to want to walk, jog, and bicycle when we have environments that contain abundant trees and greenery. The investments in trees and urban forests that we see in cities like Wellington and New York will pay health dividends both in terms of direct improvement to those environments (e.g., cooling and shading benefits) but also more indirect effects—encouraging more time out of doors, more physical exercise and activity, and more social contact and interaction, all imparting considerable health-improving value.

A biophilic city is defined by more than the presence or absence of nature; also important is the extent of the engagement residents have with that nature, and herein lies another essential aspect of the expanded vision of flourishing life. Such an expanded definition of health must include, as we have seen, a sense of meaning and purpose in life, and engagement with nature in cities can provide much of this. Many of the mechanisms and programs through which individuals learn about and engage the natural world—whether through participating in a nature walk or joining in on a Christmas bird count or joining a family nature club, to name a few—are instances of at once fostering new meaning in life and also forming new social relationships. Connections to people happen through building new connections with nature, again with important health benefits (Koss and Kingsley 2010; O'Brien, Townsend, and Ebden 2010). Many programs in cities aimed at tree planting happen through nonprofits and voluntary organizations, such the Friends of the Urban Forest in San Francisco and Vancouver Urban Forestry, in Vancouver, British Columbia. As one Vancouver volunteer recently expressed about the ancillary social value of involvement in neighborhood tree planting: "It just makes it a more beautiful place. It makes it so people want to be outside and meeting each other" (Prokop 2016).

One of the things that nature is especially suited to delivering is a sense of awe and wonder. Awe is characterized by two characteristics, according to Keltner and Haidt (2003): vastness and accommodation. A sense of vastness might be triggered by a panoramic view, an encounter with an animal doing something remarkable (the wren climbing the tree upside down), anything that pushes us to see the vastness of a larger world that exists outside ourselves. Accommodation is the way we integrate these experiences into our mental framework of the world.

We have much work to do to facilitate that sense of awe and wonder, but the raw ingredients are there in urban environments. Indeed, one measure of a biophilic city might be the number and frequency of "moments of awe," whether this is watching an orca whale visiting a city harbor (as happens sometimes in Wellington), or a diving peregrine falcon in New York City, or nesting Vaux's swifts in Portland, Oregon, and a city can do many things to "maximize" these opportunities. It is not clear what exactly are positive health-enhancing benefits of wonder, but these experiences do seem to generate deep enjoyment and pleasure, sense of connection, enthusiasm, and perhaps a greater sense of meaning and purpose. And there is some evidence that wonder and awe might serve to reduce chronic stress, as one recent study suggests that our sense of time is altered and slowed when we experience episodes of awe, and we also experience greater levels of satisfaction (Rudd et al. 2012).

It is an interesting open question how health is affected or influenced by caring and empathy for others, a behavior enhanced by biophilic cities. There is some intriguing research suggesting that when physicians are trained to develop more empathy for their patients, the patients actually experience lower levels of stress (Higgins 1979). There appear to be important health-enhancing benefits, then, from empathy and caring. A flourishing life, in our expanded view of health, is one where individuals do indeed care about and often actively care for others. And in biophilic cities this sense of empathy and caring extend to other forms of life, whether birds or other urban wildlife or domestic pets. Much of the motivation behind urban wildlife coexistence and the development in a number of cities of bird-friendly design guidelines stems from a deep sense of caring about these other forms of life and a deep ethical belief in their intrinsic value and inherent worth. These are important values irrespective of their health benefits, but it is worth noting the importance of empathy and caring to an expanded notion of health as flourishing.

And there is now growing evidence that in the presence of nature we tend to exhibit more generosity (e.g., Weinstein et al. 2015). Evidence also suggests that we are likely to be more cooperative in the presence of nature (Zelenski, Dopko, and Capaldi 2015) and more likely to make decisions that take a longer view (e.g.. van der Wal et al. 2013). Nature seems to bring out the best in us as a species and helps cultivate many of the qualities that we seem to need in order to achieve sustainability and resilience.

The challenge of addressing the profound inequalities in health, especially in the United States, is a vexing one worthy of special mention, and an issue that investments in nature might help address. In many American cities health disparities are deeply ingrained, a function of poverty and a history of segregation and discrimination. The year 2015 witnessed a marked increase in gun violence and in homicide rates in many U.S. cities, making clear and visible the differing qualities of life and disparate levels of risk different groups in

American society experience. How can nature address the health impacts of poverty and gun violence? Early work by Kuo and Sullivan (2001) found lower crime rates as a function of greater amounts of nature. Some further studies have shown how investments in greening neighborhoods—such as planting trees in vacant lots—leads to significant reductions in crime and violence. One study by Weinstein et al. (2015) finds a strong correlation between presence of nature and time spent in nature, with sense of a close and cohesive community and in turn lower crime incidence.

Urban Nature–Health Interventions:
Design for Health at Many Different Scales

In considering the elements that make up a healthy community or city, not all of them involve nature, of course, but many do, and there are a variety of different design and planning interventions that can be effective. The following list provides a set of examples organized around scale—from the interior spaces of a building to the larger region or bioregion in which that city sits, and all of the scales between.

1. Building scale: apartment buildings/single-family homes/offices/ hotels/hospitals; green rooftops; green walls/habitat walls; biophilic materials, images, furnishings; virtual or digital nature (e.g., virtual windows, virtual sky; skygardens)
2. Site/development scale: onsite gardens or edible landscaping; butterfly gardens; rain gardens and bioswales; permeable paving; dark sky compliant lighting
3. Neighborhood scale: pocket parks; greening vacant lots; green alleys and alleyways; neighborhood tree planting; stormwater features
4. City/regional scale: rivers and waterfronts; trails and walking pathways; greenbelts and bluebelts; viewsheds, watersheds, foodsheds; dark sky ordinances

Healthy home and work environments will require an emphasis on nature given that studies suggest that more than 90 percent of the average day for most Americans is spent indoors. There are a plethora of creative interior biophilic design strategies, design concepts, and products, from carpet to furniture to lighting to features such as terraria, aquaria, interior green walls, and water features, among many others (e.g., see Kellert, Heerwagen, and Mador 2008).

An important point is to understand the value of interlocking and interconnecting natural features and elements and the need for nature at level scale and in every living environment. Just as we must look creatively to bring nature inside homes, flats, offices, and hospitals, we must include nature in the design (and retrofit) of urban blocks and neighborhoods and must extend these strategies to the citywide and regional (or bioregional) scales. A parallel to the whole-of-life nature approach is a *whole-of-city approach* that sees the value and importance of nature at all scales. The green roof or living wall is important, but so also are larger regional interventions, such as a regional trail system that permits easy walking and hiking and that allows one to move from one's neighborhood and explore larger nature and networks of biodiversity. Efforts to heal and restore citywide ecosystems—for instance, in the case of the Los Angeles River—at once provide these kinds of benefits and a framework for many neighborhood-level design decisions, connections, and investments.

The kinds of nature interventions will vary, of course, depending on the scale considered and the opportunities at hand. Neighborhood tree planting delivers incredible health-enhancing value for the money (and may literally be low-hanging fruit). Initiatives such as the Philly Orchard Project have helped establish community orchards in economically struggling and food-insecure neighborhoods in the city of Philadelphia. There is research (again) suggesting that urban nature-retrofits will deliver considerable benefits. One study of the greening of vacant lots in Philadelphia found significant reductions in gun violence compared with neighborhoods where the tree planting and lot greening had not taken place (Garvin, Cannuscio, and Branas 2013). Scaling up otherwise small-scale urban greening interventions has the potential to greatly multiply these positive effects and to provide larger ecosystem benefits and values.

Retrofitting existing urban neighborhoods to bring more nature into them is a promising partial solution to urban neighborhoods experiencing social and economic distress. American cities are famous for the extent of vacant land and lots, especially of course in the economically distressed rust belt. So-called shrinking cities, such as Cleveland and Detroit, face significant challenges in stemming the tide of population and economic decline, to be sure, but the presence of land holds much promise as a viable community asset. Many such cities have discovered the power of nature—of interventions that green and grow—to shift perceptions of these spaces, to create parks and community gathering spaces in places where they are desperately needed, and also to grow food in neighborhoods where food insecurity is high and access to healthy food low. The city of Milwaukee, for instance, through the leadership of Mayor Tom Barrett, has created the HOME GR/OWN Initiative, an attempt to gradually convert many of that city's more than 2,400 vacant sites into new pocket parks and community orchards. The city recently unveiled the first

Figure 2. Urban trails and pathways are essential to a healthy, biophilic city, as shown in this segment of Singapore's Nature Connectors.

of six planned pocket parks—Sunshine Park, on the city's North Side, where most of the vacant lots are found. A prototype and model was created through the opening of the Ezekial Gillespie Park in 2014—shaped from two vacant lots and one abandoned house.

The ability to walk and hike in a city represents an important category of planning and design interventions. Facilitating walking and other forms of physical activity are an important counterpoint to health impacts of physical inactivity, but walking in outside nature should be a priority in healthy cities. One study by the UK charity MIND, for instance, compared the effects on mood from a walk in an inside shopping mall compared with a walk in nature. Not surprisingly they found significant mood enhancements in the nature walk, consistent with the forest bathing and other research. There are many things that cities can do to enhance these opportunities, and opportunities exist at every scale. Many cities have developed and are expanding networks of trails and pathways, often tying urban centers to existing parks, such as Singapore's Park Connectors (figure 2) and Rio de Janeiro's TrilhaCarioca (see Beatley 2016).

Imagining truly natural and biophilic cities will require us in some ways to go beyond the standard view of urban greening interventions. We need to re-imagine the very nature of what a city is and aspire to a more radical vision of immersive nature. Singapore, a partner city in the Biophilic Cities Project, has recently changed its motto from Garden City, to City In a Garden. This subtle

Figure 3. ParkRoyal Hotel is a living building that integrates nature throughout and re-flects Singapore's vision of a City in a Garden.

but profound shift imagines urban nature as enveloping rather than as a place that one visits or travels to. Overcoming the urban-nature divide remains a challenge, but increasingly cities are following Singapore's lead. Melbourne, for instance, recently adopted a forest plan ambitious in scope—with a goal of doubling its canopy coverage by 2020 and seeking to implement a vision of a City in a Forest (rather than of trees in the city).

Singapore is perhaps the city that has been most able to bring this vision of immersive nature to fruition. Official policy supports and in some cases man-dates nature be designed into every structure and neighborhood (a landscape replacement policy requires new buildings, at a minimum, to replace ground-level nature with vertical nature—in the form of green facades, vertical plant-ers and green rooftops, skygardens, and so forth. The results are spectacular, such as the ParkRoyal Hotel (figure 3), designed by local firm WOHA. And the building actually provides more than 200 percent of the lost ground-level nature in the form of vertical greening.

One of our most powerful biophilic pulls is water, and a feature that for many cities is pervasive and immersive and represents special health-enhancing opportunities. There have been new studies that verify the pow-erful emotional and health benefits of proximity to water. Wallace J. Nichols, from the California Academy of Sciences, writes compellingly in his book *Blue Mind* about the many ways that contact with water can heal, sooth, and connect (Nichols 2015). This book summarizes the emerging neuroscience around water and makes a strong case for finding every possibility to include water in our design and planning. Indeed, proximity to water, the sight and sounds of water, has been a widely acknowledged biophilic quality. The draw and pull of remarkable urban spaces, such as Paley Park in New York City, demonstrate viscerally the therapeutic power of water. Physical and visual access to water are important health-enhancing biophilic qualities. Cities like New York have in recent years sought to expand physical access, through the creation of new waterfront parks, for example. Richmond, Virginia, is undertaking similar steps through a new riverfront master plan that highlights the river there—the James—as the city's central park and is working to expand physical and visual connections to the river (City of Richmond 2013).

A *whole-of-city* perspective on nature and health suggest taking a hard look at the many different ways that built environments influence or provide access to or enjoyment of nature. Light and sound are two additional important considerations. Some forms of sound, noise in particular, have been associated with a variety of negative health effects (e.g. Shepherd et al. 2010), and as our appreciation of the importance of good sleep to overall health continues to grow (e.g., Jackson, Redline, and Emmons 2015), more effective control of noise becomes an important goal. Investing in nature can at once help moderate or control noise (with trees and greenery dampening the sounds of cars and roads) but also enhance the natural soundscape that serves as a health-enhancing asset in cities. Elsewhere I have argued for the need to design and plan to enhance natural soundscapes in cities (see Beatley 2013).

Light pollution represents another emerging health threat in urban settings. As cities have grown, so also has their light footprint and pervasive sky-glow, interrupting restful sleep for many and disconnecting us from the night sky. Light proliferation has many negative consequences, including wasteful energy consumption, and increasingly studies identify negative impacts on other species of life (e.g., for bats see Hale et al. 2015). Biophilic cities understand the value of connecting to the nature and wildness of the night sky, and support dark sky lighting restrictions and other efforts to control light pollution and its negative environmental and health consequences. It is a parallel set of issues to sound/noise and another example of how the urban nature agenda and community health agenda can productively dovetail.

Nature's Design for Health at Different Ages and Phases of Life

The positive impacts of having nature in our communities vary at different phases and times of life but provide important experiences and resources at *every* phase of one's life. This suggests that a key aspect of the future vision of healthy cities is the notion of a "whole-of-life" perspective on exposure to nature. Nature is beneficial and indeed essential to a healthy life at every phase, from childhood through adulthood to retirement and older age.

There is a growing body of thinking and research, for instance, demonstrating how access to nature is an essential element in growing up as a healthy, resilient child. Rich Louv has argued passionately about the importance of a childhood spent in nature, and in many ways he is responsible for igniting a national (and international) discussion about the problem of the child-nature disconnect, through his book *Last Child in the Woods* (2007; see also Louv 2011).

The emerging research supports Louv's concerns about the importance of nature in a healthy childhood. Some of this research looks, for example, at the role of play and the need for exposure to natural play experiences and settings. New research from the University of British Columbia demonstrates the value of play experiences that connect kids with trees and nature and that entail a certain degree of risk. These natural elements of playgrounds have been growing in popularity and provide an unusual degree of choices and opportunities to test, explore, and learn in ways that more conventional playgrounds (and playground equipment) provide. In the words of University of British Columbia researcher Mariana Brussoni, "We found that play environments where children could take risks promoted increased play time, social interactions, creativity and resilience. . . . These spaces give children a chance to learn about risk and learn about their own limits" (UBC, 2015).

There is now considerable research showing that kids exposed to nature reap considerable cognitive benefits. Some studies have shown a correlation between day-lit schools, schools designed to draw in full spectrum natural daylight, and increased test scores. One recent study, published in the journal *Environment and Behavior,* shows how a walk in nature, contrasted with a walk in a more hard-surfaced, nature-less urban setting, enhances so-called executive functions in kids aged four to five and seven to eight (Schutte, Torquati, and Beattie, 2015). Recent work by Li and Sullivan found that high school students did better on attention scores when in a room with window with a natural view, as opposed to a view of a parking lot or building facade (Li and Sullivan, 2016).

Nature remains important to living a healthy adult life, and there are special concerns about the negative health outcomes associated with contemporary work environments, where much time is spent indoors, sitting, and often in the absence of natural light or greenery. Sitting is now commonly described as "the new smoking," and there is growing awareness of the health implications of sedentary work patterns and settings. New research is demonstrating that even modest improvements in the nature of work environments—providing windows and natural daylight, for example—yield significant increases in productivity, and presumably happiness and health. Breaking out of the indoor work box, encouraging more outdoor walks and exercise, a practice now encouraged in some work settings, delivers significant health benefits.

Equally true, nature holds special power for enhancing health and well-being for older individuals. Elders in cities face special health challenges that nature can help address. We know, for example, that the extent of physical activity declines with age (Watson et al. 2016), and social isolation is a serious concern (Nicholson 2012). Social isolation is health-impacting by definition but also serves to put elders at greater risk of death from heat waves. More nature in cities can directly influence some of these risk factors, such as by reducing heat loads in urban neighborhoods through cooling and shading. Nature also seems to hold special power to both encourage more physical activity and also provide necessary social interaction and an important element of meaning and purpose as one ages. Gong et al. (2014) found in their study of residents over sixty-six years old a strong correlation between extent of walking and the extent of greenery in a neighborhood. Anecdotal evidence further confirms the research findings. Consider, for instance, Jane Rau, cofounder of the McDowell Sonoran Preserve, a now more than thirty-thousand-acre desert and park in Scottsdale, Arizona. Rau is in her early nineties and is very active in the preserve—clearing trails, leading school groups, generally maintaining a very active engagement in the life of the preserve, delivering for her both physical activity and social engagement and connection.[1]

Conclusions and Future Directions

I have argued here that nature can deliver significant and sustained positive benefits to health and well-being. Few aspects of city life, and few urban interventions, will have more influence on the flourishing of urbanites than investments in nature. The research and evidence is growing, and though the pathways of influence remain to be fully sorted out, the evidence is increasingly compelling and convincing. This essay has also argued that there are many kinds of nature experiences that can enhance physical and mental health—some within buildings, many outside; some very human designed, such as vertical green walls, other elements, such as birds and urban wildlife, less so. There are many different design and planning strategies and interventions,

from neighborhood gardening and tree planting to larger region-wide investments in protecting and growing nature. To obtain the full positive effects
of nature in cities it is necessary to implement a comprehensive, multiscaled
approach—from rooftop (or room) to region or bioregion. There are especially promising opportunities to retrofit many urban environments to expand
nature and to deliver new and important health benefits.

Each city and metro area will have its own unique set of opportunities to
protect, restore, retrofit, and design for new nature and natural elements. And
it is a worthy long-term goal for advocates of cities to reimagine these spaces
and places of immersive nature—of neighborhoods and urban environments
where residents don't go to visit the park or the garden or the forest so much,
but live within these enveloping forms of nature.

Consistent with this point, I have argued for an approach to urban nature
that is both *whole-of-city* and *whole-of-life*. To reap the full benefits of nature,
health, and well-being requires exposure over the entire physical space and
scales of the city, and over the course of one's life from childhood through
adulthood to older age. The precise form of emotional and health benefits we
garner may be different at different stages of life, but they are no less essential
at every stage.

Technological changes, moreover, offer promising new ways to understand
and study the health impacts of spending time in nature. The proliferation of
personal smartphones, and associated apps to go with them, has resulted in
many new ways to understand how and where people are enjoying nature,
what they feel and see, and how they react to this nature, geo-coded and in real
time. As an example, the Mappiness Project in the UK has provided some of
the largest data in support of the sense of well-being that people enjoy when
in natural settings (some 60,000 people have participated). For Mappiness
Project participants one optional step is to take a photo of where you are and to
upload that image. More generally the emergence of many new citizen science
initiatives provides new ways for individuals to feel connected to nature and
to other people (perhaps). Another technological innovation is the use of portable EEG caps in evaluating human brain response to natural and other urban
settings. There is considerable potential in the future then to be able to better
understand the specific urban nature qualities, conditions, and interactions
that seem to be the most beneficial. Roe and her colleagues have been pioneering the use of portable brain scans in this way, yielding important insights
and reconfirming the importance of nature in cities (e.g., Aspinall et al, 2015).

The connections between health, nature, and urban resilience will un-
doubtedly continue, and this represents an important trend and opportunity
in the future. Cities will be hotter, will be more prone to droughts, and will ex-

perience greater frequency and severity of severe weather events in the future. In response, there has been much needed attention to the idea of urban resilience in recent years—few terms and terminology have captured the planning and design world so quickly. The Rockefeller Foundation 100 Resilient Cities initiative is one indication of the emergence of this new framing. Under this initiative a hundred cities are each receiving a million dollars to underwrite the development of resilience capacity and specifically to hire in each city a chief resilience officer, whose job will be to think about how resilience can be expanded. Increasingly, resilience and health will go hand-in-hand in urban planning and design, and investments in nature will be understand as especially effective strategies for enhancing urban resilience and for delivering a variety of positive health benefits, including safety from floods, storms, and other natural disaster events.

Despite the growing sense of the power of nature to help communities and cities become healthier, some serious obstacles remain. Some are political, some are economic, some are perceptual. The urban-nature bifurcation remains a potent obstacle, for example. A failure to fully understand or to possess an accounting of the health and other benefits of nature has also been an obstacle. The costs associated with conservation, restoration, and new designed nature (e.g., green walls and rooftops) are typically upfront, which is sometimes an obstacle, even though they provide a relatively quick payback period.

While the public and private costs of nature investments remain an obstacle, it is worth emphasizing that these investments in urban nature pay remarkable dividends. Marc Berman, coauthor of the Toronto tree study, notes that planting ten additional trees per block involves a very modest expense for most cities ($500–$3,000), with remarkable health and well-being benefits (Netburn 2015). Few things that planners and elected officials can do will deliver greater bang for the buck.

Keyes (2007) argues, moreover, that achieving a mental health goal of flourishing will also have other health benefits and is an especially effective way to reduce the high cost of medical care. Mentally healthy individuals have fewer chronic health conditions. "In short, complete mental health—that is, flourishing and the absence of mental illness—should be central to any national debate health care coverage and costs. Rather than focusing all discussions around health care delivery and insurance, the nation must also increase and protect the number of individuals who are healthy, driving down the need for health care" (Keyes 2007, 102). A flourishing population, living in flourishing biophilic cities, holds the best hope of reducing our immense and growing health care costs.

Achieving more nature in cities, working toward the whole-of-city and whole-of-life vision, will require the good work of many different stakeholders, professionals, and different disciplinary perspectives. Roadway engineers are perhaps understandably concerned mostly about the quick movement of cars, with less natural affinity for accommodating wildlife (e.g., designing roadways for wildlife crossings). Architects, while increasingly supportive of green design, may not be fully supportive of some of the new aesthetics of building in the vision of a city in a garden. Richard Hassell, cofounder of WOHA, which designed the ParkRoyal Hotel in Singapore, pointed this out in a recent interview with the author. He explains that the building "seems to offend people who really . . . have this idea of architecture as something very pristine and clean and geometric."

There also remain some important open questions that require additional research and scholarship. One such question involves how much nature we need to be healthy. Some studies indicate that even very small amounts of exposure to nature—a few minutes outside, or a passing, occasional view of nature through a window—can have significant positive effects. Yet how long these effects last remains unclear, as does whether the full benefits of a nature-immersed life can accrue through such limited exposure. There are broader and deeper ways in which connections to nature and other living creatures can foster greater meaning in life, something that does seem associated with a healthy life, and a healthy life at different stages of life, yet these benefits are still in need of greater attention and study.

Several of these questions go to the heart of what we actually mean by nature. In the biophilic design literature and emerging practice, especially in architecture, there is appreciation for the beneficial effects of design that incorporate natural shapes, forms, images, and materials. Use of wood and stone, for instance, or incorporation of tree or fern shapes in the design of interior and exterior spaces might serve in important ways to connect us to the natural world. Many of us who advocate for biophilic design and planning believe these natural qualities and nature-like elements insert a measure of joy and connection, but the actual physical and psychological benefits are more uncertain and less established in the literature. Structures that include abundant natural daylight and fresh air and greenery clearly provide demonstrable, positive health benefits, but for other biophilic features—for instance, use of wood and stone or artwork that references the natural world—the extent of the benefit is less clear. More research is needed to fully understand the power and import of the many kinds and expressions of nature that may appear in our cities of the future.

Note

1. See the YouTube interview we conducted with McDowell Sonoran Conservancy co-founder Jane Rau at *https://www.youtube.com/watch?v=TKyDIgFERBQ.*

References

Alcock, I., White, M. P., Wheeler, B. W., Fleming, L. E., & Depledge, M. H. (2013). Longitudinal effects on mental health of moving to greener and less green areas. *Environmental Science and Technology*, 48(2), 1247–55.

Antonovsky, A. (1979). *Health, Stress and Coping.* San Francisco: Jossey-Bass.

Antonovsky, A. (1996). The salutogenic model as a theory to guide health promotion. *Health Promotion International*, 11(1): 11–18.

Appleton, J. (1975). *The Experience of Landscape.* New York: John Wiley & Sons.

Aspinall, P., Mavros, P., Coyne, R., & Roe, J. (2015). The urban brain: Analysing outdoor physical activity with mobile EEG. *British Journal of Sports Medicine*, 49(4), 272–76.

Beatley, T. (2009). *Planning for Coastal Resilience: Best Practices for Calamitous Times.* Washington, DC: Island Press.

Beatley, T. (2011). *Biophilic Cities: Integrating Nature into Urban Design and Planning.* Washington, DC: Island Press.

Beatley, T. (2013). Celebrating the Natural Soundscapes of Cities. Nature of Cities blog, January 13. http://www.thenatureofcities.com/2013/01/13/celebrating-the-natural -soundscapes-of-cities/.

Beatley, T. (2016). The Value of Urban Trails. Nature of Cities blog, January 31. http://www .thenatureofcities.com/2016/01/31/the-value-of-urban-trails/.

Bratman, G. N., Hamilton, J. P., & Daily, G. (2012). The impacts of nature experience on human cognitive function and mental health. *Annals of the New York Academy of Sciences*, 1249, 118–36.

Bullen, J. (2015). More trees on your street help you feel younger. *Sydney Morning Herald*, July 9. http://www.smh.com.au/nsw/more-trees-on-your-street-help-you-feel-years -younger-20150708-gi7t3u.html.

Cave, D. (2012). Lush walls rise to fight a blanket of pollution. *New York Times*, April 9. http://www.nytimes.com/2012/04/10/world/americas/vertical-gardens-in-mexico-a -symbol-of-progress.html?_r=2&partner=rss&emc=rss&.

City of Richmond, VA. (2013). *Riverfront Master Plan.* http://www.richmondgov.com /planninganddevelopmentreview/riverfrontplan.aspx.

Corbett, M., & Corbett, J. (2010). *Designing Sustainable Communities: Learning from Village Homes,* Washington, DC: Island Press.

Depledge, M. E., Stone, R. J., & Bird, W. J. (2011). Can natural and virtual environments be used to promote improved human health and wellbeing? *Environmental Science & Technology*, 45(11), 4660–65.

Donovan, G. H., Michael, Y. L., Butry, D. T., Sullivan, A. D., & Chase, J. M. (2011). Urban trees and the risk of poor birth outcomes. *Health and Place*, 17(1), 390–93.

Fair, D. (2016). Issues of the Environment: The 'Nature Pill' and Its Benefits to Mental Well-

Being. *Morning Edition,* NPR, January 27. http://wemu.org/post/issues-environment
-nature-pill-and-its-benefits-mental-well-being#stream/0.

Feda, D. N., Seelbinder, A., & Baek, S. (2015). Neighborhood parks and reduction in stress
among adolescents: Results from Buffalo, New York. *Indoor and Built Environment,*
24(5).

Garvin, E. C., Cannuscio, C. C., & Branas, C. C. (2013). Greening vacant lots to reduce vio-
lent crime: A randomised controlled trial." *Injury Prevention,* 19(3), 198–203.

Gong, Y., Gallacher, J., Palmer, S., & Fone, D. (2014). Neighbourhood green space, physical function and participation in physical activities among elderly men: The Caerphilly
Prospective study. *International Journal of Behavioral Nutrition and Physical Activity,*
11(40). doi:10.1186/1479-5868-11-40.

Goodyear, S. (2013). Liking your neighbors could help prevent you from having a stroke.
Atlantic Cities, September 19.

Hale, J. D., Fairbrass, A. J., Matthews, T. J., Davies, G., & Sadler, J. P. (2015). The ecological impact of city lighting scenarios: Exploring gap crossing thresholds for urban bats.
Global Change Biology, 21(7), 2467–78.

Haviland-Jones, J., Rosario, H. H., Wilson, P., & McGuire, T. R. (2005). An environmental
approach to positive emotion: Flowers. *Evolutionary Psychology,* 3(1).

Heschong Mahone Group, Inc. (2003). *Windows and Offices: A Study of Office Worker Performance and the Indoor Environment.* Prepared for the California Energy Commission.
http://www.energy.ca.gov/2003publications/CEC-500-2003-082/CEC-500-2003-082-A
-09.PDF.

Higgins, H. M. (1979). Empathy Training and Stress. PhD diss., University of British Columbia.

Holt-Lunstad J., Smith, T. B., & Layton, J. B. (2010) Social relationships and mortality risk:
A meta-analytic review. *PLoS Med* 7(7), e1000316.

Jackson, C., Redline, S., & Emmons, K. M. (2015). "Sleep as a potential fundamental contributor to disparities in cardiovascular health. *Annual Review of Public Health,* 36, 417–40.

Jiang, B., Chang, C.-Y., & Sullivan, W. C. (2014). A dose of nature: Tree cover, stress reduction, and gender differences. *Landscape and Urban Planning,* 132, 26–36.

Kahn, P. H., Severson, R. L., & Ruckert, J. H. (2009). The human relation with nature and
technological nature. *Current Directions in Psychological Science,* 18(1), 37–42.

Kaplan, K., & Kaplan, S. (1989). *The Experience of Nature: A Psychological Perspective.* Cambridge: Cambridge University Press.

Karden, O., Gozdyra, P., Misic, B., Moola, F., Palmer, L. J., Paus, T., & Berman, M. G. (2015).
Neighborhood greenspace and health in a large urban center. *Scientific Reports,* 5, article
no. 11610. doi:10.1038/srep11610.

Kellert, S. (2002). Experiencing nature: Affective, cognitive and evaluative development in
children. In: Kahn, P., & Kellert, S. (Eds.), *Children and Nature: Psychology, Sociocultural
and Evolutionary Investigations,* Cambridge, MA: MIT Press.

Kellert, S. R., Heerwagen, J. H., & Mador, M. L. (Eds.). (2008). *Biophilic Design: The Theory,
Science, and Practice of Bringing Buildings to Life.* Hoboken, NJ: John Wiley & Sons.

Kellert, S., & Wilson, E. O. (1995). *The Biophilia Hypothesis.* Washington, DC: Island Press,
Shearwater Books.

Keltner, D., & Haidt, J. (2003). Approaching awe—A moral, spiritual, aesthetic emotion.
Cognition and Emotion, 17(2), 297–314.

Keyes, C. L. M. (2003). Complete mental health: An agenda for the 21st century. In: Keyes, C. L. M., & Haidt, J. (Eds.), *Flourishing: Positive Psychology and the Life Well-Lived*. Washington, DC: American Psychological Association.

Keyes, C. L. M. (2007). Promoting and protecting mental health as flourishing: A complementary strategy for improving national mental health. *American Psychologist, 62*(2), 95–108.

Keyes, C. L. M., & Lopez, S. J. (2002). Toward a science of mental health: Positive directions in diagnosis and interventions. In: Lopez, S. J., & Snyder, C. R. (Eds.), *Handbook of Positive Psychology*. Oxford: Oxford University Press.

Koss, R. S., & Kingsley, J. Y. (2010). Volunteer health and emotional wellbeing in marine protected areas. *Ocean and Coastal Management, 53*(8), 447–53.

Kuo, F. E., & Sullivan, W. C. (2001). Aggression and violence in the inner city: Effects of environment via mental fatigue. *Environment and Behavior, 33*(4), 543–57.

Lee, K. E., Williams, K. J. H., Sargent, L. D., Williams, N. S. G., & Johnson, K. A. (2015). 40-second green roof views sustain attention: The role of micro-breaks in attention restoration. *Journal of Environmental Psychology, 42*, 182–89.

Li, D., & Sullivan, W. C. (2016). Impact of views to school landscapes on recovery from stress and mental fatigue. *Landscape and Urban Planning, 148*, 149–58.

Louv, R. (2008). *Last Child in the Woods: Saving Our Children from Nature-Deficit Disorder*. Chapel Hill, NC: Algonquin Books.

Louv, R. (2012). *The Nature Principle: Reconnecting with Life in a Virtual Age*. Chapel Hill, NC: Algonquin Books.

Mass, J., Verheij, R. A., Groenewegen, P. P., de Vries, S., & Spreeuwenberg, P. (2006). Green space, urbanity, and health: How strong is the relation? *Journal of Epidemiology and Community Health, 60*(7), 587–92.

Netburn, D. (2015). 10 more trees on your street could make you feel 7 years younger. *LA Times,* July 23.

Nichols, W. J. (2015). *Blue Mind: The Surprising Science That Shows How Being near, in, on, or under Water Can Make You Happier, Healthier, More Connected, and Better at What You Do*. New York: Back Bay Books.

Nicholson, N. R. (2012). A review of social isolation. *Journal of Primary Prevention, 33*(2–3), 137–52.

Novak, D. J., Crane, D. E., & Stevens, J. C. (2006). Air pollution removal by urban trees and shrubs in the United States. *Urban Forestry and Urban Greening, 4*(3–4), 115–23.

O'Brien, L., Townsend, M., & Ebden, M. (2010). "Doing something positive": Volunteers' experiences of the well-being benefits derived from practical conservation activities in nature. *VOLUNTAS: International Journal of Voluntary and Nonprofit Organizations, 21*(4), 525–45.

Prokop, J. (2016). Friends of Trees looks to branch out: Nonprofit wants to boost Vancouver's tree canopy. *Vancouver Columbian,* January 3. http://www.columbian.com/news/2016/jan/03/vancouver-friends-of-trees-look-onward-upward/.

Pugh, T. A. M., MacKenzie, A. R., Whyatt, J. D., & Hewitt, C. N. (2012). Effectiveness of green infrastructure for improvement of air quality in urban street canyons. *Environmental Science & Technology, 46*(14), 7692–99, doi:10.1021/es300826w.

Rudd, M., Vohs, K. D., & Aaker, J. (2012). Awe expands people's perception of time and enhances well-being. *Psychological Science, 23*(10), 1130–36.

Schutte, A. R., Torquati, J. C., & Beattie, H. L. (2015). Impact of urban nature on executive functioning in early and middle childhood. *Environment and Behavior, 49*(1), 1–28.

Selhub, E. M., & Logan, A. C. (2012). *Your Brain on Nature: The Science of Nature's Influence on Your Health, Happiness and Vitality.* New York: John Wiley & Sons.

Shepherd, D., Welch, D., Dirks, K. N., & Mathews, R. (2010). Exploring the relationship between noise sensitivity, annoyance and health-related quality of life in a sample of adults exposed to environmental noise. *International Journal of Environmental Research and Public Health, 7*(10), 3579–94. doi:10.3390/ijerph7103580.

Smith, R. (2010). Bird song "may calm" children receiving injections. *Telegraph* (London), August 24.

Spaulding Rehabilitation Network. (2013). Spaulding Rehabilitation Hospital unveils its state-of-the-art new hospital to the public. http://spauldingrehab.org/about/news -events/Spaulding-Hospital-Unveils.

Troy, A., Grove, J. M., & O'Neill-Dunne, J. (2012). The relationship between tree canopy and crime rates across an urban-rural gradient in the greater Baltimore region. *Landscape and Urban Planning, 106*(3), 262–70.

Ulrich, R. S. (1984). View through a window may influence recovery from surgery. *Science, 224*(4647), 420–21.

University of British Columbia (UBC). (2015). Risky outdoor play positively impacts children's health: UBC study. UBC News, June 9. https://news.ubc.ca/2015/06/09/risky -outdoor-play-positively-impacts-childrens-health-ubc-study/.

van den Berg, A. E., van Winsum-Westra, M., de Vries, S., & van Dillen, S. M. E. (2010). Allotment gardening and health: A comparative survey among allotment gardeners and their neighbors without an allotment. *Environmental Health, 9*, 74–86.

van der Wal, A. J., Schade, H. M., Kabbendam, L., & van Vugt, M. (2013). Do natural landscapes reduce future discounting in humans? *Proceedings of the Royal Society B, 280*(1773).

Wang, H., Tsunetsugu, Y., & Africa, J. K. (2015). Seeing the forest for the trees. *Harvard Design Magazine,* no. 40.

Ward, L. (2014). A tree-filled atrium to inspire patients: Farrow Partnership Architects created an indoor forest before digital fabrication came of age. *Architect,* July 29. http://www .architectmagazine.com/technology/detail/a-tree-filled-atrium-to-inspire-patients_o.

Watson, K. B., Carlson, S. A., Gunn, J. P., Galuska, D. A., O'Connor, A., Greenlund, K. J., & Fulton, J. E. (2016). Physical inactivity among adults aged 50 years and older—United States, 2014. *Morbidity and Mortality Weekly Report (MMWR), 65*(36), 954–58.

Weinstein, N., Balmford, A., DeHaan, C. R., Gladwell, V., Bradbury, R. B., & Amano, T. (2015). Seeing community for the trees: The links among contact with natural environments, community cohesion, and crime. *BioScience, 65*(12), 1141–53. doi:10.1093/biosci/biv151.

Wilson, E. O. (1984). *Biophilia.* Cambridge, MA: Harvard University Press.

Winterman, D. (2013). The surprising uses for birdsong. BBC News Magazine, May 8. *http://www.bbc.com/news/magazine-22298779.*

Wolf, K. L., & Flora, K. (2010). Mental health and function—A literature review. In: *Green Cities: Good Health.* Urban Forestry/Urban Greening Research, College of the Environment, University of Washington. http://www.greenhealth.washington.edu.

Zelenski, J. M., Dopko, R. L., & Capaldi, C. A. (2015). Cooperation is in our nature: Nature exposure may promote cooperative and environmentally sustainable behavior. *Journal of Environmental Psychology, 42*, 24–31.

CAN NATURE BE A
HEALTH INTERVENTION?

JUDITH H. HEERWAGEN

An expanding body of research shows that nature nurtures. Being in a natural environment or viewing nature through the window reduces stress, enhances emotional experience, and supports cognitive performance.

People everywhere seek out landscapes with large trees, flowering plants, animals, water, and views to the horizon from places of refuge. But even small spots of nature—a flower garden or a grove of trees—also delight. Our connection to nature has many faces and many ways to create positive experiences in our homes, offices, backyards, or common spaces.

Yet in many locations across the United States and in other countries, rapid urbanization is reducing opportunities for contact with the natural environment. Open spaces are being replaced by buildings, and urban neighborhoods are losing lawn space, trees, and small parks to buildings that pay little heed to the way everyday nature benefits human health and well-being. Distant views and daylight are blocked by ever-taller structures and greater density to the point where only those few citizens who live or work in tall buildings have views of natural amenities. What are the consequences of these dramatic changes in the urban landscape? How do we encourage building practices that integrate nature experience, rather than eliminating it?

This essay identifies key benefits of nature and addresses how nature can be integrated into urban settings to improve quality of life and health. But first it is useful to discuss key findings from the extensive literature on the benefits of human contact with the natural world.

What Kinds of Nature Matter Most?

This section summarizes key findings organized around the aspects of nature that affect human experience, including urban green space, water, gardens, distant views, and views of nature from indoor spaces.

Urban Green Space

A major study in The Netherlands of health outcomes linked to urban green space found benefits of nature contact, especially for green space within one kilometer of home (Maas 2009). The study was able to use an extensive national database of health linked to doctor's visits and health assessments. The study analyzed data separately for socioeconomic status (SES) and age groups. High-level findings include the following:

- Within urban environments, those closer to green space have higher perceived general health and report fewer health problems.
- Green space is important for health for all age groups.
- Those who benefit most from green space within one kilometer of their homes are the elderly, children, and those in low SES households due to their reduced mobility.
- Less green space was also associated with greater feelings of loneliness and perceived shortage of social support.

A detailed assessment of "disease clusters" in The Netherlands research also found a connection to green space, with clusters more prevalent in areas with less green space. The research revealed that the rate of disease in seven categories was lower for people living within one kilometer of a park or greenway.

The study concludes that green space is more than a luxury. It serves as a buffer for negative life events and should be equitably distributed to all urban inhabitants.

Other smaller-scale research projects have found similar outcomes, including improvements in emotional functioning and reductions in stress associated with exercising (walking, running, biking) in outdoor green spaces. Hartig et al. (1991) found that people who went for a walk in a predominantly natural setting performed better on an editing task than those who walked in a predominantly built setting or who quietly read a magazine indoors. Performance was assessed by number of errors found in the text and corrections implemented.

In a review article, Thompson and colleagues (2011) found that people who exercised outdoors experienced more positive moods, greater feelings of rejuvenation, more energy, and a reduction in negative moods (such as tension, anger and depression) compared to people who exercised indoors. Outdoor exercisers also reported greater intention to repeat the activity. None of the studies assessed measured physical health and well-being.

Barton and Pretty (2010) also conducted a multistudy analysis of the impact of green exercise on mental health. The studies they analyzed included

1,252 participants. All ten research studies assessed self-esteem and mood as indicators of mental health. Barton and Petty found both improved self-esteem and mood for those who exercised in urban green space. The largest effects were for short-duration exercise, with decreasing benefits (but still positive) with longer-duration exercise bouts. Green spaces with water had increased positive impacts.

Nearby Nature

In many urban environments, the experience of nature is close to home. Grassy areas with trees, rather than expansive greenways, become an important component of the urban environment and its potential to positively influence health and well-being.

Studies of natural spaces adjacent to public housing projects in Chicago by Kuo, Sullivan, and colleagues from the University of Illinois (Kuo & Faber Taylor 2004; Kweon et al. 1998) found multiple benefits from having large trees close at hand. Using behavioral observations and interviews, the researchers found that housing developments with large trees attracted people to be outdoors, and once there, they talked to their neighbors and developed stronger social bonds than people in similar housing projects without green space and trees. Furthermore, children in housing projects with large trees showed reduced levels of attention deficit hyperactivity disorder than children in similar projects lacking trees. The researchers concluded that providing "green time" for children may be an important supplement to medicine and behavioral therapies. The research from these studies contributed to the creation of the most extensive tree-planting program in Chicago's history.

Nearby nature can also influence the character of children's play. In an observational study of play sessions in kindergarten children during recess at a neighborhood school, Kirkby (1989) found that children playing in a small cluster of shrubs had longer play bouts, engaged in more imaginative play, and were more collaborative than children playing on typical playground equipment, who engaged in more aggressive play in shorter bouts.

Gardens and Gardening

Both active and passive contact with gardens provides psychological, emotional, and social benefits. Marcus and Barnes in their book *Healing Gardens* (1995) show that benefits of gardens include recovery from stress, having a place to escape to, and improved moods. Benefits also occur with horticulture therapy, especially in clinical settings and nursing homes. Other studies provide evidence that dementia and stroke patients show improved mobility and dexterity, more confidence, and improved social skills as a result of gardening activities (Rappe 2005).

According to Ulrich (2002), gardens are more likely to be calming and to ameliorate stress if they contain rich foliage, flowers, a water feature, congruent nature sounds (bird songs, moving water), and visible wildlife, particularly birds. Given the popularity of flowers and flower gardens, there has been surprisingly little research on the potential benefits. However, a series of experiments by Haviland-Jones and others (2005) explored the emotional response to flowers. The researchers used a similar paradigm in three related experiments. They presented people with gift of a flower or another item (such as a pen or an orange). The researchers recorded the recipient's facial expressions and comments. The results showed that only the recipients of the flower showed a "true smile"—one that engages the zygomatic muscles in the cheek and the small muscles around the eye. The true smile is considered a valid indicator of emotional pleasure.

Nonliving Natural Elements

Although the vast majority of research on the human benefits of nature focus on living organisms (trees, flowers, varied plants), nature also consists of nonliving elements that have life-like properties (such as movement, temporal changes, and seasonal variability) that can have significant effects on human well-being. These elements include daylight, water, and fire.

Daylight

We have known for a long time that people prefer daylight environments and that they believe daylight is better for health and psychological functioning than is electric light (Heerwagen and Heerwagen 1986). However, a clear delineation of the health and well-being benefits of daylight are relatively recent.

With many urban environments becoming canyons of darkness, it is important to address the impact of this situation on our physical and psychological well-being We are learning now that bright daylight has medicinal properties. It entrains circadian rhythms, enhances mood, promotes neurological health, and affects alertness. The benefits of sunlight can be experienced in even brief walks outdoors on a sunny day or through design of spaces that integrate daylight and sun into the interior.

Because we are a diurnal species, light plays a critical role in our sleep-wake cycles, and it also synchronizes numerous physiological processes from temperature regulation to hormone production. Although we can now alter our activity cycle with the use of electric light, research evidence suggests that typical indoor light is sufficient for seeing, but not for circadian health without supplementation from daylight or additional electric light designed for circadian functioning (Figueiro et al. 2017).

Research in hospital settings has looked at the relationship between room daylight levels and patient outcomes. Benedetti and others (2001) found that bipolar patients in bright, east-facing rooms stayed in the hospital 3.67 fewer days on average than those in west-facing rooms. Similar results were found by Beauchamin and Hays (1996) for psychiatric in-patients. Those in the brightest rooms stayed in the hospital 2.6 fewer days on average. However, neither of these studies provide data on the actual light levels in the patient rooms or light entering the retina, so it is difficult to draw conclusions about exposure levels.

More recent research in a Pittsburgh hospital actually measured room brightness levels. Walch and others (2005) studied 89 patients who had elective cervical and spinal surgery. Half of the patients were located on the bright side of the hospital while the other half were in a hospital wing with an adjacent building that blocked sun entering the rooms. The study team measured medication types and cost as well as psychological functioning the day after surgery and at discharge. The researchers also conducted extensive photometric measures of light in each room, including light levels at the window, on the wall opposite the patient's bed, and at the head of the bed (which presumably would have been at or near the patient's eye level). The results showed that those in the brighter rooms had 46 percent higher intensity of daylight. Patients in the brightest rooms also took 22 percent less analgesic medicine per hour and experienced less stress and marginally less pain. This resulted in a 21 percent decrease in the costs of medicine for those in the brightest rooms. The mechanisms linking bright light to pain are currently unknown.

Water

Given the importance of water to human life, studies of human experience and preferences for different aspects of water are surprisingly scarce. In fact, most landscape preference studies omit water from visual stimuli because researchers believe that water features are so emotionally powerful that they dwarf response to other aspects of the landscape. Nonetheless, available research shows that people respond very positively to specific features of water—sparkle, reflections, and surface movements (Coss and Moore, 1990). Coss and Moore suggest that early humans may have used visual sparkle, in particular, as a cue to the location of water. Sparkle can be seen in the distance, whereas reflections and water surface movement can only be seen on closer inspection. Reflection and movement may have been used as indicators of water quality.

Our biological attachment to water is reflected in the frequent inclusion of water features in or adjacent to buildings. Of special interest is how water features are created and displayed to evoke positive affordances and qualities and to reduce the negative affordances. Water can be soothing as well as terrifying. It can be calm and gently flowing or rampaging and destructive. It can be crystal clear or turgid and foul smelling.

To be aesthetically appealing, water elements should emphasize the features of water that are the best indicators of water quality, safety, and usefulness. Clarity, gentle flow, reflectivity, and shallowness (to reduce potential for drowning) are positive features most likely to be replicated in buildings. Water features across time have emphasized these very qualities in fountains and reflection pools.

The value of water is also evidenced in studies of real estate value. Realtors have long known that market prices of houses are strongly influenced by access to water. Quantitative investigations reveal how much (Benson et al. 1998). Data from 6,949 home sales from 1984 through 1993 in Bellingham, Washington, show that water frontage increased the value of a home by 26 percent compared to a comparable nonview, nonfrontage home. An unobstructed view of Bellingham Bay added 58.8 percent to the market price of a home, whereas a mountain view added only 8.9 percent to value. Distance to water also influenced market prices. A home with a full ocean view sold for a premium of 68 percent if it was located within one-tenth of a mile from the bay, a premium of 56 percent if located half a mile from the bay, a 45 percent premium if one mile from the bay, and a 30 percent premium if two miles from the bay (Benson et al. 1998).

The desire for proximity to water is creating conflicts across the country as real estate development is encroaching on public beaches and blocking access for the general public. Thus the benefits of water for well-being may be diminishing as access itself diminishes.

Fire

Research on biophilia seldom includes discussion of fire. Yet fire has been a powerful safety and social benefit across time. Prior to the use of fire, early humans used caves primarily for sleeping and were likely to have stayed close to the entry for rapid escape when necessary (Klein 1983). Fire provided protection at the mouth of the cave, particularly at night. With multiple hearths the interior of the cave could be heated and made visible for social activities.

Rolland (2004) argues that control of fire enabled not only protection but also rapid social development. Eating, sleeping, socializing, caring for infants and juveniles, ceremonial activities, and tool making could all take place in one primary and safe site, thereby "favoring the transmission of knowledge and behaviors through prolonged learning by the young of shared and transmitted technological, socio-economic and cognitive repertoires" (Rolland 2004, 263). Konner (1982) also speculates that control of fire and its use as a focal point in evening social life resulted in a "quantum advance in human communication: a lengthy, nightly discussion, perhaps, of the days events, of plans for the next day, of important occurrences in the lives of individuals and in the cultural past, and of long term possibilities for the residence and activity of the band" (50).

Fire also allowed people to see others' gestures and facial expressions that are central to communication and social understanding, and portable fire enabled deep spaces in caves to be used for ritual activities. Torches aided movement through the dark recesses of caves and provided sufficient and dramatic light for dance, music, painting, and other activities that accompanied rituals. In the absence of fire, early humans probably slept as soon as the sun went down because social interaction would have generated noise that could have alerted predators or hostile humans to the group's location.

Although there is little research on fire as a well-being amenity, we know that fire is used to increase the appeal of social settings. Campfires are common across time. Their modern counterparts—the fireplace, the backyard grill, and candlelight dinner—are integral parts of socializing and eating. Technologies are making it possible to extend the socializing to outdoor spaces even when the night gets chilly.

Compensating for Lack of Connection with Nature

Murals and paintings of flowers, foods, and animals have been used in buildings for thousands of years and continue to be a common practice today either through formal art programs or informal adaptations by occupants. A walk through any workplace today is likely to show offices and cubicles adorned with visual décor provided by the occupants. Given that these items are self-selected with the intention of enhancing the appeal of personal space, it is worth asking what types of visuals are used.

In contrast to most studies of workspace personalization that do not identify the subject matter of the personal decor, windowless spaces devoid of contact with the outdoors should be more likely to have nature decor than windowed spaces (Heerwagen and Orians, 1986).

Results showed that occupants of windowless rooms used twice as many items (primarily posters and photos) to decorate their offices than those in windowed offices (193 items vs. 82) and three times as many nature-dominant visual materials (134 vs. 45). Those in windowless offices also used three times as many surrogate views (96) compared to occupants of windowed offices (where there was a total of 32 surrogate views.) Furthermore, the majority of the posters and photos were placed directly in the field of view, where they could be seen from the desk as people were working.

The windowless office research was conducted before digital technologies and computer-generated displays were readily available. So it is worth asking: can display technologies further enhance the view from windowless spaces, and is a digital view as good as the real thing? Peter Kahn and colleagues at the University of Washington have explored this question in a series of experiments comparing the stress-reducing impacts of a real window view with the same view provided by a video camera connected to a plasma display screen or no window at all (Kahn et al. 2008).

The study investigated the effects of the three different conditions on recovery from stress induced by performing moderately complex tasks. Each subject was exposed to one of the three experimental conditions while completing the various tasks. Two outcome variables were assessed: heart rate and amount of time spent gazing up at the window, the plasma screen, or the wall. The results showed that subjects in the real window condition showed significantly greater heart rate recovery than subjects in either the plasma window or no window condition. There were no differences in heart rate recovery between the plasma screen and no window conditions.

The data on gaze also showed that subjects looked at the real window and plasma screen just as often, but they spent more time overall looking out the real window. Furthermore, the more time looking out the window, the greater the subjects' heart rate recovery. The researchers suggested that the differences in gazing time may be due to what it means for an image to be "real" versus "representational."

The Mechanisms of Impact

Benefits of contact with nature are found in multiple settings, multiple cultures, and across the age span, from early childhood to late adulthood (Heerwagen, Kellert, and Mador 2008; Maas, 2009). Furthermore, contact with nature can be purely visual or multisensory, active engagement (walking, running, gardening) or passive (viewing through a window).

Multiple methods—from cortical activation studies using fMRI to heart rate monitoring, behavioral observations, archival data collection, and surveys—all point to the same conclusion. Sensory connection with positive nature has consistent health and well-being benefits. I use the term "positive nature" specifically to separate it from nature contact that can be stressful and frightening, such as threatening animals, storms, or other natural hazards (Ulrich 1993).

The literature discussed in the previous sections identifies three key categories of benefits: physiological, cognitive, and emotional.

Stress Reduction

Measures of stress have included both subjective surveys and physiological measures including cortisol levels, heart rate measures, muscle tension, blood pressure, skin conductance, and brain electrical activity (Bratman, Hamilton, & Daily 2012).

Ulrich (1993) was the first to explore the stress-reducing effects of nature in experimental laboratory settings. His research paradigm included both subjective assessments of mood and physiological measures of stress including skin conductance, muscle tension, systolic blood pressure, and heart rate. To induce stress, Ulrich frequently showed stressful films, and immediately afterward he randomly assigned study participants to view slides or videos of everyday nature scenes versus urban scenes without nature. Results consistently showed that the nature scenes reduced stress more rapidly when viewing nature scenes or urban scenes with nature than urban scenes with no natural vegetation. Ulrich argues that contact with nature reduces stress and enhances emotional functioning as a result of autonomic generation of physiological and psychological responses (Bratman, Hamilton, & Daily 2012).

Studies of experience in actual landscapes and urban settings rather than the laboratory support Ulrich's laboratory studies on stress reduction (Park et al. 2007; Hartig et al. 1991).

Cognitive Benefits

The most widely cited area of cognitive benefits focuses on the attentional system, drawing on Attention Restoration Theory (ART) proposed by Kaplan and Kaplan (1989). ART distinguishes between two types of attention first proposed by William James. "Voluntary attention," required for most cognitive tasks, is effortful and can be easily depleted, resulting in fatigue. In contrast, "involuntary attention" causes attention to shift without conscious effort to something that is perceived as interesting or valuable. Involuntary attention is inherently less demanding and results in less fatigue than voluntary attention. Kaplan and Kaplan argue that connection with nature taps into the involuntary attention process and thus allows the directed attention system to rest, enabling people to refocus easily after short nature breaks.

Tests of predictions from Attention Restoration Theory have generally shown good support (see Bratman, Hamilton, & Daily 2012). Researchers have used various techniques to induce directed attention and mental fatigue after which participants were exposed to either a nature or urban environment. The exposure conditions vary and have included walks, window views, or slides of nature versus urban environments. After the experimental treatment, participants are tested again on mentally demanding tasks. In the studies cited in Bratman, Hamilton, and Daily (2012), participants who experienced the nature treatment performed better, which supports the prediction that they had experienced attentional rest and recovery.

The other leading hypothesis regarding the mechanisms by which nature yields cognitive benefits is proposed by Ulrich (1993). Ulrich argues that nature contact improves cognitive performance, not directly but through impacts on affective functioning. He draws heavily on research by Isen (1990) linking positive moods to improved performance on tasks requiring creative problem solving. In numerous experiments, Isen's research shows that subjects in positive moods perform better on tests of creative problem solving than those who are in neutral or negative moods. Isen speculates that positive moods increase the tendency to "break set" and to see relatedness between divergent events or appearances. Feeling good promotes diffuse rather than focused attention, and this leads people to see things differently (e.g., to notice more details) or to search more broadly for solutions and alternative interpretations.

Joseph LeDoux (1996), one of the nation's leading brain researchers, cites neurological evidence to support this hypothesis. He has found that positive feelings lead to heightened activity of the right parietal brain region—the section of the brain associated with a more global, expansive cognitive style. Thus, positive feelings directly affect brain processes related to performance on tasks requiring creativity and novel problem solving.

The link between creativity and nature contact has not been as widely studied as ART. However, positive emotional functioning is a consistent finding across studies, suggesting that the link to creativity is just waiting to be studied more closely.

Emotional Benefits

As noted in many of the research studies cited so far, the experience of positive emotions is a significant benefit of contact with nature—whether contact is direct (being in a natural setting) or indirect (experiencing nature through slides, photos, or other image presentations). In contrast, urban settings without nature tend to elicit more negative mood states. And as the flower research showed, even a single flower can automatically elicit a true smile that reflects the positive experience (Haviland-Jones et al. 2005).

Two additional studies address neurological pathways of emotional experience. A study by Bratman et al. (2015) found that participants who went for a ninety-minute walk in a natural landscape experienced less rumination than study participants who went for a walk in an urban setting. Rumination, which is associated with risk for depression, was measured by self-report and by activity in an area of the brain that is associated with self-referential thought and behavioral withdrawal.

In an article on visual information processing, Biederman and Vessel (2006) identify a neural mechanism that creates feelings of pleasure with visual scenes that aid the acquisition of new information. Landscape scenes with broad views, hidden vantage points, and elements of "mystery" (a sense that more information will be available with movement) consistently increased stimulation of mu-opiod receptors in the brain compared to landscapes with lower information processing. This result is consistent with the research showing positive emotional experience associated with being in a pleasant natural space—especially one with the characteristics identified by Biederman and Vessel.

Implementing Biophilic Design

The evidence of the health and well-being benefits of nature is so compelling that it raises the question of why natural amenities aren't incorporated into all urban environments. In many cities, buildings are beginning to use up all available space, leading to cutting down trees and eliminating green spaces to maximize profitability of the buildings.

The research on nature benefits presented in this essay and many other publications provides a compelling case for biophilic design as a health-promoting design strategy. Yet the benefits of nature in urban settings today are not equitably distributed. Many people live and work in conditions devoid of natural amenities or comforts. If connection to nature and natural stimuli is an evolved human need, as I argue in this essay, then the benefits should be universal and not distributed only to those who can afford to live and work in pleasant natural surroundings.

The potential to promote positive health and well-being outcomes and en-hance cognitive functioning has powerful economic as well as human benefits. As Terrapin Bright Green (2012) points out in *The Economics of Biophilia*:

> Implementing biophilic design into our workplaces, health care system, edu-cational environments and communities is not just a nice amenity. It has pro-found economic benefits. It is now imperative that we bring nature into our built environments.

Nature is beneficial to all, regardless of age, gender, race, or ethnicity, and it should be available to all urban dwellers, not just those who can afford to live on the edges of parks and open spaces. Connection to nature on a daily basis re-inforces the values of respect and care for the environment that are prerequisites for sustainable communities and that languish when nature is remote.

What Can We Do Now?

Translating research into practical applications should be a priority for those interested in biophilic design and biophilic urban environments. Knowing that contact with nature has health benefits is necessary, but insufficient, to promoting new practices. We need both design guidance, policy changes, and examples of what works and for whom.

An example of guidance is provided by Terrapin's *14 Patterns of Biophilic Design* (Browning, Ryan, and Clancy 2014), which offers a pallet of choices for indoor and outdoor environments. The guidance is evidence based and can be used in all building types and especially in urban environments that are lacking in green amenities.

In an article focusing on the potential to deploy nature applications as a well-being intervention, Capaldi et al. (2015) argue that nature interventions may be an easier and more cost-effective way to enhance well-being in urban environments than many more common approaches. They site two specific examples that are successful and replicable. The first is the David Suzuki Foun-dation 30x30 Nature Challenge, which supports projects that provide thirty minutes of nature a day during the month of May. To date, they have found significant increases in mood and vitality among participants. The other ex-ample is the Canadian Mental Health Association's "Mood Walks" initiative, which promotes physical activity, mental health, and social connection in the natural environment. To date, it has more than thirty mental health agencies engaged.

Other examples include Chicago's street tree project, which has dramatically increased the number of trees planted, in part, due to findings from research on the benefits of nature contact. The tree-planting service web page identifies "increase in psychological well being" as one of the benefits of city trees.

There are many ways to enhance nature experience in urban settings. While there is still much to learn about nature in the city—such as the specific designs to use, the ideal "dose" of nature, how long the benefits last—there is also an urgency to start with what we know now and continue to learn by doing.

References

Beachamin, K. M., & Hays, D. (1986). Sunny hospital rooms expedite recovery from severe and refractory depression. *Journal of Affective Disorders, 40*(1–2), 49–51.

Barton, J., & Pretty, J. (2010). What is the best dose of nature and green exercise for improving mental health? *Environmental Science and Technology, 44*(10), 3947–55.

Beneddetti, F., Colombo, C., Barbini, B., Campori, E., & Smeraldi, E. (2001). Morning sunlight reduces length of hospitalization in bipolar depression. *Journal of Affective Disorders, 62*(3), 221–23.

Benson, E. D., Hansen, J. L., Schwartz, A. L., Jr., & Smersh, G. T. (1998). Pricing residential amenities: The value of a view. *Journal of Real Estate Finance and Economics, 16*(1), 55–73.

Biederman, I., & Vessel, E. A. (2006). Perceptual pleasure and the brain. *American Scientist, 94,* 249–55.

Boubekri, M., Hulliv, R. B., & Boyer, L. L. (1991). Impact of window size and sunlight penetration on office workers' mood and satisfaction: A novel way of assessing sunlight. *Environment and Behavior, 23*(4), 474–93.

Bratman, G. N., Hamilton, J. P., Hahn, K. S., Daily, G. C., & Gross, J. J. (2015). Nature experience reduces rumination and subgenual prefrontal cortex activation. *Proceedings of the National Academy of Sciences, 112*(28), 8567–72.

Bratman, G. N., Hamilton, J. P., & Daily, G. C. (2012). The impact of nature experience on human cognitive function and mental health. *Annals of the New York Academy of Sciences, 1249,* 118–38.

Browning, W. D., Ryan, C., & Clancy, J. O. (2014). *14 Patterns of Biophilic Design: Improving Health & Well-Being in the Built Environment.* New York: Terrapin Bright Green.

Capaldi, C. A., Passmore, H. A., Nisbet, E. K., Zelenski, J. M., & Dopko, R. L. (2015). Flourishing in nature: A review of the benefits of connection with nature and its application as a wellbeing intervention. *International Journal of Wellbeing, 5*(4), 1–16.

Coss, R. G., & Moore, M. (1990). All that glistens: Water connotations in surface finishes. *Ecological Psychology, 2*(4), 367–80.

David, E. L., & Lord, W. B. (1969). Determinants of Property Values on Artificial Lakes. Department of Agricultural Economics, University of Wisconsin–Madison.

Fjeld, T., Veiersted, B., Sandvik, L., Riise, G., & Levy, F. (1998). The effect of indoor foliage plants on health and discomfort. *Indoor and Built Environment, 7*(4), 204–9.

Figueiro, M., Steverson, B., Heerwagen, J., Kampschroer, K., Hunter, C. M., Gonzales, K., Plitnick, B., & Rea, M. S. (2017). The impact of daytime light exposures on sleep and mood in office workers. *Sleep Health, 3*, 204–15.

Hartig, T., Bringslimark, T., & Patil, C. G. (2008). Restorative environmental design: What, when, where and for whom. In: Heerwagen, Kellert, & Mador, *Biophilic Design*.

Hartig, T., Evans, G., Jammer, L., et al. (2003). Tracking restoration in natural and urban field settings. *Journal of Environmental Psychology, 23*(2), 109–203.

Hartig, T., Mang, M., & Evans, G. (1991). Restorative effects of natural environment experience. *Environment and Behavior, 23*(1), 3–26.

Haviland-Jones, J., Rosario, H. H., Wilson, P., & McGuire, T. R. (2005). An environmental approach to positive emotion: Flowers. *Evolutionary Psychology, 3*(1), 104–32.

Heerwagen, J. H. (2006). Investing in people: The social benefits of sustainable design. Paper presented at *Rethinking Sustainable Construction 2006*, Sarasota, FL, September 19–22.

Heerwagen, J. H., & Heerwagen, D. (1986). Lighting and psychological comfort. *Lighting Design and Application, 16* (4), 47–51.

Heerwagen, J. H., Kellert, S. R., & Mador, M. (Eds.). (2008). *Biophilic Design: The Theory, Science and Practice of Bringing Buildings to Life*. New York: John Wiley & Sons.

Heerwagen, J. H., & Orians, G. H. (1986). Adaptation to windowlessness: A study of the use of visual décor in windowed and windowless offices. *Environment and Behavior, 18*(5), 623–29.

Isen, A. (1990). The influence of positive and negative affect on cognitive organization: Some implications for development. In: Stein, N. L., Leventhal, B., & Trabasso, T. (Eds.), *Psychological and Biological Approaches to Emotion*. Hillsdale, NJ: Erlbaum.

Kahn, P., Friedman, B., Gill, B., Hagman, J., Severson, R. L., Freier, N. G., Feldman, E. N., Carrere, S., & Stolyar, A. (2008). A plasma display window? The shifting baseline problem in a technologically mediated natural world. *Journal of Environmental Psychology, 28*(2), 192–99.

Kaplan, R., & Kaplan, S. (1989). *The Experience of Nature*. Cambridge: Cambridge University Press.

Kaplan, S. (1995). The restorative benefits of nature: Toward an integrated framework. *Journal of Environmental Psychology, 15*(3), 169–82.

Kirkby, M. A. (1989). Nature as refuge in children's environments. *Children's Environments Quarterly, 6*(1), 7–12.

Klein, R. G. (1983). The Stone Age prehistory of Southern Africa. *Annual Review of Anthropology, 12*, 25–48.

Konner, M. (1982). *The Tangled Wing: Biological Constraints on the Human Spirit*. New York: Holt, Rinehart & Winston.

Kuo, F. E., & Faber Taylor, A. (2004). A potential natural treatment for Attention-Deficit/Hyperactivity Disorder: Evidence from a national study. *American Journal of Public Health, 94*(9), 1580–86.

Kuo, B. S., Sullivan, W. C., & Wiley, A. R. (1998). Green common spaces and social interaction of inner-city older adults. *Environment and Behavior, 30*(6), 832–58.

LeDoux, J. (1996). *The Emotional Brain*. New York: Simon and Schuster.

Leather, P., Pygras, M., Beale, D., & Lawrence, C. (1998). Windows in the workplace: Sunlight, view and occupational stress. *Environment and Behavior*, 30(6), 739–62.

Lohr, V. I., Pearson-Mims, C. H., & Goodwin, G. K. (1996). Interior plants may improve worker productivity and reduce stress in a windowless environment. *Journal of Environmental Horticulture*, 14(2), 97–100.

Luttik, J. (2000). The values of trees, water, and open space as reflected by house prices in The Netherlands. *Landscape and Urban Planning*, 48(3–4), 161–67.

Maas, J. (2009). *Vitamin G: Green Environments — Healthy Environments*. Utrecht: Netherlands Institute for Health Services Research.

Marcus, C. C., & Barnes, M. (1999). *Healing Gardens: Therapeutic Benefits and Design Recommendations*. New York: John Wiley & Sons.

McMahan, E. A., & Estes, D. (2015). The effect of contact with natural environments on positive and negative affect. *Journal of Positive Psychology*, 10(6), 507–19.

Pretty, J., Peacock, J., Sellens, M., & Griffin, M. (2005). The mental and physical health outcomes of green exercise. *International Journal of Environmental Health Research*, 15(5), 319–37.

Rappe, E. (2005). *The Influence of a Green Environment and Horticulture Activities on the Subjective Well Being of Elderly Living in Long Term Care*. Publication 24. Helsinki: Department of Applied Biology, University of Helsinki.

Rolland, N. (2004). Was the emergence of home bases and domestic fire a punctuated event? A review of the middle Pleistocene record in Eurasia. *Asian Perspectives*, 43(2), 248–80.

Tennessen, C. M., & Cimprich, B. (1995). Views to nature: Effects on attention. *Journal of Environmental Psychology*, 15(1), 77–85.

Terrapin Bright Green. (2012). *The Economics of Biophilia: Why Designing with Nature in Mind Makes Financial Sense*. New York: Terrapin Bright Green.

Thompson Coon, J., Boddy, K., Stein, K., Whear, R., Barton, J., & Depledge, M. H. (2011). Does participating in physical activity in outdoor natural environments have a greater effect on physical and mental wellbeing than physical activity indoors? *Environmental Science and Technology*, 45(5): 1761–72.

Ulrich, R. S. (1984). View through a window may influence recovery from surgery. *Science* 224, 420–21.

Ulrich, R. S. (1993). Biophilia, biophobia, and natural landscapes. In: Kellert, S. R., & Wilson, E. O. (Eds.), *The Biophilia Hypothesis*. Washington, DC: Island Press.

Ulrich, R. S. (2002). Health benefits of gardens in hospitals. Paper presented at Plants for People Conference, International Exhibition Floriade.

Ulrich, R. S. (2008). Biophilic theory and research for healthcare. In: Heerwagen, Kellert, & Mador, *Biophilic Design*, 87–106.

Ulrich, R. S., Simons, R. F., Losito, B. D., Fiorito, E., Miles, M. A., & Zelson, M. (1991). Stress recovery during exposure to natural and urban environments. *Journal of Environmental Psychology*, 11(3), 201–30.

Walch, J. M., Rabin, B. S., Day, R., Williams, J. N., Choi, K., & Kang, J. D. (2005). The effect of sunlight on postoperative analgesic medication use: A prospective study of patients undergoing spinal surgery. *Psychosomatic Medicine* 67(1): 156–63.

NATURE AS PHYSICIAN

The Return of the Garden to High-Tech Medical Facilities

REUBEN RAINEY

The garden is returning to medical facilities in the United States and Europe.[1] Once regarded as irrelevant for health care by medical researchers and an unnecessary expense by hospital executives, the garden is reappearing as a significant complement to today's high-tech medicine. This reversal of the garden's fate in the United States is not grounded in "new age" superstitions or an intuitive "alternative" medicine, but in the rigor of scientific investigations yielding what is commonly referred to as "evidence-based design."

In 1984 Roger Ulrich, a professor of geography at the University of Delaware, published a study of the healing power of "nature" in the hospital environment that has become an authoritative model of evidence-based design among researchers seeking ways to create more humane and effective spaces for medical treatment.[2] Many design professionals are familiar with the general results of this oft-cited study, but given its sophistication and restraint, it is worth discussing in detail. The deceptively simple question Ulrich's study posed led quickly into the challenging field of neuroscience and the relationship between perception, stress, and the immune system. Ulrich asked: "Can patients' views from their hospital room windows affect their recovery from surgery?" The variables in such a study were exceedingly difficult to control, but Ulrich's methodology was both meticulous and comprehensive, judged by the standards of research in the social sciences.

His study examined the records of 46 patients who had undergone gall bladder surgery between 1972 and 1981 in a 200-bed suburban hospital in Pennsylvania. The sample excluded patients under twenty and over sixty-nine and those who had developed serious complications from the surgery or had a history of psychological disturbances. Patients were then divided into pairs, one with a room looking onto a brick wall, the other with a view of a small grove of trees. The criteria for matching the pairs were sex, age, smoker or nonsmoker, obese or normal weight, previous hospitalizations, and year of surgery. The final database considered records of 15 female pairs and 8 male pairs. Except for the differing window views, patients had identical rooms on the same floor, to which they had been assigned randomly. All were cared for by the same nursing staff, although their surgeons differed.

Ulrich had a nurse with extensive surgical floor experience review the records of all 46 patients without knowledge of which window view they had experienced. The nurse focused on three essential pieces of data: how much strong pain medication the patients consumed while in the hospital; how much they had complained to nurses; and how soon they were released from the hospital. The records spoke clearly. The 23 patients with the view of a grove of trees required less pain medication, complained less, and left the hospital almost one day earlier than the 23 with the view of the brick wall. Also, the cost of their medical care was $500 less. Ulrich's conclusion was restrained and cautious: "The results imply that hospital design should take into account the quality of patient window views."

He did not argue for causality, nor did he offer a theory explaining the effect of the tree view on the patients' quicker recovery. He even suggested that for patients in long-term care who were more bored than stressed "a lively street scene" might be more beneficial.

Ulrich was not the first to probe the effects of views in a medical environment, but his meticulous study was the most convincing one to date and inspired a large body of subsequent experiments producing evidence-based design guidelines. What was especially important about Ulrich's experiment was that he was able to demonstrate a measurable positive health outcome for patients with the window view of "nature" expressed in the form of a grove of trees. As a result, many new hospitals built in the last twenty years in the United States provide window views of nature for patient rooms (figure 1).

Drawing heavily upon the methods of the social sciences, such as interviews, questionnaires, randomized samples, statistical metrics, and on-site observation, this research is not what is known as "hard" science because it is incapable of meeting the exacting demands of convincing replication, strict control of variables, and precise quantification. Medical settings are difficult to work in. There are strict rules about patient confidentiality. No one medical facility is like another in terms of staff, setting, and patients. Also, there is always the possibility that an experiment could interfere with the medical treatment taking place. However, despite such problems, recent research is more and more approaching the rigor of hard science. Developments in neuroscience charting the dynamics of the brain's response to its environment through improved visualization technologies such as PET scans and fMRI imaging are producing a new body of evidence with the potential to guide the design of more effective and humane medical facilities. Also, using digital technology it is possible to create virtual medical facilities and test their

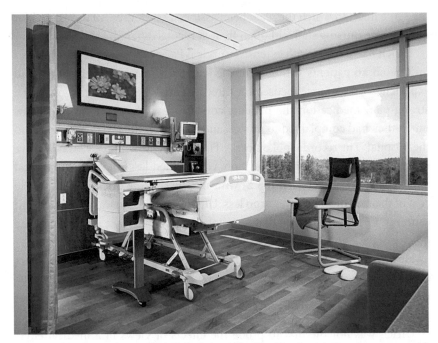

Figure 1. Shands UF Cancer Hospital, Gainesville, Florida. A typical patient room with view of a natural landscape. (UF Health, Shands)

psychological effects. Or one can use portable electroencephalography (EEG) caps to measure the response of the brain while moving through a sequence of spaces.[3] More and more such research is informing the work of landscape architects, in both the United States and abroad, commissioned to design gardens for cancer hospitals, facilities for dementia patients, children's hospitals, outpatient clinics, and centers for burn victims and other types of medical environments.

A medical facility garden is most frequently referred to as "healing" or "restorative." However, "healing" needs to be defined. In English the verb *to heal* means "to make whole." Such wholeness is psychological, physical, and social. Exposure to gardens and other forms of nature can "heal" in a physical sense in that they work together with various forms of medical care to foster recovery from illness by reducing the bad effects of stress on the immune system (Ulrich's view study is an example). Gardens can also "heal" in the more psychological sense "to make whole," by engendering feelings of calm, mental balance, and acceptance of one's situation. In some contexts, gardens "heal," but they do not "cure." A garden cannot "cure" a patient's terminal disease, but he or she will often benefit from the sense of psychological wholeness and tranquility nurtured by experiencing a garden. Finally, gardens can heal by providing a space where patients can receive social support from one another or from their families and friends.

How do these healing gardens work? Neuroscientist Esther Sternberg has insightfully discussed this question in her recent book, *Healing Spaces: The Science of Place and Well-Being*, but much remains to be discovered.[4] The most important function of gardens in medical facilities is the relief of stress. The highly damaging effect of long-term stress on the immune system has been established beyond a doubt by studies dating back to the 1930s and more recently by such scientists as Jan Kiecolt-Glaser, Ron Glaser, Sheldon Cohen, and Bruce Rabin.[5] The stress produced by hospitalization is particularly high. It is caused by loss of physical capacities, painful medical procedures, and fear and uncertainty. It is compounded by an environment that is noisy, confusing, and often invasive of privacy and lacking in emotional support. Depression, high blood pressure, and the release of potent stress-induced hormones often result. Building upon these discoveries, a host of additional researchers, including Stephen Kellert, Charles Lewis, Judith Heerwagen, Gordon Orians, Clare Cooper Marcus, Marni Barnes, Daniel Winterbottom, and Naomi Sachs have charted the positive effects of exposure to nature on human health and well-being, often with special attention to the immune system.[6] We now have convincing evidence that sustained contact with "nature," defined as plants and nonthreatening creatures, can aid the positive function of the immune system by relieving patient stress by such means as tending a plant in one's room, strolling through a fragrant garden, or simply gazing out the window at park-like scenery. Additional studies have also shown that such well-designed architectural elements as clear wayfinding systems, single-occupant patient rooms, and noise-reducing materials also can positively affect a patient's sense of well-being.[7]

Yet why is exposure to nature in the form of a garden so beneficial? Researchers have differing opinions. Most researchers define "nature" in a similar manner as "the living elements," understood as the plants and animals in the spaces they are studying. These include gardens but also larger areas such as parks or nature preserves. But here the agreement ends. Some researchers frankly admit they do not understand precisely how exposure to nature can relieve stress, but its positive results are clearly observable and can be measured. Others regard it as primarily a learned response, resulting from cultural conditioning. Others claim it to be an innate genetic predisposition, a powerful attraction and deep attachment to all living things that is an essential part of being human. This school of thought is deeply influenced by the "biophilia hypothesis" of biologist E. O. Wilson. Wilson defines biophilia as "the tendency to focus on life and lifelike processes." According to him, this tendency is encoded in our DNA: "our existence depends on this propensity, our spirit is woven from it."[8] As humans we need contact with nature to feel secure. It is essential to our well-being, and when we are deprived of it we suffer stress. This attraction to living things, plants and creatures of all sorts, is a result of the evolution of the human brain and body shaped by almost two million years of dwelling in the habitat of African savannah landscape, which enabled ancient humans to survive.[9] Many designers of gardens in healthcare facilities accept the biophilia hypothesis as a valid explanation for the stress-relieving power of gardens. So do many planners seeking to foster contact with nature in a large variety of ways in the design of cities. Tim Beatley's essay on biophilic cities provides an example of this point of view. This theoretical position is often referred to as "stress reduction theory" or SRT. Its supporters claim there is a large body of experimental evidence supporting it.[10] However, it remains controversial, especially in its claim for the encoding of the savannah habitat experience in our DNA. Opponents claim the evidence of this is not convincing. For them, positive reactions to nature are a learned response, accounted for by cultural transmission.[11]

Still other researchers understand the positive effects of nature in terms of a theory based on cognitive psychology. This second theoretical position is grounded on the work of environmental psychologists Rachael and Steven Kaplan and their followers. This position is often characterized as Attention Restoration Theory or ART.[12] According to the Kaplans and others, our brain becomes fatigued and stressed by a certain kind of mental activity and is restored by encounters with nature. This theory places more emphasis on exposure to nature as a means of renewing the mind's ability to focus on demanding tasks than on relieving stress caused by these tasks. It views the brain as a kind of muscle that becomes fatigued by a certain type of mental activity known as "directed attention." Today's highly technological society frequently demands such directed attention, which takes many forms. Examples include operating complex machinery, writing technical reports, or auditing financial statements. This kind of mental work requires intense concentration, and if it continues for a long period of time it results in fatigue and stress that can lead to mistakes and poor execution of work. For example, physicians and nurses are constantly required to perform tasks demanding directed attention and are at risk for errors and poor judgment when subjected to long periods of work. Patients and their families also can be affected, especially when they attempt to understand the technical language of medical diagnosis and complex medical procedures. For the Kaplans and others, such mental fatigue and the stress that accompanies it can be helped by what they call "indirect attention," which leads to what they call "the restorative experience." "Indirect attention" is effortless and involuntary. It can occur through many types of activities, but immersion in natural environments such as parks and gardens is especially effective. A casual stroll through a garden or simply sitting in it or even viewing it out a window can relieve the symptoms of prolonged directed attention and restore one's ability to concentrate on the demands of "directed attention." Often this kind of restorative experience can occur in a very short period of time, no more than ten to fifteen minutes. The Kaplans also claim, based on a large body of experiments, that for a garden or other type of natural environment to have effective restorative power, it needs to provide a feeling of "being away" from one's routine surroundings. It also needs to instill a sense of fascination and connection to a larger whole. Finally, it should be extensive enough to evoke a desire to explore. For a garden or other type of natural environment to produce these psychological feelings effectively it needs to exhibit in its design form "coherence," "legibility," "complexity," and "mystery." Coherence allows you to make sense of the garden. Complexity adds an aesthetic richness that keeps it from being boring. Legibility allows you to understand its complexity and decipher it. Finally, mystery attracts your attention and draws you to it.[13]

Thus the question "Why is exposure to nature beneficial?" remains unresolved. However, what is established beyond a doubt is, for whatever reason, exposure to nature can be powerful medicine. Numerous case studies of a wide range of medical facilities by Elizabeth Brawley, Nancy Gerlach-Spriggs, Sam Bass Warner Jr., Roger Ulrich, Gordon Orians, Judith Heerwagen, David Winterbottom, and others have shown just how powerful and transformative that medicine can be.[14] We may not know why nature works this way, but we can most certainly observe its positive benefits and measure them. Thus gardens are like aspirin. Physicians do not fully understand how aspirin works, but because of its many benefits they would never withhold it from patients. The same logic applies to gardens. It makes no sense to delay including them in healthcare facilities just because we have at present no agreed-upon theory of why they relieve stress and improve cognitive ability.

Why did healing gardens all but vanish from medical facilities in the United States, where once they were regarded as important? This history is long and complex, involving the close interrelationship between medical science, medical practice, and the spaces deemed best for the art and science of healing. A few highlights must suffice.

The narrative most relevant to Europe and the United States begins with the eighteenth- and early nineteenth-century pavilion hospital, a new type of facility that included healing gardens and was situated in a park-like setting (figure 2). The design of these hospitals was a response to the theory that

Figure 2. Charité Hospital, Berlin. A nineteenth-century pavilion hospital sited in a park-like setting.

all disease was caused by "miasmas," or odors produced by decaying matter, such as corpses, wounds, garbage, and human and animal waste. Given the lack of a germ theory of disease, infection still killed a large percentage of patients in these hospitals, but new hygienic practices lowered the mortality rates substantially. To counter the destructive effect of miasmas, hospitals were to be thoroughly clean, sunlit, cross-ventilated, and accessible to gardens. Physicians believed sunlight purified miasmas, while the leaves of trees filtered them from the air. The typical hospital plan consisted of low-rise pavilions with large windows for sun exposure and long hallways for cross ventilation. Beds were widely spaced in wards and located near the window bays. Gardens were either enclosed in courtyards or surrounded the entire hospital with flowerbeds and spacious lawns studded with trees to form a campus-like setting. Florence Nightingale, a British nurse, was a leader in these developments.

In the late nineteenth century, a most profound shift in hospital design resulted from the discoveries of scientists led by Louis Pasteur and Robert Koch, who developed the germ theory of disease. Infection by microorganisms, a major problem of all medical facilities, could now be dealt with decisively. Surgeons and nurses adopted antiseptic practices and advocated the design of hospitals that were easy to sanitize, often using tile and chrome materials. More and more patients were isolated in single rooms to avoid contagion. The rapid rise of specialization, following German medical practice, also meant that patients were often shuttled from physician to physician over long distances in large, centralized, high-rise medical complexes designed for efficiency and economy. At the same time, new medical theories, deeply influenced by laboratory scientists rather than practicing physicians, embraced the mistaken notion that the human immune system was unaffected by the patient's perception of the medical environment. The gardens and grounds of the old pavilion hospital were now judged irrelevant to treatment and therefore seen as dispensable costly frills. The exception was mental hospitals, which continued to employ gardens as therapeutic work spaces or places of repose for agitated patients.[15]

These new high-rise, high-tech facilities offered vastly improved medical care, but this came at a cost. Those easy-to-clean materials amplified noise, a major source of patient stress. Being shuffled from one specialist to another down long and confusing corridors created anxiety. Contact with one's physician was often too brief to allow for a meaningful discussion of one's concerns. "Sterile" in an aesthetic sense was the predominant character of patient rooms and waiting areas, as if operating rooms had become the norm for the entire hospital—which in a sense they had. In brief, the high-tech twentieth-century medical environment was becoming more stressful for staff and patients alike.[16]

However, the new research on the immune system and its relationship to the environment has recently launched a new era in medical facility design, and as a result the garden has begun to reappear along with a host of other stress-reducing architectural elements, such as noise reduction, soothing color schemes, simpler wayfinding systems, exposure to views, engaging sculpture and paintings, light-filled rooms, less sterile furnishings, and sleep sofas for a family member to stay overnight in a patient's room. The results are far fewer patient complaints and a much better working environment for physicians and staff. All of this is emblematic of a new "holistic" or "integrative medicine" combining high-tech medicine with what is called "patient-centered design."[17]

Almost all of these recent restorative gardens are a blend of science and art, with their architects and landscape architects drawing upon their own creativity and using evidence-based design data, but also with input from physicians, staff, psychologists, and patients. They are also a great design challenge, demanding a precise understanding of the specific needs of their users, the nature of their ailments, the concerns of their caregivers, and an understanding that these needs can and often will change over time. A melodious, sparkling fountain may delight children recovering from orthopedic surgery but may cause incontinence for the elderly in an adult day-care facility. It

Figure 3. Oregon Burn Center Garden. The pavilions protect sensitive skin of burn victims from direct sunlight.

simply will not do to translate an uncritical general knowledge of the pleasures of the garden for healthy individuals into a medical setting.

What this means is that the design of healing gardens must be carried out by teams and each garden tailored to address the needs of patients in a particular medical situation. There is no such thing as a "general" kind of healing garden. There are dementia sufferers' gardens, children's physical therapy gardens, cancer patients' gardens, burn victims' gardens, and many other types addressing a specific medical situation (figure 3). The design team should be composed of physicians, nurses, a landscape architect, maintenance staff, the facility's chief officer in charge of budget, and patients and their families. Physicians and staff have pressing duties and little time, so the team design process should be as brief as possible. Teresia Hazen has developed a highly effective way to implement a working system of team design that requires only three one-hour meetings.[18]

While design by a team of specialists is a necessity, it is also important to evaluate the final product of the team's effort after it is constructed. This kind of post-occupancy evaluation, or POE, is best conducted a few years after the garden has been in place. Since the medical environment is complex and frequently changes, it is difficult to create a garden that functions perfectly

Figure 4. Joel Schnaper Memorial Garden, Terence Cardinal Cooke Health Care Center, first version.

for patients and staff. Thus it is often necessary to make adjustments in a design after observing how it is used. As Clare Cooper Marcus has pointed out, these post-occupancy evaluations can vary in thoroughness.[19] The designer can interview staff and patients about their reactions to the garden, or staff can conduct the interviews. Also, teams of social scientists can more thoroughly evaluate the garden, but this is more expensive.

The fifteen-year history of the Joel Schnaper Memorial Garden illustrates the complexity and challenges of creating a successful restorative garden. The garden was specially designed to accommodate patients suffering from HIV/AIDs in the Terence Cardinal Cook Health Care Center, a large 630-bed hospital in New York City on Fifth Avenue. Sited on a rooftop, the garden is located on the sixth floor adjacent to the Discrete AIDS Unit, serving 156 "residents," as the hospital prefers to designate them (figure 4). Landscape architect David Kamp, who designed the facility in 1994, recalls its initial challenges: "The garden was a response to an emerging and largely unknown illness. That uncertainty led to a design that employed simple basic principles of flexibility, opportunity, and choice. Those principles have served the garden well over the years as our understanding of the disease, and our approach to treatment and care, has evolved."[20]

Kamp knew his first task was to consult with physicians and nurses to understand the effects of AIDS medications on patients, especially the often negative side effects, as well as the progressive nature of the disease and its treatment protocols. He also talked with the residents whenever possible to elicit their ideas for the garden and to strengthen their sense of belonging. He did not rely extensively on published evidence-based design guidelines, which were scarce at the time for HIV/AIDS patients, but trusted in careful consultation with those who would use the garden and his own ability as an experienced landscape architect.

For the hospital administrators the garden at the time was "a leap of faith." While fully supportive of the project and the use of an underutilized outdoor space, the hospital lacked the means to develop the rooftop. Funds were to be raised through private donations for the garden named in memory of a landscape architect who had died of AIDS. Built incrementally with available funds and constructed by volunteer labor, the garden required a design strategy for easy construction, including using inexpensive materials and modular elements easy to build by unskilled labor. The staff saw a need for immediacy. Time was a luxury for most of the individuals in their care. The first residents to use the garden were gravely ill, often with just weeks to live. Their conditions changed daily. They were extremely weak, and their vision was often impaired, heightening a sense of isolation and vulnerability. Depending upon their medications, they often became disoriented or developed severe reactions to varying degrees of light and shade.

Given this situation, Kamp's design emphasized palliative care under the close supervision of nurses, offering opportunity and choice to both residents and staff. Some residents could only view the garden from their rooms, but those with enough stamina to use it were afforded a welcoming bench at the entry, a fragrant plant, and a clear view of the rest of the garden to invite exploration. Kamp realized the garden needed not only to be safe, but also to be perceived as safe, if it was to offer a sense of calm and respite. The garden was divided into a series of distinctive spaces or rooms, easily accessible and understood, and connected with a very clear circulation system. All of these spaces were visible from any point in the garden, allowing full surveillance by the staff. Each room offered a different degree of protection from the elements, ranging from full sun to deep shade provided by vine-covered pavilions or lightweight tent structures. Floor tiles were smooth to allow for wheel chairs, IV poles, and walkers. A highly legible floor stencil in a decorative leaf pattern formed a path to guide individuals needing assistance into the garden and back to its entry. The abundant chairs were light enough to be easily moved to form different groupings, but secure enough to provide sup-

Figure 5. Joel Schnaper Memorial Garden, Terence Cardinal Cooke Health Care Center, second version, with more elaborate planting plan and musical performance area for patients. (Dirtworks P.C.)

port. Raised planters of varying heights were accessible from wheelchairs and walkers. The lush planting palette emphasized texture, color, and fragrance to stimulate the senses. It also served as a soothing counterpoint to the sterile hospital interior. Kamp consulted with the hospital maintenance staff and was careful to heed their concerns in his choice of materials and plants. He was acutely aware of the need for proper upkeep if the garden was to survive.

Over the next eight years more was discovered about the treatment for AIDS, and new medications prolonged life. Residents possessed more strength and stamina and could be more active in the garden. Kamp modified the garden to address the new situation, utilizing its built-in flexibility (figure 5). He expanded an area for growing vegetables and herbs to assist the program of the newly hired horticultural therapist. He added new furniture to provide for spontaneous socializing by small or larger groups and for programmed activities such as crafts and card games. An area for musical performances allowed residents to plan their own activities, introducing a much-needed sense of empowerment. Residents began to take plants inside their rooms and create small shelf gardens often containing biblical figures, playful cartoon characters, or other symbolic figures. One resident named the flowers in his room after his former women friends. This increased activity complemented the residents' medical treatment substantially, raised their morale, and resulted in fewer behavioral problems.

Figure 6. The second version of the Joel Schnaper Garden supports an enriched program of patient activities, such as horticultural therapy. (Dirtworks P.C.)

So impressed was the hospital administration with the therapeutic benefits of the garden that when the roof membrane had to be replaced in 2005 they approved the construction of a new garden built of much more expensive, durable materials designed to last twenty-five years. The new garden maintains many of the design features of the old but has a much larger musical performance area and more pavilions for various activities. The staff of the Discrete AIDS Unit noted that while the garden was out of commission during reconstruction resident morale dropped and behavioral problems increased. The garden will continue to evolve both in form and patient activities as treatment for HIV/AIDS continues to develop. Equally important, it is now open to everyone in the hospital regardless of their illness and offers a variety of new programs and activities (figure 6). A major key to its success was Kamp's acute sensitivity to changing needs of residents and staff over time and the built-in flexibility of his design to accommodate them. He continues to visit the garden to conduct his own informal post-occupancy evaluations.

Additional restorative garden types demand the same comprehensive grasp of context and careful attention to detail. A garden in a children's hospital may contain specialized play equipment, such as slides of different degrees of difficulty to challenge the children and foster recovery from orthopedic surgery. A playhouse facade may be covered in a multitude of different kinds of locks to develop digital acuity after neurosurgery. One of the most challenging gar-

Figure 7. The Life Enrichment Center, Kings Mountain, North Carolina. Spacious grounds allow for the concealment of the enclosing fence, which helps to prevent claustrophobia among dementia sufferers. (Dirtworks P.C.)

dens to design is one for dementia sufferers, and there is still much to be learned about what is and is not effective. Research has established that exposure to gardens is beneficial to dementia sufferers. They provide space for exercise, quiet their agitation, and can in some cases evoke memories supporting a patient's identity.[21] Path systems must be simple so patients will not be confused. Gardens must be as spacious as the site permits and the walls as transparent as possible to avoid feelings of claustrophobia (figure 7). Shadows cast by plants on walkways can be frightening, since they are often perceived as deep holes. The entire garden must be highly visible from the interior of the building to allow for surveillance by staff. Clearly marked entrances are essential to avoid confusion (figure 8).

Now that we know gardens do belong in hospitals, can we afford to put them there and keep them there? In today's serious situation of rapidly rising medical costs, will hospital administrators faced with tight budgets for building renovations or the construction of new hospitals be forced to remove gardens and other costlier evidence-based design features from their budgets? A recent study, "The Business Case for Better Buildings," published in the journal *Frontiers of Health Services Management,* argues persuasively that such a policy would be ill advised economically. The authors, including two hospital CEOs, an economist, and an architect, argue that including more costly yet more humane and energy-efficient design features, including healing gardens,

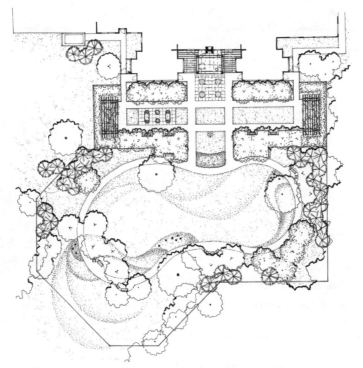

Figure 8. Plan of the Life Enrichment Center. The simple walk system helps prevent confusion among dementia sufferers. (Dirtworks P.C.)

will almost pay for themselves in a year and in the long term result in a more cost-efficient, prosperous hospital than one that does not incorporate these advances.[22] Greater patient satisfaction, fewer medical errors, less loss of staff, energy cost savings, more rapid turnover of patients, and a host of other factors will account for this.

Some highly sophisticated and successful hospitals in the United States have incorporated expensive evidence-based features in their designs, to their economic benefit, including Scripps Memorial Hospital, San Diego; The University of Florida Shands Cancer Hospital, Gainesville; St. Michael Health Center, Texarkana, Texas; and Gonda Building of the Mayo Clinic, Rochester, Minnesota. St. Michael Health Center has no fewer than seventeen different gardens for meditation, play, outdoor dining, and meetings, and they are a key element in the quality of its care and its ability to attract patients.[23]

At present in the United States, despite the economic problems of the past ten years, there is an increase in hospital construction fueled by overcrowded emergency rooms and a shortage of hospital beds, an aging population, and diminished financial investment in new and replacement hospitals in the 1990s. This presents an enormous opportunity to design more humane hospitals and other types of facilities based on the findings of evidence-based design, and gardens are a crucial part of this opportunity. The professionalism and compassion of those who staff hospitals and other types of medical facilities will always be the most important elements of outstanding health care. Yet this care deserves an environment in which it can flourish. We know how to create that environment now, and future research can only make it better. The restorative garden was once understood as being a crucial part of that healing environment. In many nations it is returning to that environment now as an ever-evolving therapeutic space informed by the latest advances in the science of healing.

However, there is much research to be done to make healing gardens more effective. Two areas of special importance are the design of gardens for sufferers of post-traumatic stress disorders and those afflicted with autism. Studies of the role of the senses, in addition to sight, in the therapeutic garden experience, such as sound, touch, taste, and smell, are also needed. Other topics are psychological responses to color and the influence of cultural tradition and memory on restorative experience in gardens. While the present evidence-based design literature is large, many experiments need to be repeated to verify their accuracy.

Yet despite the strong evidence of the positive effects of gardens on patients and staff, their future role in today's healthcare environments is not assured. They could be among the first things to be stricken from the construction budgets of today's new "leaner" healthcare facilities that are beginning to eclipse the costlier spa and resort-like hospitals of the previous decades. Recent research into patient satisfaction is becoming finer grained and has demonstrated many of these expensive design accoutrements have little influence on patients' perception of the quality of the care they receive, measured by their responses to questionnaires.[24] What matters most to them is the professionalism and compassion of their caregivers. This does not mean a well-designed environment is of minor importance, but what is becoming clearer is that certain things in this environment matter a great deal to patients and others matter very little. They highly appreciate a well-designed patient room that empowers them to control their environment and accommodate sleepovers for their family or friends. Costly, grand atria or other resort-like features appear to matter very little, although additional research is needed to replicate these findings. As researchers continue to focus on the specific design features of today's medical facilities—atria, waiting rooms, chapels, neonatal care sections, dementia units, emergency facilities, and operating suites, and so forth—the garden will be placed under the same microscope. It will be compared in terms of health outcomes and perceived patient satisfaction with other design elements, and if it does not measure up it could be dropped from the new leaner medical facilities. Staff perceptions of what features are important to their work will also be brought into the mix. In the past, credible research has clearly shown the therapeutic power of the garden. However, in today's healthcare realm of astronomically rising costs and rapid and constant change, nothing can be taken for granted. Additional research of the highest quality will be required to justify the inclusion of gardens in the medical facilities of the future.

Notes

1. Portions of this chapter were previously published in Chinese translation in *Chinese Landscape Architecture,* 31 (229) (Jan. 2015), 6–11.

2. R. S. Ulrich, "View through a Window May Influence Recovery from Surgery," *Science,* 224 (April 1984), 420–21.

3. See John Zeisel, *Inquiry by Design: Environment/Behavior/Neuroscience in Architecture, Interiors, Landscape and Planning* (New York: W.W. Norton, 2006); E. A. Edelstein, "Developing an Evidence Based Design Model That Measures Human Response: A Pilot Study of the Collaborative, Transdisciplinary Model in a Health Care Setting," in AIA College of Fellows 2005 Latrobe Fellowship (Washington, DC: American Institute of Architects, 2008), 63–132; E. A. Edelstein, "Searching for Evidence," *Health Environments Research and Design Journal, 2008,* 1(4), 40–60; Peter Aspinall, Panagiotis Mavros, Richard Coyne, and Jenny Roe, "The Urban Brain: Analysing Outdoor Physical Activity with Mobile EEG," *British Journal of Sports Medicine,* March 6, 2013, doi:10.1136/bjsports-2012-091877; M. Elen Deming and Simon Swaffield, *Landscape Architecture Research, Inquiry, Strategy, Design* (Hoboken, NJ: John Wiley and Sons, 2011).

4. Esther M. Sternberg, *Healing Spaces: The Science of Place and Well-Being* (Cambridge, MA: Belknap Press of Harvard University, 2009), 1–24.

5. Ibid., 95–99, 227–29.

6. Clare Cooper Marcus and Marni Barnes, eds., *Healing Gardens: Therapeutic Benefits and Design Recommendations* (New York: John Wiley and Sons, 1999); Clare Cooper Marcus and Naomi A. Sachs, *Therapeutic Landscapes: An Evidence-Based Approach to Designing Healing Gardens and Restorative Outdoor Spaces* (Hoboken, NJ: John Wiley and Sons, 2014); Nancy Gerlach-Spriggs, Richard Enoch Kaufman, and Sam Bass Warner Jr., *Restorative Gardens: The Healing Landscape* (New Haven, CT: Yale University Press, 1998); Judith H. Heerwagen and Gordon H. Orians, "Humans, Habitats, and Aesthetics," in Stephen R. Kellert and Edward O. Wilson, eds., *The Biophilia Hypothesis* (Washington, DC: Island Press, 1993); Charles A. Lewis, *Green Nature/Human Nature: The Meaning of Plants in Our Lives* (Chicago: University of Illinois Press, 1996).

7. R. S. Ulrich et al., "A Review on the Research Literature on Evidence-Based Healthcare Design," *Health Environments Research and Design Journal,* 2(3) (2008), 61–125. Reuben M. Rainey and Alana M. Schrader, *Architecture as Medicine: The UF Health Shands Cancer Hospital, A Case Study* (Charlottesville: University of Virginia School of Architecture, 2014).

8. Edward O. Wilson, *Biophilia: The Human Bond with Other Species* (Cambridge, MA: Harvard University Press, 1984), 1.

9. Ibid., 103–18.

10. Heerwagen and Orians, "Humans, Habitats, and Aesthetics," 138–72; Gerlach-Spriggs, Kaufman, and Warner, *Restorative Gardens*, 35–41; Roger Ulrich, "Biophilia, Biophobia, and Natural Landscapes," in Kellert and Wilson, *Biophilia Hypothesis*, 73–137; Steven R. Kellert, "The Biological Basis for Human Values of Nature," in Kellert and Wilson, *Biophilia Hypothesis*, 42–69.

11. Susan McKinnon, *Neo-Liberal Genetics: The Myths and Moral Tales of Evolutionary Psychology* (Chicago: Prickly Paradigm Press, 2005), 14–71, 120–42.

12. Rachel Kaplan, Stephen Kaplan, and Robert L. Ryan, *With People in Mind: Design and Management of Everyday Nature* (Washington, DC: Island Press, 1998); Rachel Kaplan and Stephen Kaplan, *The Experience of Nature: A Psychological Perspective* (New York: University of Cambridge Press, 1989); Gregory N. Bratman, J. Paul Hamilton, and Gretchen C. Daily, "The Impacts of Nature Experience on Human Cognitive Function and Mental Health," *Annals of the New York Academy of Sciences*, 1249 (2012), 118–36.

13. Kaplan, Kaplan, and Ryan, *With People in Mind*, 7–16.

14. Elizabeth C. Brawley, *Design Innovations for Aging and Alzheimer's* (Hoboken, NJ: John Wiley and Sons, 2006), 275–95; Gerlach-Spriggs, Kaufman, and Warner, *Restorative Gardens*; Roger S. Ulrich, "Effects of Gardens on Health Outcomes: Theory and Research," in Marcus and Barnes, *Healing Gardens*, 27–86; Kellert and Wilson, *Biophilia Hypothesis*.

15. Two excellent historical accounts of the history of healing gardens in Europe, the United Kingdom, and the United States are Edwin Heathcote, "Architecture and Health," in Charles Jencks and Edwin Heathcote, *Maggie's Cancer Caring Centers* (London: Francis Lincoln, 2010), 54–91, and Sam Bass Warner Jr., "The History," in Gerlach-Spriggs, Kaufman, and Warner, *Restorative Gardens*, 7–35.

16. Warner, "History," 21–24, 31–33; and Sternberg, *Healing Spaces*, 215–52.

17. Jencks and Heathcote, *Maggie's Cancer Caring Centers*, 81–91; Sternberg, *Healing Spaces*, 215–38; Stephen Verderber and David J. Fine, *Healthcare Architecture in an Era of Radical Transformation* (New Haven, CT: Yale University Press, 2000), 133–329.

18. Marcus and Sachs, *Therapeutic Landscapes*, 47–55.

19. Ibid., 308–15.

20. Interview with David Kamp, April 7, 2015, and five three-hour on-site observations of the garden in the fall of 2003.

21. See Marcus and Sachs, *Therapeutic Landscapes*, chap.10, and John Zeisel, "Creating a Therapeutic Garden That Works for People Living with Alzheimer's," *Journal of Housing for the Elderly*, 21(1–2), 13–33.

22. L. L. Berry, D. Parker, R. C. Coile, D. K. Hamilton, D. D. O'Neill, & B. L. Sadler, "The Business Case for Better Buildings," *Frontiers of Health Services Management*, 21(1) (Fall 2004), 3–24.

23. Sternberg, *Healing Spaces*, 237, 290–96.

24. Nicholas Watkins and Zishan Siddiqui, "Gray Area," *Healthcare Design*, 15(10) (Dec. 2015), 50–52; Zishan K. Siddiqui, Rebecca Zuccarelli, Nowella Durkin, Albert W. Wu, and Daniel J. Brotman, "Changes in Patient Satisfaction Related to Hospital Renovation: Experience with a New Clinical Building," *Journal of Hospital Medicine*, 10(3) (March 2015), 165–71.

PART III

ART AND ARCHITECTURE FOR HEALTH

THE ULTIMATE TEST FOR DESIGN

Does It Cause Health?

TYE FARROW

Sparking a Global Movement

How can we ignite a worldwide movement to achieve total health in our built environment? How can we channel our highest aspirations toward reversing nearly a century of constructed habitat degradation?

This degree of change will require fundamentally new design questions. In order to incite a campaign for design that actively makes us *feel and do* better, two questions must be planted in the mind of every politician, every decision maker, and every citizen: *"Does this place cause health?"* and *"How does it make me feel?"*

As a society, we can no longer afford to tolerate places that fail to ensure we thrive. Three generations of constructing environments that deny our deeply rooted biological needs have yielded not only a surge of lifestyle-related diseases, but also a plague on the human spirit. The design of every public space, building, campus, community, and home must be judged in terms of its capacity to *cause total health,* not simply to stop doing physical harm. We must be able to thrive and prosper; to do more than survive and sustain ourselves. The full range of design factors that influence our total health extend beyond the state of our physical well-being, such as air quality, to include qualities of place that affect our state of mind.

In other words, environmentally responsible design today cannot be isolated, placeless, careless, and rootless. The time has come to take the next leap forward by assessing factors that affect social, neural, and spiritual regeneration.

A New Design Excellence

These new design questions transcend traditional concerns for style, taste, and the creation of isolated built objects. They expand the traditional meaning of "design excellence" beyond standards of pure aesthetics to include impact on human health. The fundamental question "How does it make me feel?" looks beyond dense planning jargon and arcane theories to expose the most telling, bottom-line effects on our psyche.

Moreover, these simple questions instill the habit of paying conscious attention to the effect of every built or proposed habitat. In this way, the power of analysis becomes accessible to the people who benefit from—or suffer the health consequences of—countless design choices. When these questions become the definitive test that guides each and every design decision, they have the potential to raise expectations for design worldwide.

There is no such thing as neutral space in terms of the impact of design on our health. Every element in every space serves to either enhance or erode our capacity to thrive. In combination, these design ingredients have positive or negative consequences for our state of mind and neurological nourishment. Ultimately, these elements result in places people love, or at least feel are worth caring for, while other places have detrimental effects.

Over the past century, people have become numbed to the harmful effects of denatured, disconnected, and dismal design. In recent decades, environmental sustainability initiatives have focused primarily on physical resource damage control rather than on the full spectrum of human and natural environmental health needs. The state of our mental and physical health is an essential element of a strategy for regeneration that enables us to thrive and prosper rather than merely survive.

Instead of turning a blind eye to detrimental design, people can develop a visceral reaction to dismal places that drain their energy. Most of us today would have a strong emotional reaction if we saw a mother smoking while holding a baby. Not long ago, smoking mothers were accepted as a societal norm, along with smoking on airplanes. Major changes in sensitivity to such health issues have developed over one or two generations. Vastly reduced tolerance for these threats indicates that expectations can change quickly and dramatically.

Beyond Prevention

A global Cause Health movement aims higher than current efforts focused on disease prevention and wellness. We have been conditioned by the media and medical business interests to rarely think further than avoiding ill-health. In many ways, we live in a pathology-centric society where medical fears and phobias are fed, while research is mainly directed at finding cures for causes of disease. Very little attention is paid to discovering the causes of health.

For evidence of this imbalance, consider the term *pathogenic,* which is widely understood to mean "causing disease." A corresponding term for "causing health," *salutogenic,* is relatively unknown. If causing total health became the basis for judging every building and every public space, it would raise public aspirations beyond mere coping and prevention.

To fill this gap, we can look to the pioneering research developed by medical sociologist Aaron Antonovsky, whose books (Antonovsky 1979, 1987) formed the basis of understanding the relationship between health and illness. Antonovsky focused on the personal characteristics of individuals who were more resilient to the stressors of daily life. He claimed these qualities helped a person cope and remain healthy by providing a "sense of coherence" about life and its challenges. Antonovsky coined the term *salutogenesis,* a concept that reframes health as a positive force rather than a collection of deficiencies. Salutogenesis is derived from *salus,* a Latin word meaning "health," and the Greek word *genesis,* meaning "origin."

The distinction between causing health and preventing degradation is crucial. The Cause Health view is focused on leveraging human assets and capabilities—regardless of their current state—and engages us in building on these strengths to optimize health.

Need to Redefine Health

Today the word *health* has become synonymous with *health care.* Debates over medical care efficiencies, wait times, and delivery systems have obscured the much larger question of how to reduce overall usage of and dependence on medical services. A Google search for "cause health" yields countless variations of "cause health problems," "cause health abnormalities," "cause health risks," and "cause ill health." Any positive results on how we might actually create—or cause—health is missing from the torrent of healthcare deficiencies and disease prevention tips.

Thus we are living in a culture of negative health. It is no wonder that costs associated with keeping our society healthy have ballooned out of proportion. The movement to cause health would reduce the current burden of illness on society. It is a model of abundance and regeneration rather than scarcity because it redirects today's wasted downstream resources including human energy, capabilities, and financial assets. Instead we can create places that allow us to be and to do our best, mentally, physically, and socially.

While ongoing research aimed at pinpointing what is bad for us will continue to yield crucial medical breakthroughs, it is time to balance pathology-oriented discoveries with an entirely different pursuit. In order to minimize the burden of illness on society, we need to launch a quest to discover the causes of health and how this will affect our social and economic prosperity.

Such a shift in thinking is not about placing a positive spin on intractable medical and social problems. When we understand the causes of health through research that identifies factors in the built environment associated with wellness we will more clearly see what kinds of places give us emotional energy and what elements feed our spirit. We will discover how places communicate messages about self-esteem and mutual respect. These life-enhancing qualities are not "nice to have;" rather, they determine whether we face a future of degradation and depravation or fulfill our biological need for a nurturing habitat.

The World Health Organization defines health as "a state of complete physical, mental, and social well-being and not merely the absence of disease or infirmity" (World Health Organization 1946). This broader concept of health indicates a higher aspiration than to live out our lives with the primary goal of preventing illness.

"I learned a lot of pathology, and a lot about medicines. We were taught virtually nothing about health," writes Richard J. Jackson, chair of the Department of Environmental Health at UCLA and host of the popular PBS television series *Designing Health Communities*. "I had to learn a whole lot more about the embedded health in the world around me if I was to make an impact" (Jackson 2012). This dismal situation presents an opportunity for the design profession to assume a greater leadership role in creating regenerative places. We have an opportunity to change the definition of health so that it is no longer centered on illness and prevention.

An Appetite for Something Better

The basis of a movement needs to draw on more than sensible, good intentions; to spark a new demand we need to understand how change really happens. Major shifts in norms and values occur when people see themselves as benefiting personally, rather than being coerced by laws, lectures, and frightening news stories. The current shift to healthier eating, for example, reflects how society's evolving values and self-images have progressed from beyond the fringe to mainstream.

On one end of the food spectrum, demand is dominated by unhealthy diets, fast food, and lack of social engagement associated with cooking and eating. These conditions are coupled with unsustainable food sources and practices. The negative side effects of this soulless, empty calorie approach to food consumption range from obesity and chronic disease to families that lack the socially unifying aspects of eating together. For some, food and cooking have become a sensory-deprived, unfulfilling, utilitarian exercise. By contrast, we also see evidence of increased appreciation for food origins and preparation by people with higher expectations for what and how they eat. Rather than merely consuming unhealthy and boring meals, these individuals see themselves as part of a movement that not only cares about food sustainability and nutrition; they also seek to enhance the social and sensual experience of cooking and eating. This higher level of appreciation reflects changing values across all boundaries of society.

Similar to the healthy food movement, expectations for the quality of our habitat are beginning to rise, and this consciousness must be actively supported. More than eighty examples of suburban shopping mall transformations have been documented by Ellen Dunham-Jones, AIA, director of the urban design program at the Georgia Institute of Technology, and June Williamson, associate professor of architecture and urban design at the City College of New York/CUNY. Their case studies (Dunham-Jones and Williamson 2011) include a former 100-acre mall in Lakewood, Colorado, that has been redeveloped over a ten-year period into twenty-three walkable urban blocks, publicly owned streets, LEED-certified buildings, and sustainable site design. This example has inspired eight of the thirteen area malls to move forward with plans for applying urban design principles to their suburban settings. A recent National Association of Realtors survey found that Americans prefer walkable communities more so than they have in the past (NAR 2015).

It may seem like an overwhelming task to raise awareness about the impact of our built environment. But in a knowledge-based economy, we cannot afford to settle for facilities that starve our spirits rather than feed our minds.

The Science of "Enriched" Places

While few people would choose to dine in a café overlooking a parking lot or live next to a highway exit ramp, the full psychological effects of such places are not yet understood. However, for anyone who seeks evidence of the ways in which a person's surroundings can positively or negatively affect that individual, the study of "enriched environments" is well underway (Hebb 1947; Krech, Rosenzweig, and Bennett 1960; Gould et al. 1999).

Recent research in neuroplasticity and neurogenesis (Gould et al. 1999) is beginning to raise awareness that learning capacity and memory can be improved by our surroundings. Not all aspects of the brain are fixed, or destined to deteriorate over time, as previously assumed. Instead, the brain is changeable (or "plastic") throughout adulthood, with the potential to create new neural networks under "enriched" conditions. For example, research on rodent brains indicates that environmental enrichment (being raised outside standard cages) leads to increased cognitive development. Such discoveries could be applied to the treatment of brain-related dysfunctions, including Alzheimer's disease, while a lack of stimulation may be proven to impair cognitive development (Chuang 2010; Verret et al. 2013; Murrell et al. 2013).

Judith Heerwagen, program expert at U.S. General Services Administration, Office of Federal High Performance Green Buildings, has studied the evolution of zoo design over recent decades in relation to environmental design for humans. Tight cages in zoos have generally been replaced by more spacious natural habitats. As in nature, better habitat designs offer more options for playing, resting, and retreating from public view. She explains the incentive for this change: "A key factor was concern over the animals' psychological and social well-being. Zoos could keep animals alive, but they couldn't make them flourish" (Heerwagen 2008).

Neurotic behavior due to unnatural design is more obvious in zoos than in human habitats. Animals pace back and forth, pick fights, and exhibit obsessive behaviors when they must cope with deprivation design. Diagnosis of human deprivation design is more challenging, yet the consequences are too costly to ignore.

The study of biophilic design explores our innate need to connect with nature, natural elements, and forms. This field of enquiry emphasizes the restorative role design can play in coping with stress and mental fatigue. Natural connections to land and place occur through local materials, layers of history, cultural identity, and indigenous plants and landscape forms. Places of protection, refuge, and overview offer a primal sense of comfort that can be traced back to early hunter-gatherer societies on the savannas. Natural shapes such as curves convey feelings of ease and friendliness, while sharp angles convey tension and hostility (Bar and Neta 2006; Vartanian et al. 2013).

The opposite of biophilic design is design that causes feelings of alienation and boredom, which drain our energy and cause disease. These two fields of study—biophilic design and neurogenesis—can be brought together in the public's mind by asking, Does this place cause health? How does it make me feel?

Health at the Heart of Democratic Design

Rather than being restricted to society's elite, "enriched environments" can be widely accessible as a nourishing *luxury for all*. Democratic design conveys our shared values. Over the past century our shared values have been allowed to deteriorate. Citizens must instead be motivated to care and become stewards of places that cause health and prosperity.

Thomas Jefferson's democratic concept of an academical village at the University of Virginia was viewed as a healthy alternative to the model of "one immense building" at his alma mater, the College of William and Mary. His plan for several decentralized, human-scaled, more democratic buildings, "a small one for every professorship, arranged at proper distances around a square, to admit extension, connected by a piazza . . . (in a) village form, would be "preferable to a single great building for many reasons, particularly on account of fire, health, economy, peace and quiet" (Conant 1962).

The academical village as described by Garry Wills, professor of history at Northwestern University, "combines the expectable with the surprising," allowing for "regimentation and individual expression, of hierarchical order and relaxed improvising," ultimately encouraging "a mixture of central control, faculty supervision, private enterprise, and individual initiative" (Wills 2006). It is apparent that Jefferson believed the built environment could transform the quality of life and improve health for every citizen.

Setting a Bigger Agenda

The profession of architecture and landscape architecture is rooted in issues of health, welfare, safety, and pursuing a social agenda. The American Institute of Architects' Center for the Value of Design has stated that no greater challenge and opportunity is worth pursuing for the profession than public health (Center for the Value of Design 2012). But as mentioned earlier, architects must aim higher than conventional definitions of health that relate to health care and disease prevention. Meanwhile, the sustainability movement is also hampered by politics and disagreements regarding the best way forward. Given this reality, the intersection between individual and public health can be a unifying cause that serves to accelerate progress. In order to succeed, the criteria must be easily understood and embraced through a shared, critical eye by all of us.

The focus of public health concerns can be seen to evolve through three historical eras. The first era was the industrial period up into the 1800s, when cities were overcrowded and overwhelmed by communicable diseases. Lack of sanitation and access to clean air and other basic human survival needs led to the establishment of public health authorities. At that time, architects and urban and landscape designers naturally worked together with public health officials to create healthier environments, including the park system. Urban design guidelines were created to reduce overcrowding and improve air circulation and sanitation as a means to reduce communicable diseases.

Lester Breslow (1915–2012) was an American psychiatrist and pioneer in thinking about positive public health for all members of society regardless of economic circumstances. He was able to see the history and progress of public health, believing that health and healthy habits should be regarded as a resource for everyday life, as opposed to merely a means to prevent disease (Martin 2012).

As a result of public health improvements, people began to live longer, which led to the second era of public health concerns. Since the 1940s, the tides of noncommunicable, chronic disease and toxic pollution health threats have risen. During this era, soulless places were zoned, planned, and designed that take us away from nature and true community.

Our quest in today's third era of public health is to expect more from the places where we live, learn, and work. We can pursue a thriving habitat by uniting the interests of public health with sustainability and the regenerative potential to cause health.

Expanding the Criteria

Recent efforts to create healthy design criteria, such as Active Design Guidelines (Center for Active Design 2010) and the Sustainable Sites Initiative are aimed at reducing obesity. Improvements to physical health are encompassed by green building design criteria (e.g., controlling air quality and toxins) and highlighted by such tools as Walk Score (2017). Energy conservation and regeneration have been focused almost exclusively on the technical end of the sustainability spectrum. Attention to environmental responsibility from a placemaking and life-enhancing point of view has been nearly absent. A building might therefore attain LEED Platinum status while being extremely unhealthy in terms of its social, cultural, and psychological impact. The Living Building Challenge expands this eco-evaluation scope to include health, equity, and beauty as well as site, water, energy, and materials (International Living Future Institute n.d.).

When we look around today we see too many streetscapes that fail to supply our need for brain food. Walkable neighborhoods are becoming widely recognized for offering many health and economic advantages. However, in order to reap their full benefits, it is vital to understand that distance, safety, and access are only part of the recipe for healthy living. Boring, repetitive streets make even a short walk unappealing—whether in the city or the suburbs. We need "walk-worthy" as well as walk-able streets.

Five Vital Signs

While evidence-based design will continue to have its place in decision making, people also need to develop a gut reaction—rather than numbness and tolerance—to the health aspects of design in their everyday lives. How can more people be encouraged to diagnose the condition of their built environment? The following "Vital Signs" make it easy for anyone to become a better critic by assessing some of the most basic elements that make a place feel better. Of course, there are many overlapping factors on the spectrum of healthy to unhealthy habitats, but all of the following five elements tend to be present in places that cause total health:

1. Nature: Design that is inspired by the natural world. We feel better and less anxious when we can see living and growing things, as well as natural materials. Layouts that echo natural shapes encourage us to move beyond rigid boundaries.
2. Authenticity: Design that draws on meaningful local influences. These are places that reflect the values and aspirations of the people who work there. They motivate citizens to care and become stewards with a personal interest in its ongoing revitalization.
3. Variety: Design that offers a range of experiences and a sense of discovery. Diverse places stimulate the mind. Interesting spaces motivate people to walk and interact with others.
4. Vitality: Energetic, regenerative space that facilitates flow of people and ideas. Healthy places reflect the way people really function in today's active, connected world: providing choices and drawing people together for various activities.
5. Legacy: Design that makes a lasting contribution to health, by being responsible and durable beyond basic requirements for sustainability. People gain a sense that they are part of something bigger than themselves.

These five vital signs are exemplified by Barcelona's Santa Caterina Market and France's national pavilion at the 2015 Milan Expo.

Listed below are project examples designed by Farrow Partners that demonstrate these Vital Signs.

Nature

The design for Credit Valley Hospital (CVH) (figure 1), located in Ontario, is rooted in the client's aspiration to be "first in the hearts and minds of the

Figure 1. Natural forms and materials at Credit Valley Hospital near Toronto, Ontario, Canada, covey the sense of a safe haven. (Tom Arban Photography)

people we serve." This statement emerged from an intense period of soul searching and internal dialogue by the hospital's senior management. Credit Valley's new ambulatory care and cancer center facility presented a rare opportunity to raise expectations internationally for healthcare design and delivery.

It was clear that "first in the hearts and minds" design would not be achieved through generic elements derived from corporate office park and hospitality design. Recognizing that people are at their most emotionally vulnerable in a hospital setting, the design draws on a range of elements and concepts from nature that overcome stress and worry. Every aspect of the experience is designed to make patients, staff, and visitors feel better. It was agreed that this legacy project would communicate the message "you are in good hands here." CVH's strong new identity was also intended to motivate donors and attract the best staff.

Everyone understood that an anonymous steel structure would reduce Credit Valley's vision to empty words. Two fundamental questions kept everyone focused: "What are the most basic needs when patients are worried or feeling vulnerable?" and "Do we have the courage to advocate for human-centric places that truly provide healing and hope?" When we asked cancer patients what is important to them, they responded, "Cancer is a devastating illness; the space we come to for treatment should give us hope." When asked what gives them hope, they said, "Something that is alive!" Such insight, gained through conversations with patients, reinforced the hospital's resolve to carry through with a design inspired by nature.

Implementing this breakthrough design required not just perseverance and vision, but also the ability to attract champions who could envision Credit Valley Hospital as more than a "healing environment." It could be a place that causes health.

When you walk in the front door, the soaring tree-like shapes create feelings of both protection and inspiration. These shapes look like trees as well as function like trees. Similar to a walk in the forest, there are places of canopied refuge as well as open spaces that provide visual orientation. The clustered seating areas promote social interaction in natural safe havens with openings to a larger field of vision.

The plan has organic aspects while overall being a clear and logical arrangement of space. The prevailing sense of being sheltered ("in good hands") in this enduring biophilic space is reassuring. Other health-causing elements are the "lanterns" that bring natural light down into the radiation treatment area.

The curved lines of the dynamic wood elements convey the energy of life. All of the structural components are glulam Douglas fir, which, in addition to being a warm, natural material, truly improves with age. In contrast to sterile finishes that are manufactured to be perfect and therefore subject to damage, wood has a genuine quality and texture that gains character with imperfections over time. As imperfect beings, human are comforted by such natural imperfections.

The combination of nature-derived materials, shapes, and spaces achieves Credit Valley's vision to be "first in the hearts and minds" of its community. This dramatic architectural and social centerpiece for the hospital provides a special identity that appears on recruitment advertising and the hospital's website. Unique character, in contrast to placelessness, gives meaning and a healthy sense of being part of something bigger and more transcendent than the individual.

The project was built within a publicly funded healthcare system, at the same cost or less than any other building of a similar type that was being built.

Figure 2. The design of the National Oncology Centre, Port-of-Spain, Trinidad and Tobago, evokes a local bird as a means to lift the human spirit.

By investing in the design of the main lobby and public areas that had the most
human impact while identifying savings in the cost of basic construction, this
project was completed for $10 million under budget.

Another example of how nature can be infused in a design to cause health
is the National Oncology Centre in Port-of-Spain, Trinidad and Tobago
(figure 2). Here the image of a local bird inspired a design that seeks to literally lift our spirits under its wings. The goal was to communicate a place of
comfort that people will care about, and also where they will feel cared for.
There is an overlap between spaces of enclosure and exposure, indoors and
outdoors, which support a range of activities and emotional states by patients,
staff, and visitors.

The Grip Global Tower in London (figure 3) is the first of its kind to use
cross laminate timber reinforced with Grip Metal to create a shape that appears to grow naturally in the forest of towers on the skyline.

Authenticity

In the field of hospital design there is often a stated goal to make the facility
feel"home-like." The reality is that individuals' ideas of what exactly a home
should look like differ depending on cultural background and other factors. In

Figure 3. The Grip Global Tower in London is the first to use cross laminate timber re-inforced with Grip Metal to create a shape that appears to grow naturally in the forest of towers on the skyline.

order to create a place that will cause health, we must look at the intent behind a desire for home-like design.

In a healthcare setting people want to be comforted by design elements that are personally meaningful. Also, as in a home setting, people want to feel that "we care" is not simply a management slogan. St. Mary's Hospital in British Columbia (figure 4) was conceived as a long-term asset to the community in terms of both conservation of resources and its therapeutic effect. Strong visual themes connect native spiritual and physical worlds. Located on the Sunshine Coast, northwest of Vancouver, the land was donated by the Sechelt Indian Band nearly fifty years ago. It was the site where misguided government policies created hardship and abuse that devastated this once proud nation.

Members of the Sechelt Indian Band played an important role in the design process by advising on the most meaningful and enduring elements of native tradition to incorporate. The shape of the building was inspired by the cedar bent-box, which is unique to the coastal First Nations. In this concept, the bent-box holds our most precious possession—our health.

Themes and symbols convey reassuring stories of a coherent life, with healing and afterlife as part of a natural process. Major artworks tell stories and depict well-known cultural symbols, such as the three totem poles that mark

Figure 4. The design of St. Mary's Hospital in Sechelt, British Columbia, is rooted in local traditions and the spiritual world.

the main entrance. The lobby is animated by a spectacular mural that spans the entire seventy-foot length.

Authenticity is therefore present in this project through familiar imagery and artworks that communicate that you are in good hands with people who care. Patient rooms have large operable windows with spectacular views of the Strait of Georgia, offering a restorative opportunity to reflect on the enduring qualities of nature.

Variety

When you approach the main entrance building at Kaplan Medical Center (figure 5), located south of Tel Aviv, Israel, you are in an extraordinary spot, a place where sweet oranges are grown. Our memorable design for the academic center was inspired by the shape of orange blossoms, which provide a welcoming entry for this large healthcare campus. When you are inside the blossom, you can look out to the lawn and a eucalyptus garden beyond. At the Mission

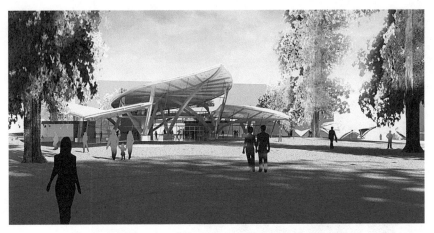

Figure 5. Locally renowned orange blossoms inspired the welcoming design of this entrance at Kaplan Medical Center in Rehovot, Israel.

Complex Continuing Care Centre (figure 6) on Canada's west coast, the plan was inspired by a radiating sun symbol from the Haida culture. Residential areas extend outward from the entrance and public areas to create welcoming places for social interaction that maximize access to natural daylight. The facade offers variety through natural color selections that begin in the warm range on one side of the building and become cooler on the other side. These colors were inspired by the effect of circadian rhythms and colors of the forest that were cooler in the morning and warmer later in the day.

Vitality

Thunder Bay Regional Health Sciences Centre (figure 7) was created as a symbol of regional revival and to attract staff to this far northern Ontario location. A dramatic, light-filled, wood-framed main circulation concourse brings people together for events and informal social interaction. The striking design celebrates a renewed pride in the distinctive culture and heritage of the region's lumber industry and railway connections.

At the time the Thunder Bay hospital was designed, the prevailing question in the hospital architecture field was whether to make the facility feel hotel-like or more like an academic campus. Rather than this false choice, we considered the real human feelings that would be embraced here. Our answer was that the design needed to exude self-confidence and a sense of abundance. It should be optimistic, engaging, and health-centric.

Colchester Regional Hospital in Nova Scotia (figure 8) has a circulation

Figure 6. Mission Complex Continuing Care Centre on Canada's west coast was inspired by a radiating sun symbol from the Haida culture, which serves to maximize access to daylight.

Figure 7. Thunder Bay Regional Health Sciences Centre in Thunder Bay, Ontario, Canada, celebrates the region's lumber industry and railway heritage. (Peter Sellar Photography)

Figure 8. Circulation corridors at Colchester Regional Hospital in Nova Scotia are connected to exterior court-yard and gardens.

Figure 9. The adaptable design for a series of Health Promoting Lifestyle Centers in South Africa are intended as a democratic legacy project.

plan that similarly brought the corridor to the outside of the building. As people move through the hospital, they are always connected to exterior courtyards and nature. Instead of the traditional main lobby, an exterior garden forms the primary circulation route.

Legacy

The design for a series of Health Promoting Lifestyle Centers (HPLCs) (figure 9) was inspired by a South African flower, the protea, which was named after the Greek god Proteus, who had the power to change his form at will. The project was in response to an international competition by the Ministry of Health of South Africa to create a design that could be adapted to urban areas, rural areas, and the townships. The intent was to bring together education, job training, food education, home skills, sustainability, sustainable farming, and clinics.

The concept was envisioned as a catalyst to support total health for South Africa's most vulnerable people, including youth and, in particular, young women. The building has the ability to grow or shrink programmatically over time and depending on location.

The legacy aspect of this project is that it underscores health as an enduring symbol of democracy, with the HPLCs as centers of influence. Health would thus become woven into the social fabric for the benefit of current and future generations.

At Bishop Strachan School in Toronto, Canada (figure 10), the student center is visually connected to the original stone building and the enduring values that stately building represents. Natural materials and donor names

Figure 10. The student center at Bishop Strachan School in Toronto, Ontario, Canada, connects visually with the original school's 1915 structure.

embedded in a terrazzo leaf floor pattern provide further connections with the school's legacy.

Conclusion

The symptoms of ill-health and emotional dis-ease are all around us, consuming resources that could be redirected to positive improvements in our environment. Hostility, alienation, obesity, drug abuse, and chronic disease are diverse symptoms with a root cause. That root cause can be addressed through the design of a restorative environment. We need places that give us energy, social connection, and enhanced self-esteem. We need places that are loveable, not just sustainable. To accelerate a public demand for these higher standards requires conscious awareness. Anyone can become a better critic of our built environment and join the ongoing movement to cause health.

References

Antonovsky, A. (1979). *Health, Stress and Coping.* San Francisco: Jossey-Bass.
Antonovsky, A. (1987). *Unraveling the Mystery of Health: How People Manage Stress and Stay Well.* San Francisco: Jossey-Bass.

Bar, M., & Neta, M. (2006). Humans prefer curved visual objects. *Psychological Science,* 17(8), 645–48.

Berardi N., Braschi, C., Capsoni, S., Cattaneo, A., & Maffei, L. (2007). Environmental enrichment delays the onset of memory deficits and reduces neuropathological hallmarks in a mouse model of Alzheimer-like neurodegeneration. *Journal of Alzheimer's Disease,* 11(3), 359–70.

Center for Active Design. (2010). *Active Design Guidelines: Promoting Physical Activity and Health in Design.* New York: Departments of Design and Construction, Health and Mental Hygiene, Transportation, and City Planning. Accessed February 16, 2016. http://centerforactivedesign.org/dl/guidelines.pdf.

Center for the Value of Design, American Institute of Architects. (2012). Remarks by Markku Allison, AIA. Accessed February 16, 2016. http://www.aia.org/practicing/AIAB088657.

Chuang, T. T. (2010). Neurogenesis in mouse models of Alzheimer's disease. *Biochimica et Biophysica Acta (BBA)—Molecular and Cell Biology of Lipids,* 1802(10), 872–80. Accessed February 16, 2016. http://www.ncbi.nlm.nih.gov/pubmed/20056145.

Conant, J. B. (1962). *Thomas Jefferson and the Development of American Public Education.* Berkeley: University of California Press.

Dunham-Jones, E., & Williamson, J. (2011). *Retrofitting Suburbia: Urban Design Solutions for Redesigning Suburbs.* San Francisco: Jossey-Bass for John Wiley & Sons.

Gould, E., Reeves, A. J., Graziano, M. S. A., & Gross, C. G. (1999). Neurogenesis in the neocortex of adult primates. *Science,* 286(5439), 548–52.

Hebb, D. O. (1947). The effects of early experience on problem solving at maturity. *American Psychologist,* 2: 306–7.

Heerwagen, J. H. (2008). Psychosocial value of space. *Whole Building Design Guide,* National Institute of Building Sciences. http://www.nibs.org.

International Living Future Institute. (N.d.). Living Building Challenge. Accessed February 16, 2016. http://living-future.org/lbc.

Jackson, R. J. (2012). *Designing Healthy Communities.* San Francisco: Jossey-Bass for John Wiley & Sons.

Krech, D., Rosenzweig, M. R., & Bennett, E. L. (1960). Effects of environmental complexity and training on brain chemistry. *Journal of Comparative and Physiological Psychology,* 53(6), 509–19.

Martin, D. 2012. Lester Breslow, who tied good habits to longevity, dies at 97. *New York Times,* 14 April.

Murrell, W., et al. (2013). Expansion of multipotent stem cells from the adult human brain. *PLoS One,* 8(8), e71334.

National Association of Realtors. (NAR) (2015). NAR 2015 Community Preference Survey. July 28. Accessed February 16, 2016. http://www.realtor.org/reports/nar-2015-community-preference-survey.

Vartanian, O., et al. (2013). Impact of contour on aesthetic judgments and approach-avoidance decisions in architecture. *Proceedings of the National Academy of Sciences of the United States of America,* 110, supp. 2 (June 18), 110.

Verret, L., Krezymon, A., Halley, H., Trouche, S., Zerwas, M., Lazouret, M., Lassalle, J. M., & Rampon, C. (2013). Transient enriched housing before amyloidosis onset sustains cognitive improvement in Tg2576 mice. *Neurobiology of Aging,* 34(1), 211–25.

Walk Score. (2017). Live Where You Love. https://www.walkscore.com/.

Wills, G. (2006). *Mr. Jefferson's University.* Washington, DC: National Geographic Press.

World Health Organization. (1946). Preamble to the Constitution of the World Health Organization as adopted by the International Health Conference, New York, 19–22 June, 1946; signed on 22 July 1946 by the representatives of 61 States (Official Records of the World Health Organization, no. 2, p. 100) and entered into force on 7 April 1948.

CREATIVITY AND COMPASSION

The Influence of the Arts and Design on
the Healthcare Environment

REUBEN RAINEY AND CHRISTINA MULLEN

Enter just about any acute care urban hospital built in the last ten years. You are likely to encounter a high, light-filled lobby more reminiscent of a resort hotel than a medical facility (figure 1). Natural materials abound on walls, furniture, and elevator doors—wood paneling here, limestone there. Warm-toned carpets and wood acoustical ceilings absorb sound to a remarkable degree. Soft, live piano music wafts through the quiet atmosphere, to be followed by Renaissance harp melodies a few hours later. An eye-catching calendar of events announces a dramatic performance at 2 p.m. in the outdoor healing garden and a rehearsal of the staff orchestra at 6 p.m. As you walk down the quiet, carpeted hallway to your friend's patient room, the walls are covered with original artworks that aid your wayfinding. Serene landscapes of the local region abound, mixed with a few nonfigurative works in muted pastel colors. When you enter your friend's private room, she introduces you to the artist in residence, who has just led her through a drawing exercise to aid her in expressing her feelings about her recent surgery and the life changes it may require. The room looks out on the public park across the street. Many of its high-tech components—such as emergency oxygen access and blood pressure monitors—are concealed in cabinets, the headboard of the bed, or behind the Plexiglas framed digital images of flowers or birds. The easily sterilized vinyl floor looks like the hardwood version in a domestic bedroom. On the far side of the bed, opposite the door, is a sleep sofa chair to accommodate overnight stays by family and friends. The overall atmosphere is more home-like than hospital, yet beneath this domestic surface lies a high-tech facility with the latest in clinical protocols and equipment, and expertly trained staff to provide extraordinarily effective medical care (figure 2).

Time travel back a half century, and one's experience of an acute care hospital would have been quite different: low ceilings, monotonous white walls, tile and chrome surfaces reverberating with noise, confusing wayfinding, little, if any, artwork, and no music or healing gardens. Most patient rooms would

Figure 1. Shands UF Cancer Hospital, Gainesville, Florida. Natural light-filled, hotel-like entry lobby.

Figure 2. Sentara Martha Jefferson Hospital, Charlottesville, Virginia. The low-rise residential appearance of the building is less intimidating than a multi-story tower.

have been two- or four-bed wards with steel furniture reminiscent of a spartan navy aircraft carrier. High-tech medical equipment would crowd the hallways and rooms. Very little, if any, natural light would reach the passageways and waiting rooms, and window views of natural scenery from patient rooms would be rare. The main impression was of a depressing sterile environment with unpleasant medical aromas, glaring lights, and noise. One could almost feel one's blood pressure rise when paying a visit to a friend, as well as a strong desire to depart this stress-inducing realm as soon as possible. It was an intimidating environment organized to operate like a well-tuned machine to cater to the functional needs of staff and the latest technology more than the needs of patients.

While there is some simplification and hyperbole in this comparison, it is quite apparent that in the past thirty years medical facilities have undergone a remarkable and much welcome change. They are more patient centered and less stressful and intimidating. Much of this humane alchemy is a result of the inclusion of the arts in the medical environment. Indeed, the employment of various arts in medical settings as a complement to high-tech clinical care has increased dramatically in the past generation, especially in the United States and Europe. This application takes two basic forms: the design of a better environment for the delivery of medical care through the arts of architecture and landscape architecture and programmed activities for patients and staff involving interaction with various art forms at the bedside or in other venues. These interactive arts include music, drama, poetry, painting, sculpture, storytelling, and literature. This dual ensemble of the arts has transformed the environment in which medicine is practiced and substantially contributes to the individual health and well-being of staff and patients.

The most recent survey of hospitals in the United States, conducted in 2004–7, revealed 43 percent of the responding 2,333 healthcare institutions had some form of arts programs for patients and staff. Jointly conducted by the Global Health Alliance and Americans for the Arts, two nonprofit organizations promoting the use of the arts in medical settings, the survey sorted out the different nuances of the various arts programs. The majority of programs, 73 percent, focused on the permanent display of graphic art, such as paintings, murals, and sculpture; 49 percent included musical and dramatic performances in public spaces, and 32 percent had healing gardens. The largest number of artists engaged in healthcare contexts were musicians (82 percent), followed by actors (46 percent) and visual artists (40 percent). Twenty-two percent of arts programs were conducted at the bedside of patients, and 11 percent involved specific arts activities for staff. Twelve percent of hospitals had staff orchestras or choral groups (State of the Field Committee 2009, 3–11). As

John Graham-Pole, M.D., a pivotal leader in the modern arts in health movement, notes: "The increasing interest in arts in healthcare is a manifestation of the global acceptance of the movement. Arts in healthcare are complements to medical science rather than substitutes. The creative arts help patients reclaim power over their lives and their health" (Graham-Pole et al. 1991).

What has brought about this ever-increasing use of the arts in healthcare facilities? Why are today's hospitals, outpatient facilities, and other settings for clinical practice so much more attractive and humane than those of a half century ago? What precisely is the purpose of the arts in medical practice? What contributions do they make, and how do we know they are effective? The narrative is complex, rich, and not without elements yet to be explained.

Major Trends Accounting for the Presence of the Arts in Healthcare Settings Today

There are four major interrelated trends accounting for the important role the arts are playing in medical care today in the United States (Sadler and Ridenour 2009). They are a powerfully catalytic ensemble, each aspect of which is equally important. They include (1) a better understanding of the relationship between the immune system, stress, and the environment; (2) the dynamics of healthcare economics; (3) demographic shifts in attitudes and expectations of the American public toward medical care; and (4) the rise of what is called "evidence-based design" as an important factor in shaping the environment of care.

Scientific experiments have proven beyond a doubt the immune system is profoundly affected by perceptions of the environment (Felten 1993, 213–27). A generation ago this was not thought to be the case. Medical science understood the immune system to be mostly autonomous. What the patient felt or perceived about his or her surroundings was thus basically irrelevant to health outcomes. What this meant for the design of medical facilities was that as long as they were adequately functional and kept free of germs, high-tech surgery and pharmacology would meet patient needs. This accounts for those dismal, intimidating, and aesthetically sterile hospitals and outpatient facilities of yesteryear. With the exception of veterans' rehabilitation hospitals and those for children, the presence of the arts in medical treatment spaces was regarded as a useless frill or at best a value-added embellishment to be quickly stricken from the budget when cost overruns loomed large. The dramatic turnabout in medical science's understanding of the immune system revolutionized the design of medical facilities and the activities that took place in them. It also gave rise to holistic or integrative medicine based on an understanding of the interaction of the mind and the body and its effects on health outcomes.

One finding of the new science of the immune system documented the negative effects of continuous stress on a patient's recovery, stress especially common among patients in long-term acute care facilities or subject to repeated visits to outpatient facilities such as cancer treatment centers. Of course, just about any medical procedure or treatment is stressful. However, when that stress is compounded by what is perceived as a grim, aesthetically sterile medical facility, a patient's recovery rate can be prolonged. This is not some sort of naive new age fantasy. It has been substantiated by rigorous and credible scientific research (Sternberg 2009, 226–30).

Some of the many factors contributing to a highly stressful healthcare environment. Some involve the actual physical design of the space itself. Others involve a lack of meaningful social contact between patient and staff and the loss of autonomy and freedom experienced when one is thrust suddenly and unexpectedly into an institutionalized setting replete with plastic ID wristbands, one-size-fits-all hospital gowns, and a fixed regimen of eating, sleeping, and medication.

Given the highly damaging effects of stress, the critical issue then is how best to relieve patient and staff stress by creating a more humane environment both in terms of its physical design and the activities that occur within it. The arts can play a major role in meeting this challenge.

The second factor, the dynamics of healthcare economy, is also an important reason for the increased presence of the arts in healthcare facilities. Many of these facilities may be nonprofit, but they still compete with one another for patients to remain solvent. Also healthcare costs are constantly rising. One may agree that improving the medical environment is a humane goal but wonder whether better design and additional arts in medicine programs will be too costly in today's situation of rapidly rising healthcare expenses. This issue is not completely resolved, but credible research provides substantial evidence that these admittedly more expensive improvements are as economically sound as they are humane (Sternberg 2009, 238–40). A good stress-relieving environment for patients is a good workplace for staff. This means less staff turnover. One of the most expensive items in a medical facility budget is staff replacement, which in a large acute care hospital can cost millions of dollars per year. Today replacement costs for one registered nurse are about $65,000. Furthermore, in a less stressful environment staff work better, have higher morale, and make fewer mistakes. Errors, of course, can frequently result in extremely costly lawsuits. Better-designed facilities with arts in medicine programs will often attract staff seeking positions, creating a larger employment pool from which to choose and affording more selectivity (Berry et al. 2004).

Not only will staff be attracted, but so will patients. Some research has shown that in choosing a facility patients regard the attractiveness of the environment as the most important factor other than the medical expertise of the staff and physicians (Harris et al. 2002, 1276–99). For many, a well-designed building with an extensive arts in medicine program is emblematic of both high-quality technical medical expertise and a caring staff. In the highly competitive market for patients, such architectural and programmatic amenities are a considerable advantage.

The recent trend to quantify and openly publish surveys of patient satisfaction with medical care received in specific hospitals also is a factor influencing the choice of prospective patients. A prominent example is the HCAHPS (Hospital Consumer Assessment of Healthcare Provider and System Survey) initiated by the federal government in 2008 to establish a nationwide, consistent standard for hospital evaluation. The results of the survey are published yearly by the Centers for Medicare and Medicaid Services, allowing comparison of hospitals within one's state. The survey focuses on such things as the quality of the specific medical care received and the ability of staff to communicate with the patient. It includes questions pertaining to design, such as the quietness of the hospital environment and its perceived cleanliness, but it does not otherwise focus on design features or the inclusion of programs involving interaction of patients with various arts. However, hospitals with sophisticated design elements such as clear wayfinding or abundant exposure to natural light along with various bedside programs enabling patients to engage with the arts tend to score higher than facilities lacking those. Studies have shown attractive and efficient patient room design is especially important (Watkins and Siddiqui 2015). Such higher scores serve as magnets for privately insured individuals seeking the best possible healthcare venues. These younger, "paying customers," more so than those on Medicaid or Medicare, are the wellspring of almost every hospital's economic success (Pollitt 2015). Also, to motivate hospitals to improve their quality of healthcare, 25 percent of the Centers for Medicare and Medicaid Services' incentive payments to foster better service are linked to patient satisfaction scores.

Certain demographic and cultural developments in the United States comprise the third factor. These revolve around the baby boomer generation, whose impact is just beginning to be felt as they cross the threshold of age sixty-five. About 78 million people were born between 1946 and 1964, and they are on the verge of flooding the healthcare system with their prospects of living longer with more demanding and complex medical needs. For many of this generation, especially the more affluent, attitudes toward medical care have changed. They are inclined to view themselves no longer as "patients" in an authoritarian medical milieu but as "consumers" of health care, entitled to receive the highest-quality medical services possible. Their perception of quality includes a humane environment of well-designed facilities replete with the best high-tech and holistic medicine: the privacy of single rooms, the latest MRI and CAT scanners, world-class surgeons and radiologists, and a bevy of arts in medicine programs. This is why so many of the newer healthcare facilities radiate the ambience of posh resorts or spas. In fact, some architectural firms specialize in the design of both. This more educated and affluent majority will be choosing what they consider the best by word of mouth and the Internet, and eventually they will be the ones filling out those Medicare patient satisfaction surveys. CEOs and the governing boards of medical facilities will be constrained to respect their wishes or in all probability suffer the economic consequences.

Finally, the increase over the past thirty years in what is known as "evidence-based design" is a major cause of the ever-growing presence of the arts in the medical environment. Evidence-based design is the deliberate attempt to base design decisions for medical facilities on high-quality research in order to achieve the best possible health outcomes for patients, staff, and families (Center for Health Design 2008). Such an approach is primarily grounded in the social sciences, especially psychology and sociology. While it has focused on generating principles for the physical design of the medical environment, its methods have also been used to document the positive effects of interactive programs involving music, dance, drama, poetry, and storytelling on patients, staff, and families. Like all social science, it has its limitations and often does not measure up to the strict criteria of natural science, such as precise quantification, strict control of variables, randomization, and replication. Although such research cannot establish strict causality, it can document association. At its best, it can produce strong circumstantial evidence for how to design and program a humane and functional acute care hospital, outpatient clinic, or any other type of medical facility. Often it relies on qualitative data derived from surveys, interviews, questionnaires, and on site observations. These are subjective perceptions, yet nonetheless valuable ones. One needs to know what patients think and feel about such things as the design of their rooms or their participation in a bedside drawing exercise supervised by an artist in residence. How else can one make improvements or establish what benefits patients?

At times evidence-based design combines these qualitative studies with more precise quantitative ones involving physiological measurements of stress hormones, heart rate, skin conductivity, and brain waves. When such research is done with rigor and combined with documented best practices, nonsubjective quantitative studies, and the sensitive intuition of the architect or artist, the result can be a highly useful and formative body of knowledge. A classic and oft-cited example of evidence-based research was done thirty-one years ago by Roger Ulrich, who showed that among patients having the same operation, those in rooms with views of a grove of trees required less pain medication, complained less, and left the hospital almost a day earlier than those whose rooms looked into a brick wall. His elegant study exhibited statistical rigor, had excellent control of variables, was double blind, and demonstrated a positive health outcome. It helped set the gold standard for subsequent research in evidence-based design (Ulrich 1984). Imagine a CEO and board of directors of a healthcare institution given the task of overseeing the design of a new acute care hospital. If the design team tells them their building should have larger, more expensive windows and be resited to allow patients to view an adjacent park, they will want to know if the additional expense is worth it. Merely relying on an intuitive appeal to the wonders of nature will almost surely fail. A good evidence-based design study like Ulrich's suggests the changes will result in a quicker turnaround of beds, less expensive medication, and, in all probability, greater patient satisfaction. This has the power to persuade since it combines good economic sense with an ethic of humane care. The literature on evidence-based design is vast and growing. However, it varies in quality, so one must be cautious in applying it (Ulrich et al. 2008; Marcus and Sachs 2014).

Given these four factors accounting for the increase in arts in medicine programs, how precisely do the arts benefit patients, and what methods do they employ? The primary goal of the use of the arts in medicine is to reduce suffering and to foster health. In order to achieve this, various arts are employed in a number of ways.

The Art of Architecture

The design of a healthcare facility combines the aesthetic sensibility of the architect with the strict functional demands of the medical environment. It is one of the most demanding and complex types of commission, one that has been likened to the design of a city with various interrelated specialized communities (Tanzer 2014). Numerous federal and state codes and guidelines require strict compliance. Medical protocols are changing constantly, fueled by new scientific research and discovery. Existing equipment is subject to frequent upgrading, and totally new medical devices are constantly appearing. The typical acute care hospital is a complex amalgam of very specific functional spaces: operating suites, emergency rooms, neonatal care units, post-anesthesia care areas, bone marrow transplant facilities, patient rooms, waiting rooms, chapels, gift shops, pharmacies, examination rooms, chemotherapy cubicles, radiation treatment areas, and staff and physician offices. Given this complexity, most medical facilities are created by architectural firms specializing in their design. These tend to be among the larger firms, often with in-house engineering and interior design capabilities. Also, the complexity of the work demands a team design approach involving a broad range of specialties, including crucial input from the physicians and nurses. Furthermore, the design challenge encompasses a broad spectrum of project types, from large medical campuses to the smallest neighborhood clinic. It includes acute care hospitals, long-term care facilities, teaching hospitals, outpatient clinics, children's hospitals, veterans' hospitals, primary care centers, hospices, and a diverse assortment of facilities for the elderly. While each of these facilities consists of highly varying spatial organizations and technical demands, the various projects emerging from the drawing boards and computer screens of architectural firms over the past thirty years tend to share a common core of fundamental design principles. These principles are partially the result of the sheer intuitive talent of those involved mixed with the findings of the better evidence-based design research, proven precedent, and input from medical staff (Ulrich et al. 2008). Peruse the latest magazines and books on the design of medical facilities, and these principles will emerge in sharp focus. Their common purpose is to create less stressful spaces combining compassionate care with economic and functional efficiency. The following list is not all encompassing, but it contains many of the most important fundamentals.

Noise Abatement

Noise is the number one stressor of patients and staff. Acoustical ceiling tiles, anti-microbial treated carpets, and other sound-dampening materials are essentials in the new medical facilities (Toph 1988; Toph and Thompson 2001; Hill and LaVela 2015).

Exposure to Natural Light

Natural light has been shown by highly reliable design research to hasten healing and reduce stress in several healthcare contexts. The newer medical facilities are replete with transparency. Entry lobbies, atria, hallways, waiting rooms, and patient rooms are situated as much as possible to allow natural light to penetrate (Beauchemin and Hayes 1996; Benedetti et al. 2001; Shepley et al. 2012; Zadeth et al. 2014) (figure 3).

Figure 3. Shands UF Medical Campus Plan, Gainesville, Florida. The garden and adjacent lake in the center of the Medical Campus will be visible from many patient rooms. (UF Health, Shands)

Exposure to Nature Both Real and Virtual

Evidence-based design attests to the healing potential of exposure to nature in a medical context. Gardens are the most frequent source for this and are discussed in more detail in a separate essay of this book (see Rainey's essay in Part II). Also, natural landscape views from patient rooms have been shown to be possible catalysts of significant positive health outcomes, as numerous replications of Roger Ulrich's pioneering study of 1984 have demonstrated. Where direct exposure to plants and water is a medical risk, as in an outpatient cancer center where chemotherapy and radiation treatment weaken immune systems, virtual nature in the form of paintings, prints, and sculpture can also be therapeutic (Ulrich 1984, 2009; Domke 2009, 15–30; Vincent et al. 2010; Pati, O'Boyle, et al. 2014).

Clear Wayfinding

Confusion while navigating the health environment is highly stressful for patients and is expensive since extra staff have to be employed to direct patients and visitors. The circulation systems of the newer medical facilities are for the most part highly legible, employing various types of landmarks, simpler spa-

Figure 4. Shands UF Cancer Hospital, Gainesville, Florida. Large oil paintings of well-known natural springs provide an experience of virtual nature while serving as landmarks for wayfinding.

tial design, color codes, and clear, well-placed signage (Carpman, Grant, and Simmons 1984, 1985) (figure 4).

Excellent Ventilation and Air Filtration

Highly effective ventilation systems are required to reduce the danger of infection for patients and staff as well as to avoid the unpleasant and often nauseating smells of the facilities of the past (Ulrich et al. 2004).

Private Patient Rooms

The present trend is toward private patient rooms, and many states now require them in their building codes. They reduce contagion and allow more frequent visitation and overnight accommodation for a family member, providing important social support. The better designed rooms empower a patient to control lighting and provide a full array of electronic devices, including CD players, televisions, and computers. Single rooms have been shown to improve patient morale and to lessen the time of one's stay in the facility (Ulrich et al. 2004; Pati et al. 2009; Lavender et al. 2015).

Anti-Microbial Surface Finishing

Staph infections and the so-called super bugs are a plague that is ever increasing. Anti-microbial finishing of furniture, counters, rugs, and other surfaces helps prevent infection (Ulrich et al. 2004; Sharpe and Schmidt 2011; Kirk 2013).

Such features as these combined with the latest and most sophisticated energy-saving technology will increase the initial construction cost of medical facilities of whatever type. However, when measured by a long-term perspective, such initial expense pays for itself in just a few years and makes a major contribution to the economic health of the facility over the long term, as noted previously, by attracting patients, decreasing staff turnover, and reducing medical errors (Berry et al. 2004).

These major architectural design principles are evident in the new construction and retrofitting of leading medical facilities in the United States, such as the Mayo Clinic, Johns Hopkins Hospital, Duke University Medical Center, Parkland Memorial Hospital (Dallas), Massachusetts General Hospital (Boston), Brigham and Women's Hospital (Boston), the Cleveland Clinic, the University of Florida and Shands Medical Campus (Gainesville), the University of Virginia Medical Center (Charlottesville), and a host of other institutions varying in scale and complexity across the nation.

The Visual, Performing, and Literary Arts

While the arts of architecture, landscape architecture, and interior design create a stress-relieving physical setting for patients and staff, the arts of painting, music, drama, dance, storytelling, and poetry through various programs can directly engage the patient or staff member on a personal level within that setting to relieve suffering and create hope. In some cases participation in these arts can actually relieve symptoms and hasten the physical healing process, and, in situations where recovery is not possible, they can help a patient meet death with greater self-understanding and calm, in a manner similar to the experience of a garden (Sternberg 2009, 18–21; Nainis et al. 2006). The particular use of the visual, performing, and literary arts in medicine is firmly grounded in the understanding of the close interrelationship of body and mind and the innate potential for all humans to be creative.

Arts in health programs have two distinct ways of stimulating the creative, health-giving spirit of patients and staff. One way is more "passive," involving such things as observing a dramatic performance or listening to a musi-

Figure 5. Shands UF Cancer Hospital, Gainesville, Florida. The playing of familiar music in a patient's room can relieve stress and boredom. (UF Health, Shands)

cal event in a public space (figure 5). It can also involve viewing paintings or other modes of graphic art in a hallway or examination room (Rollins 2011). The more "active" way is to actually engage in the process of creativity itself, to make a drawing, compose a poem or song, create a dance, or take part in a dramatic performance. Both ways can have remarkable positive influences on the health of patients and staff. Research has shown listening to familiar songs on an iPod can revive Alzheimer's sufferers from their torpor (Sacks 2007, 335–47). Access to music for patients undergoing stem cell transplants decreases depression and mood disturbances (Cassileth, Vickers, and Magill 2003). Dancing can for a time activate the muscular coordination of those with Parkinson's disease (Hackney et al. 2007). Viewing landscape paintings and photographs of nonthreatening animals in waiting rooms, corridors, and patient rooms can substantially lessen the stress of both patients and staff. Dental patients perceive less pain in offices with landscape paintings (Ulrich 1984). Burn victims experience less pain when shown video images of scenic nature (Miller, Hickman, and Lemasters 1992). These are but a few examples of the many ways the arts have been shown to be beneficial.

Also, passive engagement with the arts can lead to more involvement. Passing an image of a familiar landscape in a hospital corridor might bring back a pleasant memory, or hearing a song might evoke feelings of connection to one's personal history. While these can be valuable stress-relieving encounters in themselves, they may lead to deeper creative expression through active engagement in some art form of interest. For example, when a trained arts in medicine practitioner is with a patient, the song just heard may lead to a serious conversation about the patient's life experience. The patient might then create a story or painting expressing a deeper psychological understanding of the medical issues confronting him or her beyond the bare facts of the diagnosis and prospects for recovery. There are benefits for staff as well. Medical students can improve their diagnostic skills by developing an ability to closely observe the significant details of paintings (Staricoff 2004). Staff can also participate in orchestras or choral groups to build a sense of team spirit as well as to enjoy a welcome relief from stress (Hond 2015).

Neuropsychologist Jeffery E. Evans notes the latest behavioral and biological research into the effects of personal creativity has established its powerful and lasting benefits for health and well-being. It has demonstrated that whatever art media in which an individual engages has the potential to develop a strong sense of "harmony" or "coherence" between patients and their outer world. Such involvement can also foster "abilities" and "competencies," promoting feelings of self-worth. For patients, this can reduce boredom and depression, two very common problems. The result is a better functioning immune system as well as other markers of physical and mental health. In some instances, intense absorption in the creation of art has been shown to enhance the connectivity of the brain's neurons in several of its areas, such as those governing action, perception, degrees of conscious control, and wider and narrower focus of attention. Also, the feelings of pleasure and relaxation often following the completion of a work of art are additional relievers of stress (figure 6). Thus when a patient or staff member translates a thought into a physical medium—a sketch, poem, song, story, concerto, or dance—the result can be a cascade of health-inducing processes (Evans 2007).

Arts in medicine programs vary in size from the small rural clinic with its modest collection of catalog posters of old cars, farmhouses, and nature scenes to the extensive programs of large medical centers with their large collections of original paintings and sculptures and numerous artists in residence, as well as credentialed art therapists. The largest, precedent-setting program is at UF Health at the University of Florida in Gainesville. This program founded in 1990 by physicians, nurses, and community artists consists of twenty-two artists in residence, a collection of over a thousand works of original art, a

Figure 6. University of Virginia Children's Hospital, Charlottesville. The personal creativity involved in forming a mosaic from rotating blocks can provide a welcome form of
stress relief.

research division, and a master's degree program and undergraduate certifi-
cates in arts in medicine and dance in medicine (Rainey and Schrader 2014,
26–36). However, this program hardly stands alone. An Internet search of the
home pages of the nation's hospitals, outpatient facilities, and children's hospitals reveals large arts in medicine programs in a considerable number of healthcare complexes (State of the Field Committee 2009). Programs such as those
at the Mayo Clinic, the University of Virginia Medical Center, the Cleveland
Clinic, Massachusetts General Hospital, and the University of Iowa Hospital,
while not as extensive as the University of Florida's, still are quite impressive.

The methods these programs apply to benefit patients and staff vary and
are quite flexible, but many somewhat resemble the procedures employed by
the innovative University of Florida artist in residence program. In this program, depending on what art form is employed, activities may take place in
the patient's room or in public areas such as waiting rooms or lobbies. The
artists in residence are local professional artists under contract, capable of
utilizing a wide variety of art forms in a range of clinical settings. They strive

to empower the patient through creative engagement, either active or passive. The desired outcome is for the patient to achieve greater self-awareness or control over his or her circumstances. Artists in residence undergo rigorous training for their work and adhere to the same institutional policies that apply to all hospital professionals. For all, patient safety is the primary focus.

While those who perform this work are highly skilled in their craft, this alone is not a qualification for success. Empathy and the ability to communicate are the most important capacities. The artist's task is not to teach the patient technical skills; rather, the artist must be willing to put personal artistic goals aside and focus on the needs of the patient in a process known as "the patient-driven experience." This type of experience is specially designed to aid a patient in regaining a sense of control that is so often lost when recovering from a traumatic injury or being treated for a serious illness. Also, in communicating with the patients, one must allow them to say, "No, thank you" to the art experience offered. The artist then quietly and politely excuses himself or herself. This is one of the critical differences between an "arts in medicine experience" and an "art therapy intervention," where artists in residence and art therapists have different responsibilities. Art therapists are clinical professionals educated in both art and therapy. They help diagnose and chart the progression of a patient's illness. They are knowledgeable about human development, psychological theories, clinical practice, and multicultural religious traditions. They interpret a patient's artistic expression in various media, consult with other medical specialists, and chart the progression of a patient's disease. In contrast, artists in residence listen empathetically to the patient and engage the patient in a creative activity of the patient's own choosing. They do not interpret their patient's artwork or record the progress of a patient's illness. While both professions strive to use the arts to provide patients with a better understanding of self during illness or injury, the two disciplines differ in credentialing and basic working procedures. Both are essential for a comprehensive arts in medicine program.

A more detailed examination of an artist in residence approach reveals there is no one fixed method to foster a patient's creativity. However, there are typical things that often occur. Artists Jill Sonke-Henderson and Rusti Brandman, both highly experienced artists in residence and cofounders of the University of Florida's Center for Arts in Medicine, suggest a frequently occurring process they call the "four bridges." However, they emphasize these "bridges" are often observed "tendencies" or phases and not a "fixed method to apply." They designate these phases as "moving into relationship," "moving into creativity," "moving into the patient's creative process," and "moving towards closure." (Sonke-Henderson and Brandman 2007). Basically, the process involves as a first and essential step the establishment of trust and communication between the artist and patient. Following this, the patient may choose to engage in some form of creativity, such as making a drawing, performing a dance, or writing a poem. In this phase the artist usually takes the lead, and the patient follows his or her suggestions. Next the roles are reversed; the patient initiates the creative activity, and the artist may echo it or respond to it with his or her own creative improvisations. The process ends with "closure," in which the patient moves from absorption in creativity to return to everyday life and his or her present medical situation. The artist may then encourage further creativity by leaving the patient with some kind of suggestion to engage in further art production, such as a sketchpad or poetic phrase. In no case do the artists judge the patients' creative expressions; neither do they interpret them. However, if the patient engages in an interpretation, the artist listens with empathy.

The field of arts in medicine is not without controversy. While there is general agreement about the benefits of both passive and active engagement in the arts, there is some dispute over what type of graphic art is appropriate for a medical facility. Some researchers insist only figurative art depicting positive subject matter, such as calm landscapes, nonthreatening animals, people engaged in pleasant activities, and fresh flowers, is appropriate. For them, nonfigurative or "abstract" art is taboo, for it increases the anxiety and stress of patients in an already stressful situation. Their argument is based on studies of popular taste, mostly in the United States and Europe, which indicate a dislike of nonfigurative or "abstract" art and a preference especially for depictions of calm landscapes. Further evidence is provided by a few studies indicating nonfigurative art can be deeply disturbing for mental patients or patients recovering from surgery. This polemic against nonfigurative art is further bolstered by a psychological theory known as "emotional congruence," which holds that already anxious patients in a medical setting will experience the ambiguity and unfamiliarity of nonfigurative art as stressful. They will tend to read into it some figurative meaning that is depressing or frightening. A jagged line becomes a threatening knife, or the color red a representation of blood. The unfortunate result is an even greater compounding of their stress (Ulrich 2009, 134–41). Other researchers disagree (Karnik et al. 2014). Based on their own research, they assert that certain types of nonfigurative art characterized by pastel colors and more harmonious compositions with soft-edged amoeboid shapes and graceful curving lines can have therapeutic qualities. Such works can serve as positive distractions by stimulating flights of the imagination or attempts to translate them into figurative depictions. In many cases, the viewer may simply enjoy their color harmony or captivating

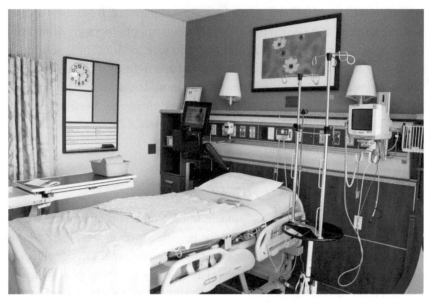

Figure 7. Each patient room at UF Health in Gainesville contains two large-scale photographs of some aspect of the Florida landscape.

compositions. Representatives of this position argue one should match the graphic art in a medical facility with the constituency of its patients. In many rural areas with a population with little exposure to nonfigurative art, such art is mostly inappropriate and should be little used. They affirm that in more urban settings it can be appropriate to mix it with figurative art to provide variety and appeal to a more heterogeneous patient population (Domke 2009, 55–78; Camp 2015). One thing is certain: this issue calls for more research (Nanda et al. 2009).

While this controversy remains unresolved, the medium of photography, especially depicting nature scenes, has proven to be an effective reliever of stress among patients and staff. There are even instances in healthcare facilities where the staff contribute their own photographs for display with very positive results. At UF Health's medical campus, staff, including not only professional caregivers but also maintenance workers, IT specialists, and administrators, have contributed photographs of the Florida landscape to the art collection on display. The result is each patient room contains two large-scale photographs of some aspect of the Florida landscape, such as seascapes, wetlands, flowers, and birds (figure 7). Next to each photograph is a small plaque identifying the photographer and his or her position in the medical complex—janitor, nurse, physician, or parking attendant. These small plaques act as a bridge between healthcare worker and those being cared for, and that

bridge leads to the emotional space of common experience. It builds an awareness for families that their nurse also participates in photography or that the
IT specialist took a picture at a place they too love to visit. These seemingly
unrelated thoughts are, in fact, at the heart of arts in health. The arts are employed to create a climate of human-to-human understanding. They nurture
and expand the notion that we are all connected through experience regardless of which side of the hospital bed we find ourselves (Rainey and Schrader
2014, 32–33).

Conclusion

Over 150 years ago, Florence Nightingale, in her pioneering efforts for a better
healthcare environment, championed the healing power of art: "The effect in
sickness of beautiful objects, of variety of objects, and especially of brilliancy
of color is hardly at all appreciated. . . . People say the effect is only in the
mind. It is no such thing. The effect is on the body, too" (Nightingale 1969, 59)
Today such design features are beginning to be more than "appreciated." They
are becoming essentials in a humane medical environment. There is a bit of
irony in this, for the early twentieth-century medical science that downplayed
the arts or regarded them as superfluous frills now has helped establish their
importance. Today the arts in medicine are undergoing a renaissance, a true
rebirth, for until their neglect during the first two-thirds of the twentieth century, they were always a part of healing practices as far as we can gaze back
into the mists of earliest humanity. The drums of Inuit Shamans, the sand
paintings of Navaho healers, the statues in Ancient Greek healing shrines,
the ornate, colorful ceilings in Medieval hospitals, and the soothing music for
mental patients in Ottoman Empire hospitals (Sonke-Henderson 2007) testify
to the pervading presence of the arts in medicine throughout most of human
history. Today what art can do for patients and staff in concert with the clinical
work of physicians and staff is powerful medicine. We live in a world where
the medical sciences and technology continue to create solutions to almost
unimaginable problems and draw the world closer than ever before to the notion that most of the diseases of our time can be cured. This broadening vision
of health care includes hospitals and other types of care facilities that surround
their patients and staff with creativity in both the arts and sciences. The arts
in health programs and the design of more humane healthcare environments
across the nation have grown out of that vision. What began as an investigation into the possible benefit of using art to relieve stress has now become a
major part of the culture of care at many medical facilities in the United States
and throughout much of the world.

References

Beauchemin, K. M., & Hayes, P. (1996). Sunny hospital rooms expedite recovery from severe and refractory depression. *Journal of Affective Disorders,* 40(1–2), 49–51.

Benedetti, F., Colombo, C., Barbini, B., Campori, E., & Smeraldi, E. (2001). Morning light reduces length of hospitalization in bipolar depression. *Journal of Affective Disorders,* 62(3), 221–23.

Berry, L. L., Parker, D., Coile, R. C., Hamilton, D. K., O'Neill, D. D., & Sadler, B. L. (2004). The business case for better buildings. *Frontiers of Health Services Management,* 21(1), 3–24.

Camp, Reba (2015). Administrator, Environment of Care, University of Virginia Medical Center. Interview with authors, September 15.

Carpman, J., Grant, M. A., & Simmons, D. A. (1984). *No More Mazes: Research about Design for Wayfinding in Hospitals.* Ann Arbor: University of Michigan Hospitals.

Carpman, J., Grant, M. A., & Simmons, D. A. (1985). Hospital design and wayfinding: A video simulation study. *Environment and Behavior,* 17(3), 296–314.

Cassileth, B, Vickers, A., & Magill, L. (2003). Music therapy for mood disturbance during hospitalization for autologous stem cell transplantation: A randomized controlled trial. *Cancer,* 98(12), 2723–29.

Center for Health Design. (2008). *An Introduction to Evidence-Based Design.* EDAC Study Guide no. 1. Concord, CA: Center for Health Design.

Domke, H. (2009). *Picture of Health: Handbook for Healthcare Art.* New Bloomfield, MO: Henry Domke Fine Art.

Evans, J. E. 2007. The science of creativity and health. In: Serlin, E. A. (Ed.), *Whole Person Healthcare,* vol. 3, *The Arts and Health,* 86–105. Westport, CT: Praeger.

Felten, D. (1993). The brain and the immune system. In Moyers, B. (Ed.), *Healing and the Mind,* 213–37. New York: Doubleday.

Graham-Pole, J., Lane, M. R., Kitakis, M. L. & Staacpoole. L. (1991). Re-storying lives, restoring selves: The arts and healing. *International Journal of Arts in Medicine,* 1(1), 34–38.

Hackney, M. E., Kantorovich, S., Levin, R., & Earhart, G. M. (2007). Effects of tango on functional mobility in Parkinson's disease: A preliminary study. *Journal of Neurological Physical Therapy,* 31(4), 173–79.

Harris, P. B., McBride, G., Ross, C., & Curtis, C. (2002). A place to heal: Environmental sources of satisfaction among hospital patients. *Journal of Applied Social Psychology,* 32(6), 1276–99.

Hill, J. N., & LaVela, S. L. (2015). Noise levels in patient rooms and at nursing stations at three VA medical centers. *Health Environments Research and Design Journal,* 9(1), 54–63.

Hond, P. (2015). The Hippocratic overture. *Columbia Magazine,* Spring/Summer,18–27.

Karnik, M., Printz, B., & Finkel, J. (2014). A hospital's contemporary art collection: Effects on patient mood, stress, comfort, and expectations. *Health Environments Research and Design Journal,* 7(3), 60–77.

Kirk, H. D. (2013). Facility design to reduce hospital-acquired infection. *Health Environments Research and Design Journal,* 6(2), 93–97.

Laursen, J., Danielsen, A., & Rosenberg, J. (2014). Effects of environmental design on patient outcome: A systematic review. *Health Environments Research and Design Journal,* 7(4), 108–19.

Lavender, S. A., Sommerich, C. M., Patterson, E. S., Sanders, E. B. N., Evans, K. D., Park, S., Umur, R. Z. R., & Li, J. (2015). Hospital patient room design. *Health Environments Research and Design Journal*, 8(4), 98–114.

Marcus, C. C., & Sachs, N. A. (2014). *Therapeutic Landscapes: An Evidence-Based Approach to Designing Healing Gardens and Restorative Outdoor Spaces.* Hoboken, NJ: John Wiley & Sons.

Miller, A. C., Hickman, C., & Lemasters, G. K. (1992). A distraction technique for control of burn pain. *Journal of Burn Care and Rehabilitation*, 13(5), 576–80.

Nainis, N., Paice, J., Ratner, J., Wirth, J., Lai, J., & Shott, S. (2006). Relieving symptoms in cancer: Innovative use of art therapy. *Journal of Pain and Symptom Management*, 31(2), 162–69.

Nanda, U., Chanaud, C. M., Brown, L., Hart, R., & Hathorn, K. (2009). Pediatric art preferences: Countering the "one-size-fits-all" approach. *Health Environments Research and Design Journal*, 2(4), 46–61.

Nightingale, F. ([1859] 1969). *Notes on Nursing, What It Is, and What It Is Not.* New York: Dover.

Pati, D., Harvey, T. E., Jr., Reyers, E., Evans, J., Waggener, L., Serrano, M., Saucier, R., & Nagle, T. (2009). A multidimensional framework for assessing patient room configurations. *Health Environments Research and Design Journal*, 2(2), 88–111.

Pati, D., Harvey, T. E., Willis, D. A., & Pati, S. (2015). Identifying elements of the health care environment that contribute to wayfinding. *Health Environments Research and Design Journal*, 8(3), 44–67.

Pati, D., O'Boyle, M., Amor, C., Jiancheng, H., Valipoor, S., & Fang, D. (2014). Neural correlates of nature stimuli: An fMRI study. *Health Environments Research and Design Journal*, 7(2), 9–28.

Pollitt, B. (2015). Vice-president of facilities, UF Shands Cancer Hospital, Gainesville, FL. Interview with authors, October 14.

Rainey, R. M., & Schrader, A. M. (2014). *Architecture as Medicine: The UF Shands Cancer Hospital, A Case Study.* Charlottesville: University of Virginia School of Architecture.

Rollins, J. A. (2011). Arousing curiosity: When hospital art transcends. *Health Environments Research and Design Journal*, 4(3), 72–94.

Sacks, O. (2007). *Musicophilia: Tales of Music and the Brain.* New York: Alfred A. Knopf.

Sadler, B. L., & Ridenour, A. (2009). *Transforming the Healthcare Environment through the Arts.* San Diego: Aesthetics.

Sharpe, P. A., & Schmidt, M. G. (2011). Control and mitigation of healthcare-acquired infections: Designing clinical trials to evaluate new materials and technologies. *Health Environments Research and Design Journal*, 5(1), 94–115.

Shepley, M. M., Gerbi, R. P., Watson, A. B., Imgrund, S., & Sagha-Zadeh, R. (2012). The impact of daylight and views on ICU patients and staff. *Health Environments Research and Design Journal*, 5(2), 46–60.

Sonke-Henderson, J. (2007). History of the arts and health across cultures. In: Serlin, I. A. (Ed.), *Whole Person Healthcare*, vol. 3, *The Arts and Health*, 22–41. Westport, CT: Praeger.

Sonke-Henderson, J., & Brandman, R. (2007). The hospital artist in residence programs: Narratives of healing. In: Serlin, I. A. (Ed.), *Whole Person Healthcare*, vol. 3, *The Arts and Health*, 67–86. Westport, CT: Praeger.

Staricoff, R. (2004). *Arts and Health: A Review of the Medical Literature*. London: Arts Council of England.

State of the Field Committee. (2009). *State of the Field Report: Arts in Healthcare*. Washington, DC: Society for the Arts in Healthcare.

Sternberg, E. M. (2009). *Healing Spaces: The Science of Place and Well-Being.* Cambridge, MA: Harvard University Press.

Tanzer, K. (2014). Former dean of the School of Architecture, University of Virginia. Interview with authors, April 14.

Toph, M. (1988). Noise-induced occupational stress and health in critical care nurses. *Environmental Behavior,* 21(6), 717–33.

Toph, M., & Thompson, S. (2001). Interactive relationships between hospital patients and noise-induced stress and other issues with sleep. *Heart & Lung,* 30(4), 237–43.

Ulrich, R. S. (1984). View through a window may influence recovery from surgery. *Science,* 224(4647): 420–21.

Ulrich, R. S. (2009). Effects of viewing art on health outcomes. In: Frampton, S. B., & Charmel, P. A. (Eds.), *Putting Patients First: Best Practices in Patient-Centered Care,* 2nd ed., 129–49. San Francisco: Jossey-Bass.

Ulrich, R. S., Zimring, C., Quan, X., Joseph, A., & Choudhary, R. (2004). The role of the physical environment in the hospital of the 21st century: A once-in-a-lifetime opportunity. Center for Health Design. https://www.healthdesign.org/chd/knowledge-repository /role-physical-environment-hospital-21st-century-once-lifetime-opportunity-0.

Ulrich, R. S., Zimring, C., Zhu, X., DuBose, J., Seo, H. B., Chol, Y. S., & Quanix, J. A. (2008). A review of the research literature on evidence-based health care design. *Health Environments Research and Design Journal,* 2(3), 61–125.

Vincent, E., Battisto, D., Grimes, C., & McCubbin, J. (2010). The effects of nature images on pain in a simulated hospital patient room. *Health Environments Research and Design Journal,* 3(3), 56–69.

Wakins, N., & Siddiqui, Z. (2015). The gray area of healthcare design. *Healthcare Design,* 15(0), 50–52.

Zadeh, R. S., Shepley, M. M., Williams, G., & Chung, S. S. E. (2014). The impact of windows and daylight on acute-care nurses' physiological, psychological, and behavioral health. *Health Environments Research and Design Journal,* 7(4), 35–61.

DESIGN FOR AGING

New Models in Senior Living

EMILY CHMIELEWSKI AND J. DAVID HOGLUND

The Age Wave: Why We Need to Plan for the Elder Consumer

As of January 1, 2011, baby boomers (the generation of Americans born between 1946 and 1964—the largest generation in our country's history to date) began turning sixty-five. At an estimated rate of approximately ten thousand Americans reaching this age each day, this population of seniors will continue to grow until 2030, when all boomers have reached the age of sixty-five.[1]

The rapid aging of America will shift the country's demographics, from 12 percent (37 million people) age sixty-five or older in 2005 to a projected 19 percent (81 million) in 2050.[2] This demographic shift is occurring alongside changes in the traditional multigenerational family. More older adults are living alone and are relying on informal means to meet their needs for services, or they are relying on primary-care healthcare service providers who are often lacking in their ability to meet seniors' special requirements. Like many other countries, the United States is also experiencing greater diversity in our population. Minority ethnic groups, especially the growing number of Hispanics and Asians, will present unique cultural requirements. More people will also be looking for like-minded communities, uniting around such affinities as religion, lifestyle, and sexual orientation.[3]

Just as the baby boomers have influenced American culture their entire lives, this population will continue to affect the economy, politics, technology, religion, and the country's social behaviors and values as we move toward the future. Taken as a whole, this generation of seniors is more tolerant of change, more technologically savvy, less religious, and more liberal than older generations.[4] They are also more ethnically diverse and come from a variety of personal experiences, with more divorced couples as well as late-in-life marriages, greater visibility and acceptance of same-sex relationships, and generally better health, plus higher levels of education (and therefore typically higher incomes and standards of living) than previous generations.[5]

In sum, the drivers of change in the senior living industry include:

- Significant growth and rapid aging of the over-sixty-five population, worldwide
- Longer life expectancies with better health and active lifestyles
- More seniors are living alone, plus fewer professional caregivers
- Product acceptance is rising, though needs to be flexible and appeal to a large but diverse audience

The senior living industry must recognize and plan for the different needs and expectations of this generation. In the near future, programs and services geared toward elders will need to have greater flexibility and appeal to a large but varied audience. The way in which senior living care providers, architects and designers, and businesses in general attract older adults and support their needs and interests is inherently changing as we respond to changing consumer demands. The aging population in the United States, and around the world, will impact many facets of our lives, from the delivery of healthcare services to cultural beliefs. It should also influence the way we design our homes and cities.

The State of Senior-Friendly Housing in America

According to a report released in 2014 by the Joint Center for Housing Studies of Harvard University, the United States needs to support aging in the community by "taking immediate steps to address the deficiencies in the housing stock, community preparedness, and the health care system [that] are vital to our national standard of living."[6] Through extensive research in the field of environment-behavior, we also know that the design of the physical environment can affect the quality of life and well-being of all people and has an even greater impact on vulnerable populations who need more environmental support, such as older adults.

Seniors need special design consideration for many reasons. Although each person's life and personality are unique, everyone experiences different physiological and psychological changes as they age. Designing senior-friendly environments accommodates such changes to facilitate everyday activities and minimize obstacles to a good quality of life. "If properly designed, a senior living facility can contribute positively to an older person's independence, dignity, health, and enjoyment of life. If poorly planned and detailed, it can imprison, confuse, and depress."[7]

When designing for an elderly population, the main objectives are to provide the following:

- A safe and comfortable environment that is supportive of the residents' need to maintain independence

- A design that seamlessly incorporates environmental supports in an unobtrusive manner
- Spaces that encourage good nutrition, physical fitness, and social connections
- A design that addresses the six characteristics of aging that have the largest impact on older adults' relationship to their environment: loss of balance, cognitive impairment, loss of strength, visual impairment, hearing impairment, and increased sensitivity to cold, drafts, and direct sunlight

In the United States, roughly one-quarter of adults aged fifty and older have an age-related impairment (e.g., difficulty with hearing, vision, cognition, or mobility); by the age of eighty-five, the proportion increases to 68 percent.[8] Unfortunately, many American homes do not have "basic accessibility features, preventing older adults with disabilities from living safely and comfortably in their homes."[9] Without a supportive residential environment, many older adults find themselves needing to relocate to more supportive housing, be it a stand-alone facility or by entering into a continuum of care within a Life Plan Community (formerly known as continuing care retirement communities, or CCRCs).

In addition to designing environments that address older adults' basic physical, psychological, and socio-emotional needs, we also should be exploring ways to support aging-in-place and leverage existing community resources so that seniors can stay in their homes longer. Focusing on wellness and creating real homes for people—not simply "home-like" settings—are becoming the industry norm these days. But as we look to the future, there are many additional ways designers can respond to the growing senior market, improve people's quality of life, and address their varied interests.

Senior Living Design Trends

Today's seniors are not looking for "home-like" settings; they want *real* homes in *real* communities that just so happen to offer senior-friendly services and supportive environments. They are looking for very different housing products, elder-specific supportive services, and lifestyle options than what past generations had or were interested in. Choice, options, and variety are now the concepts guiding design, financial structures, and development.

Seeing this shift in the market, senior living providers are experiencing (or are planning for) changes in their models of care and/or the way they deliver supportive services. Seniors expect, and designers are providing, a variety of interior styles, spatial layouts, and finishes that are commonly found in market-rate housing or hospitality settings. The following is an overview of these senior living design trends.

Aging-in-Place

Seniors typically want to remain connected to their community, established social network, and family, rather than move to a senior-specific care facility. Aging-in-place occurs when an older adult chooses—and is able—to continue living in his or her own home and adapt it for the services and support required. In fact, given the choice, 73 percent of Americans would rather stay in their homes and age-in-place than move to a senior living facility, and 67 percent want to stay within their communities.[10]

Unfortunately, millions of seniors are living in homes that are not accessible, lacking essential features such as "a no-step entry, single-floor living, extra-wide doorways and halls, accessible electrical controls and switches, and lever-style door and faucet handles. Indeed, the 2011 American Housing Survey reports that just [1 percent] of US housing units have all five of these universal design features. Roughly two in five housing units in the country have either none or only one of these features."[11] Aging-in-place is not just about housing, though; integrated services are critical, and sound urban planning is essential.

Thus, aging-in-place relies on a supportive physical environment, community-based programs and services, and technology that allow for at-home care and assistance. This can occur within one's home and the surrounding neighborhood, or within a senior living community.

The issue of aging-in-place is so important because older adults' day-to-day feelings of competence, relatedness, and autonomy influence their emotional well-being.[12] Fortunately, there are more and more ways that aging-in-place is being supported today, including naturally occurring retirement communities, age-friendly cities, Life Plan Communities without walls (when at-home services are provided beyond the campus), hub-and-spoke projects (where a senior living provider—the hub—has one or more satellite sites—the spokes), and even aging-in-place within a Life Plan Community.

Leveraging Resources and Connecting to the Greater Community

When creating a senior living community there are two main ways to offer services and amenities: provide everything on campus or within the building, or take advantage of existing resources in the surrounding neighborhood. Not too long ago, the former was prevalent. Large-scale Life Plan Community de-

Figure 1. Central Village Demonstrator Project, Apple Valley, Minnesota. Perkins Eastman. Creating age-friendly communities is becoming more common, such as this age-friendly demonstration project to create a Central Village in an underutilized part of Apple Valley, with access to transportation hubs and central to the city's core services and retail. (Perkins Eastman)

velopments would provide residents with everything on-site, from dining venues to a bank branch. Many of today's seniors, however, are not as interested in living within this kind of gated, one-stop-shop community. They want variety and choice, options and connectivity to the world around them. So, to respond to this demand, senior living communities are leveraging existing resources and connecting to the greater community (see figure 1).

The primary ways a senior living community can leverage resources and connect to the greater community include the following:

- Supporting residents' existing relationships and life patterns
- Having a close proximity to local services and amenities and/or easy access to public transit
- Creating opportunities for intergenerational interactions
- Developing urban models or hub-and-spoke communities that integrate into the surrounding neighborhood
- Offering programming to members of the greater community or hosting others on-site
- Developing partnerships with non-senior providers, such as integrating retail on-site (a mixed-use development) or becoming affiliated with an institute of higher learning

According to the World Health Organization's *Global Age-Friendly Cities: A Guide,* "Participating in leisure, social, cultural, and spiritual activities in the community, as well as with the family, allows older people to continue to exercise their competence, to enjoy respect and esteem, and to maintain or establish supportive and caring relationships."[13] *Housing America's Older Adults,* a report of the Joint Center for Housing Studies of Harvard University, also states that these connections can "lower the risk of isolation, while access to amenities, health care, supportive services, and retail stores enhances [elders'] ability to remain independent."[14]

Unfortunately, many seniors live in lower-density suburban or rural areas where neighborhood resources can only be accessed by car. Since many older adults' ability to drive is limited or taken away, it can be difficult to go shopping, visit friends and family, or access senior-specific services and programs. In fact, the AARP's *Home and Community Preferences of the 45+ Population* explained that about 20 percent of people over the age of fifty occasionally or regularly missed an activity they wanted to do because they could not drive to the event.[15] So, if older adults cannot drive, they need to be able to walk to the services and amenities offered by the greater community. Thus, in addition to safe and walkable sidewalks and other senior-friendly pedestrian infrastructure, a major factor to consider is proximity. Seniors need to be close to the services and amenities in the greater community in order to make use of them.

Accordingly, urban senior living communities are a growing trend. These urban developments are highly integrated with their surrounding neighborhood, allowing residents to walk or take mass transit to a variety of existing resources found in the neighborhood. Urban developments are not the only ones that can be integrated into the neighborhood, though. Suburban and even rural senior living communities can also be sited to take advantage of neighborhood resources. For instance, a small hub-and-spoke satellite community could be located within several blocks of a senior-friendly shopping center, pedestrian mall, or thriving small town that boasts a vibrant network of shops and unique events.

Another trend is to build a mixed-use development that integrates retail within the senior living residential campus or building (figure 2). In addition, more and more senior living communities are connecting to the surrounding neighborhood by inviting people in and by becoming a resource to members of the greater community. Today's senior living facilities are more commonly offering services, programs, and amenities that are open to the public. Some senior living communities are also serving as a host for outside events and organizations. In this scenario, the senior living community becomes the venue for outside groups' presentations, meetings, weddings, community or school theater performances, home-based healthcare services, social services, counseling, and so forth. Beyond providing the necessary space, programs, and

Figure 2. Christie Place, Scarsdale, New York. Perkins Eastman. Senior living developments in town centers and near public transportation, dining, and services/amenities are popular with many older adults. (Sarah Mechling/Perkins Eastman)

amenities, if a senior living community invites in the public or acts as a host, the campus or building also needs to have an inviting and welcoming entry, easy wayfinding, secure and clear divisions between publicly accessed and resident-only spaces, and adequate parking for the visiting public. By becoming a neighborhood resource and/or by hosting others, a senior living community can use its common spaces and programming to affirm the presence of its residents while also inviting in members of the greater community. This can promote a stronger and broader sense of community, as well as develop a synergy with the surrounding neighborhood.

Senior living communities are also establishing relationships with other senior-friendly service providers, such as entertainment venues or educational institutions. In a recent study, the three most common types of partnerships were focused on music, theater, or art programs, medical or rehab services, and continuing education or lifelong learning classes.[16] University affiliations are also a popular trend and are becoming more so as seniors want to stay cognitively active, pursue personal interests further, and interact in an intergenerational environment. There are multiple senior living communities located near institutes of higher learning, with arrangements for residents to audit classes, visit university medical facilities, use amenities like the campus fitness facilities, and even mentor students or volunteer in school-run programs.

Wellness

Whatever form new developments will take, they must accommodate the specific "wellness" needs of an aging population. These must include appeals to personal interest and higher levels of care. Such needs will require a variety of architectural responses. Wellness is a multidimensional state of being, describing the existence of positive health in an individual as exemplified by "quality of life" and a "sense of well-being." The concept of wellness taps all the senses—vision, hearing, taste, touch, smell, balance, and motion. According to Dr. Bill Hettler, cofounder of the National Wellness Institute, there are six dimensions of wellness: occupational, physical, social, intellectual, spiritual, and emotional.[17] However, many also add on environmental and financial, for a total of eight dimensions of whole-person wellness.[18]

Holistic wellness can be supported by the physical environment in many different ways, such as the provision of fitness and clinic facilities; communal dining rooms; venues for social gatherings; a connection to the greater community; places to stimulate the mind, such as libraries, lecture halls, meeting spaces, and classrooms; opportunities for choice, privacy, and control; places for reflection, meditation, or spiritual worship; areas to practice or learn new skills and hobbies; ways to connect with nature; and incorporating ecologically sustainable design practices. A growing trend in the marketplace is to offer a center for healthy living that brings all of these elements together under one program or roof (figure 3).

Connecting to nature is also important for seniors—from having good views of the outdoors to having easy access to walking trails, outdoor patios or balconies, and other exterior common spaces. Ecological sustainability, or "green" design, is also part of whole-person wellness. By living in a green building and/or practicing ecological sustainability, an older adult not only enriches his or her own life but also the lives of others—from next-door neighbors to people living on the other side of the globe.

Appealing to Personal Interests

Today's senior consumers have some clear opinions on what they are looking for and want to customize their living experiences. Like anyone else, seniors want to shape their day-to-day lives and choose how their needs are met. This includes having access to an extensive array of amenities, a variety of floor plans and customizable residential units, the ability to pursue personal interests and surround oneself with like-minded peers, and the opportunity to care for others, not just be cared for.

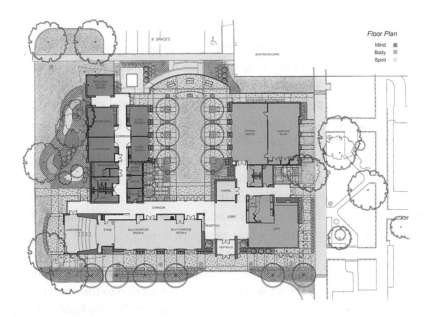

Figure 3. C.C. Young—The Point, Dallas, Texas. Perkins Eastman. Providing spaces that support whole-person wellness goes beyond well-designed fitness areas. Mind, body, and spirit all must be considered. (Perkins Eastman)

In regard to residential units, older adults want to tailor their homes to their own aesthetic tastes and functional needs. In 2010, when Perkins Eastman polled 128 senior living providers and industry consultants about senior living trends, 93 percent felt that new and emerging lifestyles and choices would dictate customization of residential unit spaces.[19] Some senior living providers are going so far as to design residential units as empty shells that can be finished as each resident desires.

Another way senior living residents are looking for choice is in how they spend their days. In the 2014 *Design for Aging Review 12,* "Insights and Innovations: The State of Senior Housing," it was reported that when providers and designers were asked what was more critical to the success of the project, 63 percent stated that the common spaces were more important than the units/private spaces. In this same study, when providers and designers were asked what design elements were included specifically to attract the targeted market, common features reported included offering multiple dining venues, with casual to formal options, and fitness, spa,/ and/or wellness amenities to meet market demand (figure 4).

There are also specialized senior living communities that are designed to

Figure 4. Spring Lake Village, Santa Rosa, California. Perkins Eastman. Today's seniors tend to take a proactive approach to their health and well-being. Fitness and wellness spaces should be functional and inviting, as they are more than just marketing showpieces. (Chris Cooper)

attract a particular type of resident, whether it is people who share a personal interest (i.e., gourmet food and wine, gardening, or art), a personal affiliation, or a common background (figure 5). Providers are finding a market for environments that attract like-minded adults. Examples include Veterans' Homes, The Lillian Booth Actors Home in New York City, religion-based communities, ethnic or culturally based communities, as well as LGBT communities.

The practice of aging-in-place within an intentional community is also becoming more common.[20] In fact, senior cohousing is now being more widely developed in the United States, though has a long history in other countries such as Denmark. These small communities allow residents to engage in meaningful social roles, which help prevent loneliness, depression, and isolation.[21] Residents of cohousing are not expected to become primary caregivers for their neighbors (as one might do for a family member), but they do develop neighborly relationships that support aging-in-place.

In fact, in the entire senior living industry, the concept of seniors solely as care *recipients* is being questioned, with more programs enabling seniors to play an active and meaningful role as care *givers*—a good thing since a strong sense of meaning has been correlated with an extended number of years of life.[22]

Figure 5. NewBridge on the Charles, Dedham, Massachusetts. Perkins Eastman. From a love of art to wine, professions to personal affiliations, specialized senior living communities attract residents who share personal interests and/or similar past histories. (Hebrew SeniorLife)

Higher Levels of Care

Until about twenty-five years ago, housing for the elderly—especially frail elderly needing long-term care—was provided in traditional, institutional facilities. The approaches to care and the physical environment usually did not support providing person-centered care. "Person-centered care promotes choice, purpose, and meaning in daily life. Person-centered care means that nursing home residents are supported in achieving the level of physical, mental, and psychosocial well-being that is individually practicable. This goal honors the importance of keeping the person at the center of the care planning and decision-making process."[23]

More recently, however, a new industry perspective has brought about the culture change movement, which has resulted in significant changes to both models of care and the way physical environments support staff, residents, and the families of residents.

Culture change can be seen in the person-centered care practices being

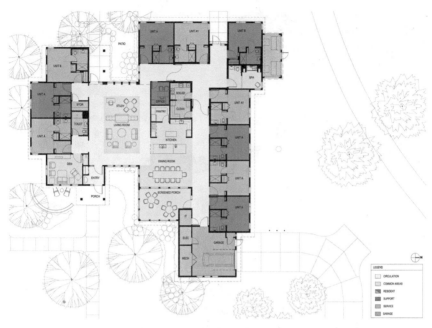

Figure 6. U.S. Department of Veterans Affairs—Danville, Danville, Illinois. Perkins East-man. A small house is typically defined as ten to twelve private residential bedrooms organized around a shared living/dining/kitchen area. This could be built as a stand-alone home (typically with four or five homes grouped together), or as a floor or wing in a larger building. (Perkins Eastman)

adopted by providers and is also evidenced by the changes in the physical environment, such as the development of the small house model (figure 6). Adopting a person-centered approach results in a community in which residents and professional caregivers all have choices and can make meaningful contributions to their environment. This is important because operational and design decisions that empower people and that offer resident-centered care can influence building occupants' mental, social, emotional, and physical well-being—which, therefore, affects their quality of life (figure 7).[24]

Another trend is the convergence of the healthcare and senior living sectors. Lines of accountability and responsibility in the healthcare and senior care industries will continue to blur, due in part to the shift to reimbursement by the federal government and the insurance industry. The goal is for care providers to offer proactive programs and services and, in some cases, living environments that allow seniors to remain independent and thrive.[25]

One area where senior living and health care naturally converge is in short-term rehabilitation settings. Short-term rehab is a cost-effective way to enable patients with injuries, acute illnesses, or post-operative care needs to recover

Figure 7. Abe's Garden, Nashville, Tennessee. Perkins Eastman. Carefully designed programming and physical environments can support residents' higher quality of life, promote social interactions, and maintain—even extend—higher functioning with activities of daily living. (Sarah Mechling/Perkins Eastman)

outside a hospital environment. The high cost of hospital stays has driven insurance providers to move patients out of the hospital as quickly as possible, creating a demand for short-term rehab and spurring its growth. Also, it is not unusual for those who can live at home, even with the support of family and/or visiting nurse services, to require ongoing outpatient rehab.[26]

Short-term care focuses on patient rehabilitation, as opposed to centering on residents' quality of life, which is at the center of long-term care. In addition, since patients are expecting to return home after staying in the facility for only a few weeks, they are less interested in being made to feel at home or create social connections in the community. Thus, the length of stay, the differences in care needs, and expectations about returning home are the key distinctions between the short-term patient and the long-term resident. These distinctions drive the program and service (as well as the physical environment), resulting in short-term rehab facilities that tend to be styled more like hospitality and healthcare environments than residences (figure 8).

Addressing the need for programs and spaces that support people with cognitive issues is also a growing trend since between 2010 and 2050 "it is projected that the number of individuals in the U.S. aged 65 years and older with [Alzheimer's] disease will triple, from 5 million to 13.8 million. During this same time, the number of persons aged 85 years and older with the dis-

Figure 8. MorseLife: Sondra & David S. Mack Pavilion, West Palm Beach, Florida. Perkins Eastman. Tightly bound to the healthcare industry, short-term rehabilitation facilities are a cost-effective way for patients with injuries, acute illnesses, or post-operative care needs to recover outside a hospital environment and have emerged as a critical component to the continuum of care. (Tom Hurst)

ease is projected to reach 7 million, accounting for half (51 percent) of the 65+ population with Alzheimer's."[27]

The evolution of care for people with dementia has come a long way in the last few decades, with meaningful initiatives taking root across sectors to promote health, wellness, and a high quality of life for this population. Given the increasing costs of formal and informal dementia care, the heavy financial burden on family caregivers, and the Affordable Care Act, it is important to also consider the financial benefits that can derive from a well-designed physical environment. As seen in the studies conducted on The Green House Project Small Houses, residents living in these environments have lower Medicare and Medicaid expenditures as a result of staffing and operational efficiencies, fewer or shorter lengths of stays in hospitals, and residents maintaining their functional status longer.[28]

The Promise of Healthy Environments and Communities for Seniors

It is clear that change is underway. A recent Perkins Eastman survey (2015) polled nearly two hundred senior industry providers and consultants and produced the following results:

- 61 percent felt that the Great Recession had permanently changed people's outlook for their retirement choices
- 61 percent believed that the traditional continuing care retirement community model (now known as Life Plan Communities) needs to be rethought
- While only 10 percent currently have a direct partnership with a healthcare provider, 50 percent felt they would have one in the future

The senior demographic will represent an increasingly large influence over communities and will shape how they respond to new needs, demands, and services. Seniors will have an increasing political influence and will drive policy by their sheer numbers, use of disposable retirement income and benefits, and health needs accompanying aging. In addition, current conversations about population health management are intriguing because of the holistic approach it takes to creating healthy communities across all age spectrums. Future solutions will look broadly at housing and services rather than just age-specific solutions.

New models will emerge that build on the types of partnerships and community resources discussed in this essay. Hopefully partnerships will emerge that bring different talents, expertise, and insights to the table. For instance, the Vitalocity consortium is forming to advise cities on age-friendly planning and design. Vitalocity is an interdisciplinary planning group taking a broad look at senior options, nutrition, technology, city planning, and design. The partnership includes Ecumen, BusinessLab (UK), Kendal Corporation, IBM, Sodexo, Nestle, and Perkins Eastman.

We are already seeing a boomer receptivity to the product offerings and the experiences companies like these bring. But there is no one solution. The demographics, personal experiences, and lifestyles of aging Americans argue for a growing diversity of ideas and options. This essay has captured some of the current leading-edge thinking about healthy environments, models, and opportunities. However, they still fall in a narrow range and only begin to touch the challenges of affordability and an expanding longevity. More is yet to come.

Notes

1. Cohn and Taylor, Baby Boomers Approach 65.
2. Passel and Cohn, U.S. Population Projections: 2005–2050.
3. Perkins Eastman, *Building Type Basics for Senior Living*, 3.
4. Cohn and Taylor, Baby Boomers Approach 65.
5. Federal Interagency Forum on Aging-Related Statistics, *Older Americans 2012*.

6. Joint Center for Housing Studies of Harvard University, Housing America's Older Adults, 1.

7. Perkins Eastman, *Building Type Basics for Senior Living,* 4.

8. Joint Center for Housing Studies of Harvard University, Housing America's Older Adults, 11.

9. Ibid., 1.

10. Keenan, *Home and Community Preferences of the 45+ Population,* 2, 7.

11. Joint Center for Housing Studies of Harvard University, Housing America's Older Adults, 4.

12. Reis et al., Daily well-being, 419–35.

13. World Health Organization (WHO), *Global Age-Friendly Cities,* 38.

14. Joint Center for Housing Studies of Harvard University, Housing America's Older Adults, 24.

15. Keenan, *Home and Community Preferences of the 45+ Population.*

16. Perkins Eastman, *Design for Aging Review 10.*

17. Hettler, Six Dimensions of Wellness Model.

18. Substance Abuse and Mental Health Services Administration, Eight Dimensions of Wellness.

19. Hoglund, et al., Look at the External Market Influences on Senior Living.

20. Thomas and Blanchard, Moving beyond place, 12–17.

21. Jang et al., Role of mastery and social resources in the associations between disability and depression in later life, 807–13.

22. Krase, Meaning in life and mortality, 517–27.

23. National Nursing Home Quality Improvement Campaign, Person-Centered Care.

24. Gabriel and Bowling, Quality of life from the perspectives of older people, 675–91.

25. Perkins Eastman, *Convergence of Healthcare and Senior Living.*

26. Perkins Eastman, *Building Type Basics for Senior Living,* 33, 44–47.

27. Hebert et al., Alzheimer disease in the United States (2010–2050) estimated using the 2010 census, 1778–83.

28. Oliva, Green House model gains traction as providers see payoff.

References

Aronson, L. (2014). New buildings for older people. *New York Times,* November 1. http://www.nytimes.com/2014/11/02/opinion/sunday/new-buildings-for-older-people.html?smid=nytcore-iphone-share&smprod=nytcore-iphone&_r=0.

Attitudes about Aging: A Global Perspective. (2014). Pew Research Center, Global Attitudes & Trends. Accessed October 6, 2017. http://www.pewglobal.org/2014/01/30/attitudes-about-aging-a-global-perspective/.

Chmielewski, E. (2014). Design for Aging Review 12: Insights and Innovations—The State of Senior Housing. In A. D. Community, *Design for Aging Review 12* (pp. 210-237). Mulgrave, Victoria, Australia: The Images Publishing Group.

Chmielewski, E., Steinberg, C., Rosenbaum-Cooks, K., & Cribbs, K. (2014). *Excellence in Design: Optimal Living Space for People With Alzheimer's Disease and Related Dementias.*

Cohn, D., & Taylor, P. (2010, December 20). *Baby Boomers Approach 65—Glumly | Pew*

Research Center's Social & Demographic Trends Project. Retrieved September 29, 2014, from PewResearch Social & Demographic Trends: http://www.pewsocialtrends.org /2010/12/20/baby-boomers-approach-65-glumly/

Federal Interagency Forum on Aging-Related Statistics. (2012). *Older Americans 2012: Key Indicators of Well-Being.* Washington, D.C.: U.S. Government Priniting Office.

Feng, Z., Coots, L., Kaganova, Y., & Wiener, J. (n.d.). *Hospital and emergency department use by people with Alzheimer's disease and related disorders: Final report. U.S. Department of Health and Human Services.* Retrieved April 7, 2014, from http://aspe.hhs.gov /daltcp/reports/2013/ADRDhedes.shtml

Gabriel, Z., & Bowling, A. (2004). Quality of life from the perspectives of older people. *Aging & Society, 24,* 675-691.

Glass, T. A., Mendes De Leon, C., Marottoli, R. A., & Berkman, L. F. (1999). Population based study of social and productive activities as predictors of survival among elderly Americans. *BMJ, 319,* 478-483.

Harris-Kojetin, L., Sengupta, M., Park-Lee, E., & Valverde, R. (2013). *Long-Term Care Services in the United States: 2013 Overview.* National Center for Health Statistics.

Hebert, L. E., Weuve, J., Scherr, P. A., & Evans, D. A. (2013). Alzheimer disease in the United States (2010-2050) estimated using the 2010 Census. *Neurology, 80*(19), 1778–83.

Hettler, B. (1976). *The Six Dimensions of Wellness Model.* Retrieved October 10, 2014, from http://c.ymcdn.com/sites/www.nationalwellness.org/resource/resmgr/docs/six dimensionsfactsheet.pdf

Jang, Y., Haley, W. E., Small, B. J., & Mortimer, J. A. (2002). The role of mastery and social resources in the associations between disability and depression in later life. *The Gerontologist, 42*(6), 807-813.

Joint Center for Housing Studies of Harvard University. (2014). *Housing America's Older Adults: Meeting the Needs of an Aging Population.*

Keenan, T. A. (2010). *Home and Community Preferences of the 45+ Population.* Washington, D.C.: AARP.

Koren, M. J. (2010). Person-centered care for nursing home residents: The culture-change movement. *Health Affairs, 29*(2), 1-6.

Krase, N. (2009). Meaning in life and mortality. *Journal of Gerontology: Social Sciences, 64B*(4), 517-527.

Lee, G. R., & Ishii-Kuntz, M. (1987). Social interaction, loneliness, and emotional wellbeing among the elderly. *Research on Aging, 9*(4), 459-482.

NORC Service Programs. (2014). Retrieved October 8, 2014, from New York City Department for the Aging: http://www.nyc.gov/html/dfta/html/services/retirement.shtml

Ogden, C. L., Fryar, C. D., Carroll, M. D., & Flegal, K. M. (2004). *Mean body weight, height, and body mass index: United States 1960-2002.* U.S. Department of Health and Human Services, Centers for Disease Control and Prevention, National Center for Health Statistics, Hyattsville, Maryland.

Oliva, J. (2014, April 21). *Green house model gains traction as providers see payoff.* Retrieved May 7, 2014, from Senior Housing News: http://seniorhousingnews.com/2014/04/21 /green-house-gains-senior-care-traction-providers-see-payoff/

Passel, J. S., & Cohn, D. (2008, February 11). *U.S. Population Projections: 2005-2050 | Pew Research Center's Hispanic Trends Project.* Retrieved September 29, 2014, from

PewResearch Hispanic Trends Project: http://www.pewhispanic.org/2008/02/11/us-population-projections-2005-2050/

Payne, L. L., Orsega-Smith, E., Roy, M., & Godbey, G. C. (2005). Local park use and personal health among older adults: an exploratory study. *Journal of Park and Recreation Administration, 23,* 1-20.

Pennix, B. W., van Tilburg, T., Kriegsman, D. M., Deeg, D. J., Boeke, A. J., & van Eijk, J. T. (1997). Effects of social support and personal coping resources on mortality in older age: The longitudinal aging study Amsterdam. *American Journal of Epidemiology, 146*(6), 510-519.

Perkins Eastman. (2009). *Design for Aging Review 9: Data Mining Findings.* Retrieved from http://www.aia.org/aiaucmp/groups/aia/documents/pdf/aiab079905.pdf

Perkins Eastman. (2010). *Design for Aging Review 10: Insights and Innovations—The State of Senior Housing.* Retrieved from http://www.aia.org/groups/aia/documents/pdf/aiab087283.pdf

Perkins Eastman. (2013). *Building Type Basics for Senior Living* (2 ed.). Hoboken, New Jersey: John Wiley & Sons.

Perkins Eastman. (2013). *Design for Aging Review 11: Insights and Innovations—The State of Senior Housing.* Retrieved from http://www.aia.org/aiaucmp/groups/aia/documents/pdf/aiab096294.pdf

Perkins Eastman. (2014). *The Convergence of Healthcare and Senior Living.*

Pew Research Center. (2014). *Attitudes about Aging: A Global Perspective.*

Pinquart, M., & Sörensen, S. (2003). Differences between caregivers and noncaregivers in psychological health and physical health: a meta-analysis. *Psychology and Aging, 18,* 250–67.

Reis, H. T., Sheldon, K. M., Gable, S. L., Roscoe, J., & Ryan, R. M. (2000). Daily well-being: The role of autonomy, competence, and relatedness. *Personality and Social Psychology Bulletin, 26*(4), 419-435.

Reker, G. T. (1997). Personal meaning, optimism, and choice: Existential predictors of depression in community and institutional elderly. *The Gerontologis, 37*(6), 709-716.

Schulz, R., & Martire, L. M. (2004). *Family caregiving of persons with dementia prevalence, health effects, and support strategies.* Retrieved April 7, 2014, from http://www.ucsur.pitt.edu/files/schulz/ajgpfamilycaregiving.pdf

Segmiller, D. J. (2014). *The State of Senior Living in the Carolinas.*

Severson, K. (2014, September 7). *Grandma's Meat Loaf? Hardly. Her Retirement Home Now Has a 3-Star Chef.* Retrieved September 9, 2014, from The New York Times: http://www.nytimes.com/2014/09/08/dining/grandmas-meat-loaf-hardly-her-retirement-home-now-has-a-3-star-chef.html?_r=0

Sugiyama, T., Ward Thompson, C., & Alves, S. (2009). Associations between neighborhood open space attributes and quality of life for older people in Britain. *Environment and Behavior, 41*(1), 3-21.

The Advancing Excellence in America's Nursing Homes Campaign. (n.d.). Retrieved March 17, 2014, from http://www.nhqualitycampaign.org/star_index.aspx?controls=personcenteredcareexploregoal

The Eight Dimensions of Wellness. (n.d.). Http://www.samhsa.gov/wellness-initiative/eight-dimensions-wellness

The Green House Project. (n.d.). *A New Pilot Study Finds Meaningful Savings in THE GREEN HOUSE® Model for Elder Care.* Retrieved May 7, 2014, from http://thegreen houseproject.org/doc/9/cost-saving-summary.pdf

Thoits, P. A. (1983). Multiple identities and psychological well-being: A reformulation and test of the social isolation hypothesi. *American Sociological Review, 48,* 174-187.

Thomas, W. H., & Blanchard, J. M. (2009). Moving beyond place: Aging in community. *Generations - Journal of the American Society on Aging, 33*(2), 12-17.

United Nations Department of Economic and Social Affairs, Population Division. (2006). *Population Ageing.* Retrieved October 6, 2014, from http://www.un.org/esa/population /publications/ageing/ageing2006.htm

Vitaliano, P. P., Zhang, J., & Scanlan, J. M. (2003). Is caregiving hazardous to one's physical health? A meta-analysis. *Psychological Bulletin, 129,* 946–72.

World Health Organization. (2007). *Global Age-Friendly Cities: A Guide.* Geneva, Switzerland: WHO Press. Retrieved from http://www.who.int/ageing/publications/Global_age _friendly_cities_Guide_English.pdf.

PART IV

CREATING A HEALTHY COMMUNITY FOOD SYSTEM

COMMUNITY FOOD INFRASTRUCTURE

A Vital Consideration for Planning Healthy Communities

SAMINA RAJA AND JENNIFER WHITTAKER

Planners and designers lay claim to creating places where people can lead full and healthy lives. A key characteristic of such a place is a well-functioning food system. Yet until recently the food system was "a stranger to the planning field" (Pothukuchi and Kaufman 2000). Although scholars and practitioners have outlined strategies for rebuilding community food systems (Caton Campbell 2004; Born and Purcell 2006; Raja, Born, and Kozlowski Russell 2008; Hodgson 2012), mainstream planning practice, especially through the agency of local government, falls short. Planners continue to undermine public health by failing to strengthen community food infrastructures (CFIs), which are essential to ensuring public health and well-being.

In this essay, we describe the workings of a CFI and emphasize the need for local governments and planners to invest fully in CFIs to create healthy places to live, work, and play. The essay details planning strategies that communities and their local governments can use to strengthen CFIs.[1] The essay concludes with cautionary notes about planners' engagement in this new area of planning.

A CFI is a complex network of practices, resources, processes, and policies that enables community inhabitants to grow, process, distribute, and acquire food, and enables the management, reduction, and disposal of food-related waste. We use the term *community food infrastructure* in lieu of the more common phrase *community food system* for two reasons (figure 1). First, the term emphasizes that the arrival of food—in whatever form it takes—at our tables is not a matter of chance nor the result of an invisible hand but of an intricate infrastructure that has become largely invisible to U.S. consumers.

Second, and perhaps more important, we emphasize CFI as a public infrastructure that supports the provision of an essential good for human and community well-being: food. In addition to providing food, nutrition, and their attendant health benefits for residents, a CFI supports numerous jobs and generates a sizeable portion of earned wages in communities. The economic activity triggered by CFIs also generates revenue for local governments, through sales and property taxes and licenses or fees. Of course, CFIs also

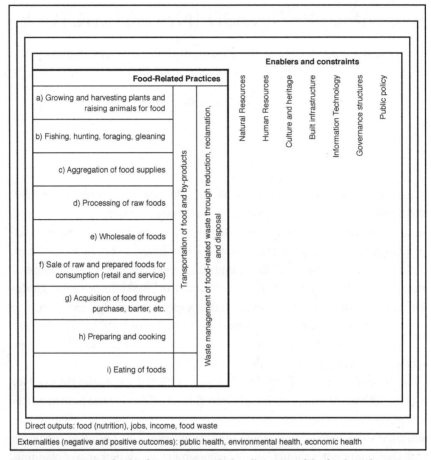

Figure 1. Community food infrastructure includes all aspects of the food production process to the consumption.

result in public expenditures, as food-related business sectors—like all other sectors—demand from local governments services such as roads and police. Still, a well-functioning CFI can indirectly help to reduce public expenditures. A population that has access to and consumes healthier, affordable foods is more likely to prevent chronic disease, thereby reducing healthcare costs. For local governments and planners, developing a fuller understanding of the fiscal impacts of investing in CFIs is crucial for reasons spanning public health and economic development. Much like other public infrastructure, such as transportation, whose responsibility we now assign to local governments, CFIs require local governments' and planners' deliberate public investment.

Although a holistic view of CFIs as an essential public infrastructure does not yet exist, local government policies and plans nonetheless inadvertently undermine or support CFIs. Land-use plans and zoning ordinances influence CFI practices such as farming by influencing the amount and location of farmland preserved in a community. Building codes regulate the design of CFI physical structures, such as public markets, supermarkets, and restaurants. Public transportation networks determine physical access to food stores, farms, and markets for populations with limited access to automobiles and, therefore, influence where individuals can shop for food. Economic development programs incentivize particular food-related businesses. Tax rates, licensing, and fee structures influence the ease with which a food-related business can start up, operate, and survive. Municipal capital budgets are used to develop or repair CFI-relevant structures such as public markets, and operating budgets may fund staff that oversee the permitting, licensure, and inspection of food businesses. Publicly funded food-assistance programs facilitate low-resource individuals' access to foods.[2] In sum, countless local government policies influence the workings of a CFI, albeit with little reflexivity.

Until about a decade ago, few local governments and planners in the United States viewed the health of food systems as central to their responsibility. To our knowledge, even today no "departments of food" exist within local governments, and only a few cities, such as Baltimore, Maryland, Portland, Oregon, and Seattle, Washington, have staff charged explicitly with strengthening their CFIs. Part of the explanation is that CFIs are not yet viewed as public infrastructure in the way as, for example, transportation infrastructure is. Indeed, Americans expect local governments (and other levels of governments) to provide roads for their mobility, but they hold limited or no expectations for infrastructure that provides food essential for their survival and health. In short, food—or food-related infrastructure—is not yet viewed as an explicit concern of local government planners and policy makers.

Facets of a CFI: Practices, Resources, Culture, and Technology

A CFI is the soil-to-soil infrastructure that enables food to move from field to fork and delivers the remnants back to soil (see table 1). A CFI functions is enabled and constrained by many interlinked factors, including natural and human resources, cultural practices, the built environment, and technological, information, and public-policy regimes. We explore each of these facets of a CFI in turn.

Food-related practices include the production, aggregation, processing, and distribution of food; the acquisition, preparation, cooking, and consumption of food by people; and the reduction and management of food-related waste in all food practices (see table 1 on food practices). Food production includes growing plants, raising animals, fishing, hunting, or gleaning and

Table 1. The spaces and structures where community food practices unfold

Community food practices	Spaces and structures
Growing and harvesting, hunting, foraging, gleaning, and fishing	Rural farmland, urban farmland, community gardens, backyard gardens, aquaponics facilities, forests, rivers, oceans, and seas
Aggregation and distribution of food	Warehouse and storage facilities, aggregation hubs
Processing of food	Processing plants, factories, abattoirs, food incubators
Wholesaling of raw and prepared foods	Public markets, farmers' markets, farm stands, community supported agriculture drop-off locations, wholesale hubs, terminal markets
Selling of raw and prepared foods	Retail: supermarkets, convenience stores, bodegas Service: restaurants, cafeterias, canteens
Acquisition/procuring, preparing, cooking, eating	Home kitchens, community kitchens, institutional kitchens, etc.
Disposing, reclaiming food waste	Landfills, incineration and composting facilities
Transporting	Waterways, roads, airways

foraging edible plants or fungi for human consumption. After production, raw foods are aggregated and/or processed into value-added products before they are sold to wholesalers, retailers, or directly to end consumers. All of these practices span increasingly large geographies in the contemporary food system, and food must travel farther distances, or food miles, from farm to table.

A CFI depends on various resources, including natural and human resources. Natural resources include soil, water, energy, and pollinators. These resources may be depleted because of fossil-based energy sources and extreme weather events (Oleson and Bindi 2002; von Blottnitz and Curran 2007). Several communities are trying to maximize the use of environmentally sustainable practices in their CFIs. *Multnomah County Food Action Plan: Grow and Thrive 2025* (2010), for example, includes several goals related to encouraging sustainable resource stewardship. The plan promotes diversion of food waste away from landfills into compost and includes the creation of a regional seed library to protect species diversity and provide access to seeds for local farmers. Additionally, emphasis is placed on consumer education surrounding toxic chemical alternatives, water conservation, and protection of native pollinators.

A CFI depends on the human resources of those who engage directly in food-related practices, such as farmers, gardeners, fishermen, hunters, bakers, and retailers, and those who indirectly influence a CFI's functioning, such as policy makers, planners, and hunger advocates (Caton Campbell 2004). CFIs in the United States face significant human resource challenges, especially in the area of food production. The number of individuals engaged in food production is declining (and the average age of farmers is rising), as farming remains an economically unsustainable occupation. Fewer than a quarter of all farms in the United States report net financial gains higher than the poverty line for a family of four (U.S. Department of Agriculture 2012; U.S. Department of Health and Human Services 2012). Six in ten principal farm operators also hold an off-farm job to make ends meet (USDA 2012). Overall, there are insufficient human resources for rebuilding CFIs.

Technological regimes also influence the workings of a CFI. Mechanical sowing and harvesting, the "invention" of chicken fingers in the 1960s, refrigeration and freezing, and numerous other developments have changed how food is delivered from farm to fork (Spaargaren, Oosterveer, and Loeber 2012). The adoption of particular technologies has short- and long-term ramifications for the quantity and quality of nutrition that CFIs provide. For example, widespread pesticide use may increase crop yield by reducing crop loss but may result in contaminated air, water, and soil in the long run (Arias-Estevez et al. 2008). In short, technology plays a critical role in how CFIs function.

Cultural practices are a key characteristic of CFIs. People's experience of their CFI is shaped by these cultural experiences and by the meaning they attribute to them. Without understanding this cultural heritage, planners, designers, and policy makers cannot support a thriving CFI nor maximize its potential in creating a sense of well-being and a sense of place in communities. Worse, despite a desire to improve public health, policy makers rebuilding CFIs run the risk of imposing a food hegemony rooted in the cultural preferences of a dominant class.

These facets of a CFI are all shaped by, and in turn shape, prevalent public policies and governance structures.

Community Health and CFIs: Many Pathways

The World Health Organization describes health as "a state of complete physical, mental and social well-being and not merely the absence of disease or infirmity." CFIs influence all of these facets of health, and they impact physical health most directly by making food available for sustenance and nourishment. In the United States, CFIs are not, in fact, fulfilling this key function. One symptom of this malfunction is the low prevalence of retailers selling healthy foods (e.g., supermarkets) and the high prevalence of retailers selling

high-calorie, low-nutrition foods (e.g., convenience stores) in many neighborhoods (Raja, Ma, and Yadav 2008; Caspi et al. 2012). Such food environments, commonly (if somewhat inaccurately) labeled as food deserts, tend to
be concentrated in neighborhoods of low-income minority populations (Raja,
Ma, and Yadav 2008). For example, in Erie County, New York, predominantly
black neighborhoods have about one-half (0.43 times) the number of supermarkets as compared to the number available within a five-minute walk of
white neighborhoods (Raja, Ma, and Yadav 2008).

Studies, especially within the field of public health, have linked the prevalence
of these so-called food deserts with poor dietary behaviors (Sohi et al. 2014), poor
dietary intake (Lamichhane et al. 2012), and increased diet-related disease (Ahern,
Brown, and Dukas 2011). As a result, the limited public policy effort around food
systems focuses on bringing fresh, healthy foods to these food deserts.

Although this scholarship and its attendant public policy measures have
merits, several concerns remain. First, existing studies are unable to demonstrate unequivocal causal links between neighborhood food environments
and health outcomes. Second, and more important, the singular focus on
neighborhood retail food environments has drawn attention away from the
factors leading to poor food environments in the first place. For instance, the
limited prevalence of apples in a neighborhood retail store may have more to
do with upstream problems in the supply chain that limit the quantity, quality, affordability, and availability of apples grown, harvested, aggregated, and
distributed to a retailer than with a retailer simply failing to stock or sell or
consumers failing to buy or eat apples. Ignoring the underlying problems in
the CFI makes it near impossible to create healthy food environments that can
support healthy food purchasing and eating behaviors.

Second, even if a food retailer sells healthy foods in a low-income neighborhood, residents may not be able to afford it. Monsivais, Aggarwal, and
Drewnowski (2010) note that the price of low-calorie, high-nutrition foods
in the United States tends to be higher than the price of high-calorie, low-
nutrition foods. For example, grains cost approximately $0.5 per 100 calories
compared to vegetables, which cost about $3.75 per 100 calories (Carlson and
Frazao 2012). Therefore, poverty-reduction public policies, such as a living
wage, that increase consumers' purchasing power and enable them to buy
healthful foods are crucial in supporting healthy food practices (see practices
g, h, and i in figure 1) within a CFI.

A CFI also impacts public health indirectly, as outlined below.

- CFIs are a significant source of employment for residents. Yet many
  jobs within a CFI, such as in the food-service industry, pay poorly

(Maloni and Brown 2006). Low-wage workers within CFIs have limited ability to purchase expensive healthful foods. A well-functioning CFI maximizes both the number and quality of jobs in a community.

- A well-functioning CFI in which different community food sectors, such as farming, processing, wholesale, and retail, are interlinked or networked generate a greater economic multiplier from consumer expenditures on food, compared to a CFI in which food wholesalers and retailers purchase from nonlocal or nonregional growers and suppliers (Halebsky 2010).

- The physical spaces of a CFI, such as traditional markets, can potentially enhance a sense of place where visitors experience an affective bond between themselves, others, and the physical place, a feeling often blurring racial, ethnic, and socioeconomic lines (Tuan 1974; Anderson 2004). Consider the Pike Place Market in Seattle and Reading Terminal in Philadelphia, which, as sources of food, not only serve a functional need but are also signature destinations (Anderson 2004; Aiello and Gendelman 2008). Such destinations attract tourists and locals alike and are hubs of economic activity.

- In addition to being sources of fresh food, the physical spaces of CFIs promote social exchange and interaction. Farmers' markets, for example, are places where people go not only to purchase food directly from farmers but also to gather with friends and neighbors (Oberholtzer and Grow 2003). A well-functioning CFI maximizes opportunities for social interaction and fosters social capital.

- A CFI that maximizes food production while compromising environmental health may promote food security in the short run but may adversely impact public health in the long run. For example, the use of synthetic fertilizers to maximize crop yield and the animal waste generated from concentrated feedlot operations (CAFOs) negatively impact waterways and airways, with adverse effects on human health (Schulze et al. 2011; Lockhart, King, and Harter 2013).

In short, there are numerous direct and indirect pathways by which CFIs can influence public health.

Case Example: Healthy Kids, Healthy Communities Partnership in Buffalo, New York

Although local governments and planners have been slow to recognize the potential of CFIs to promote community health, community groups have not. In the last decade, civic groups and social entrepreneurs have revitalized CFIs through on-the-ground food-related practices. Public-health considerations are often, although not always, central to these efforts. We draw on the example of Buffalo, New York, to untangle the possibilities and challenges of using a CFI to improve public health. The case example is based on the synthesis of previously published data from interviews, site visits, and document reviews collected by the authors through community-based participatory research (Raja, Picard et al. 2014).

Efforts to revitalize Buffalo's food infrastructure can be traced in part to the efforts of not-for-profit groups and community advocates who have long engaged in practices to rebuild Buffalo's CFI. Key among these is the Massachusetts Avenue Project (MAP), a nonprofit established formally in 2000 by residents on Buffalo's west side.[3] MAP's mission is to empower youth to be agents in rebuilding their city's food system (Raja, Picard et al. 2014). MAP operates an urban farm on former vacant lots on the city's west side; runs a capacity-building program to teach youth to grow, process, cook, and eat healthful foods; and conducts community outreach to raise awareness and induce policy change (Raja, Picard et al. 2014).

MAP's work has translated into several positive benefits. Since the early 2000s, MAP has trained about forty youth per year. Surveys completed by youth before and after their participation indicate the program's transformative impact. Youth report greater knowledge and awareness of the food system and view themselves as leaders within the local community. Despite these promising outcomes, the survey results also point to the need for public investment in CFIs so that programs like MAP can be fully effective. For example, the young people's self-reported fruit and vegetable consumption did not appear to change measurably following participation in MAP's programming (Raj et al. 2016). In open-ended conversations, the youth reported other impediments to eating well, such as limited family income, limited time, and the unavailability of affordable, healthful foods in their neighborhoods. Even when youth are motivated to eat well, a malfunctioning food infrastructure hinders healthy behaviors.

Most of MAP's food-related practices occurred within a public policy context that offered limited or no support for Buffalo's CFI. Some examples of this oversight are noteworthy. The city's comprehensive plan, adopted in 2006, made no reference to the city's food infrastructure (City of Buffalo 2006). The local government offered no systematic economic development to food entrepreneurs. Food-related practices, such as community gardening and, more broadly, urban agriculture, were not recognized as a land-use category in the zoning ordinance. Community gardens that have existed on vacant public parcels—of which there are nearly fifteen thousand—exist without formal lease agreements. There was no systematic effort to address the absence of or limited healthy food retail sources in low-resource neighborhoods. In short, until recently, as in many cities, food was simply absent from the public policy and planning agenda in Buffalo (Raja, Picard et al. 2014) (table 2).

In part to seek greater public policy recognition for food-related activities, in 2009 several organizations, including MAP, joined forces to seek policy support for Buffalo's CFI. Although the impetus for formalizing this partnership came from a grant, several organizations had collaborated since 2002 and had intermittently discussed the need for policy reform. A formal partnership was established in 2009 after the group won a multiyear partnership grant from the Healthy Kids, Healthy Communities (HKHC) Program of the Robert Wood Johnson Foundation (RWJF), resulting in the coalition's formalization into the Healthy Kids, Healthy Communities–Buffalo partnership. Although the RWJF grant period ended in 2013, the partnership continues informally with partial financial support from a local foundation and from the lead organization, Buffalo Niagara Medical Campus, Inc., a not-for-profit group that oversees the development of a medical campus.

The partnership includes a food-advocacy organization (MAP), a local university (University at Buffalo), a bicycling advocacy group (Go Bike Buffalo), a health-promotion organization (the Wellness Institute), and public sector representatives, including from the city government (Office of Strategic Planning), the county government (Department of Public Health), and the Buffalo Public School District (director of health-related services for the district).[4] A staff member of the Buffalo Niagara Medical Campus, Inc., coordinates the partnership.

The partnership focuses on coordinating efforts to advocate for food policy reform in Buffalo (Neuner, Kelly, and Raja 2011). In part due to the HKHC-Buffalo partnership's work, a clear shift in public policy regarding food is evident in the city. In 2010, to follow the directives of the city's 2006 Comprehensive Plan, the mayor's office launched a process to prepare a new land-use plan and zoning code for the city. The new land-use plan and the zoning ordinance squarely address food-related public health concerns. In 2013, city and county lawmakers created a joint city-county food policy council (FPC) to advise the lawmakers on food-policy issues. An advisory board under the county's Board of Health, the FPC includes public and private sector representatives from across the food system. Finally, in 2013, the regional transportation agency launched a planning process to prepare a regional sustainability plan and included food and public health as considerations. The One Region

Table 2. Food systems in comprehensive plans

Date of adoption/release	Jurisdiction	Treatment of food in comprehensive plan
2005	City of Seattle, WA	*City of Seattle Comprehensive Plan: A Plan for Managing Growth* includes planning for food systems as a part of community vitality.
2007	Dane County, WI	The *Dane County Comprehensive Plan* includes sections on local food-system support as both agricultural and economic development issues.
2007	Marin County, CA	The *Marin Countywide Plan*'s subsection on agriculture and food considers current conditions, key trends, and issues, to create policies and implementation strategies.
2008	Boston Metropolitan Region, MA	*Metro Future: Making a Greater Boston Region* references food systems in its vision, goals, objectives, indicators, strategies, and recommends actions, within the community vitality section.
2008	Southern California Region, CA	The *2008 Regional Comprehensive Plan*'s subsection on agricultural lands describes current conditions, goals, and outcomes for eating locally.
2008	Harrison County, MS	The *2030 Harrison County Comprehensive Plan* section on public health includes goals, strategies, and actions to increase healthy food access.
2008	Cabarrus, NC	*Cabarrus County Central Area Plan* addresses agricultural land protection in one of the plan's goals.
2010	City of New Orleans, LA	The *Plan for the 21st Century: New Orleans 2030* includes a subsection on urban agriculture and open space.
2010	City of Boise, ID	*Blueprint Boise* includes goals to promote community-based and local food production in a subsection on environmental stewardship.
2010	City of Boulder, CO	The *Boulder Valley Comprehensive Plan* has a chapter on agriculture and food through the lenses of community resiliency, health, the economy, and the natural environment.
2010	City of Dillingham, AK	The *City of Dillingham Comprehensive Plan Update and Waterfront Plan*'s section on energy addresses food-related goals, strategies, timeline, and actors for implementation.
2011	City of New York, NY	*PlaNYC: A Greener, Greater, New York*'s 2011 update encourages access to healthy foods in multiple chapters but does not contain a chapter solely dedicated to food.
2013	Lexington-Fayette County, KY	The Lexington-Fayette Urban County Government *2013 Comprehensive Plan* identifies existing challenges in access to food and addresses them by designing goals, objectives, and actions to tackle food insecurity.
2014	Chicago Metropolitan Region, IL	The *Go to 2040 Comprehensive Regional Plan* allocates a subsection to promoting sustainable local food.
2014	Regional Transportation Agency of Buffalo Niagara, NY	*One Region Forward*'s regional sustainability plan addresses food and includes a technical report (*Growing Together*) focused on agricultural viability and food access.

Source: Adapted from Neuner, Kelly, & Raja (2011, 39).

Forward plan is supported by a food assessment that outlines strategies for promoting regional agricultural viability and food access (Raja, Hall, et al. 2014). The plan, completed in 2014, is the region's first official public plan to squarely address food and public health. It includes a call for prioritizing food system–based economic development, instituting long-term lease agreements for community gardens on public land, establishing a regional food policy board, ensuring farm worker representation in policy decisions, and mandating institutional purchasing of local agricultural products.

Although much work remains to be done in strengthening the region's CFI, food and public health concerns now have a place at the policy and planning table (Pothukuchi and Kaufman 2000). The arrival of food on the local government planning and policy agenda in Buffalo was not by chance. In all of the food policy victories described here, HKHC-Buffalo partners played a prominent role in making a collective impact on policy (Neuner, Kelly, and Raja 2011). They served on working groups, drafted policy language, and were actively engaged in shaping planning discourse to include food and health. Whether proposed public policies to strengthen the food infrastructure and improve public health in Buffalo will actually be implemented through laws, public investments, and public programs remains to be seen.

Local Government Planning Tools for Improving CFIs

Fortunately, Buffalo is not alone in its journey to strengthen its CFI through planning and public policy. A growing number of communities around the United States now view food as a public policy concern. Indeed, many local governments have implemented public policies and plans to strengthen CFIs. Many of these efforts are driven by concerns for public health. This section describes some of these policy tools. Because the tools depend on the type of food concerns that a community faces, their categorization is difficult. Nonetheless, for ease of understanding, we offer two broad categories of public policy tools that can potentially strengthen CFIs for public health: plans and implementation tools.

Public Plans to Strengthen CFIs

Local governments in the United States adopt various plans charting out courses of action to guide development and public investment. The plans address a diverse set of issues impacting communities' well-being, such as land use, housing, transportation, and so forth, or they focus narrowly on a single issue, such as a land-use plan. As noted earlier, however, the issues of food and public health have been largely absent from official planning documents until recently. Although food is still not part of mainstream planning practice, communities have begun to develop plans that address food.

Comprehensive (or General) Plans that Address Food

Comprehensive plans, sometimes called general plans, offer the broadest guidance for a community's future. Comprehensive plans, which (in theory) result from extensive public engagement, describe a vision for a community's future and recommend strategies for achieving this vision. Comprehensive plans address diverse topics, sometimes called elements, such as land use, housing, economic development, and natural resources. Ideally, comprehensive plans provide guidance for public programs, regulations, and investments. Recent comprehensive plans in the United States have not explicitly addressed the state of CFIs. An exception is worth noting. Plans have long been concerned with protecting farmland. Admittedly, these farmland-preservation planning efforts have focused largely on protecting land rather than helping farming remain viable (Whittaker, Clark, and Raja forthcoming).

Beginning in the late 1990s and early 2000s, a handful of local governments responded to communities' concerns by developing strategies to strengthen their CFIs. Comprehensive plans for the cities of Seattle, Washington (City of Seattle 2005) and Madison, Wisconsin (City of Madison 2006, updated 2012) are among the earliest plans in the United States to address food. Seattle's updated plan calls for the creation of sustainable urban forests that include food sources, an increase in sourcing from local agricultural producers, and expanded access to farmers' markets and a wider range of grocery stores. In Madison, concerns for the food system are evident in two sections of their 2006 comprehensive plan: the natural resources and economic development sections, where they advocate for the establishment of a food policy council, creation of a food hub, and promotion of local food purchasing.

Higher levels of government, such as county and regional governments, have also begun to address food in their comprehensive or regional plans. In some ways, these governments are better suited to tackle systemic disconnects in the food system, as they traverse urban, peri-urban, and rural areas. Dane County in Wisconsin, for example, is home to many rural farms and to the capital city of Madison, where there is significant consumer demand for locally grown foods. The county's 2006 comprehensive plan, soon due for an update, builds on this opportunity through extensive language supporting a countywide food system that connects urban and rural areas. The plan's goals include the following: "Continue to support the Dane County Food Council to (a) help capitalize on Dane County's exceptional assets; (b) coordinate efforts to build a stronger local food system; (c) advise county government to address food system issues, particularly aimed at strengthening the capacity of the local and regional food system; (d) assist in food-related education; (e) gather relevant data and information; (f) play a coordinating role among groups in the local food system; and (g) develop policies to address food system issues" (Dane County, Department of Planning and Development 2007, 7). Specific policy proposals include implementing fees to create a disincentive for conversion of agricultural land and providing loans, referrals, and business counseling to farmers.

A few local and regional governments have prepared stand-alone plans that focus exclusively on strengthening CFIs. These stand-alone food systems plans are a relatively recent development (see table 3 for recent examples). The plans typically include a baseline assessment of conditions in the food system and outline strategies for strengthening the system. Stand-alone food system plans generally address all sectors of the system, including how food is produced, aggregated, distributed, processed, and acquired in a community and how food-related waste is minimized, reused, or disposed.

Stand-alone food systems plans have been developed by different levels of governments, including state, regional, county, and city governments. At the regional scale, the most well-known plan was prepared for the greater Philadelphia region by the Delaware Valley Regional Planning Commission (DVRPC). The plan, published in 2011 following an extensive regional food assessment (DVRPC 2010) and public engagement, describes six core values: farming and sustainable agriculture, health, ecological stewardship and conservation, fairness, economic development, and collaboration. The plan outlines fifty-two implementation strategies that public and private sector entities can undertake to strengthen different components of the food system and ten indicators for monitoring progress (DVRPC 2011). In an unusual move, the plan does not identify specific actors for implementation. Instead, planners left the potential for implementation open to any community actor, both known and those yet to emerge. Planners judged that the newness of the region's food systems work would allow the participation of new actors who might wish to implement the recommendations.

County governments have also prepared and adopted food systems plans. The earliest known plan, *Recipe for Success,* was prepared by the Dane County Local Food Policy Advisory Subcommittee (2005). The plan made several recommendations, including the creation of a countywide food council that

Table 3. Food systems assessments and plans prepared or adopted by local/regional governments

Date of publication/ adoption	Scope and goals of food system plan	Type of government (lead agency)
2005	*Recipe for Success* promotes the purchase of local and fresh food and the establishment of food hubs and a food council.	County (Dane County Local Food Policy Advisory Sub-Committee)
2010	*Food Works: A Vision to Improve NYC's Food System* addresses production, processing, distribution, consumption, and postconsumption.	City (New York City Council)
2010	*Transforming the Oakland Food System: A Plan for Action* describes current conditions and outlines goals for strengthening the food system.	City (Oakland Food Policy Council)
2010	*Multnomah Food Action Plan: Grow and Thrive 2025* describes sixteen goals to promote local food, healthy eating, social equity, and economic vitality; indicators provided.	County (Multnomah County Office of Sustainability)
2010	The twelve-county *Central Ohio Food-Systems Assessment and Plan* includes twenty-four recommendations for strengthening the food system; implementation is underway.	Regional (Mid-Ohio Regional Planning Commission)
2011	*Eating Here: Greater Philadelphia's Food-Systems Plan* outlines six core values: farming and sustainable agriculture, health, ecological stewardship, fairness, economic development, and collaboration.	Regional (Delaware Valley Regional Planning Commission, Department of Planning)
2011	*Urban Agriculture Policy Plan*, part of the city's Homegrown Minneapolis initiative, aims to improve growth, sales, distribution and consumption of healthy, locally grown foods.	City (Minneapolis City Council)
2012	*Food Action Plan* promotes healthy, local food for everyone, reduction of food waste, and promotion of the food economy.	City (Seattle City Council)

Source: Adapted from Neuner, Kelly, & Raja (2011, 39).

would advise the local government on strengthening the food system. The council has since been established and works to strengthen the county's food system.

Plans Focused on a Particular Component of the Food System

Some local governments are also developing plans (or feasibility studies) for discrete sectors of the food system, such as urban agriculture. For instance, the City of Minneapolis was among the earliest local governments to prepare and adopt a plan for urban agriculture. The plan, adopted in 2011, outlines a series of recommendations, including modifying the city's land-use plan and zoning code to facilitate urban agriculture, selling or leasing city-owned property for urban agriculture, allowing green space set-aside requirements for developers to include urban agriculture space, modifying the green building requirements and incentive programs to dedicate space for gardening, integrating farmers' markets into the city's development plans, and improving nonmotorized and public transportation options to increase access to food markets (City of Minneapolis 2011). In 2014, the San Francisco Planning Department published a plan to strengthen the city's economic cluster of food and beverage industries (City of San Francisco 2014). The plan describes four strategies to enhance the city's food and beverage sector: increasing affordable and suitable spaces for the industry, providing business, technical, and workforce development and retention assistance, improving employees' transportation access to production and distribution job sites, and supporting efficient mobility for distributors.

Implementation Tools to Strengthen CFI for Public Health

Local governments have access to planning/policy implementation tools to support of CFIs. Use of these tools may be recommended in a preceding plan or policy document or may be enacted independently of a plan. We classify implementation tools into five broad categories: (1) programmatic support, (2) regulatory action, (3) fiscal actions, (4) physical infrastructure provision, and (5) human investment. These implementation tools are not independent of one another and may best serve CFIs when deployed together.

Programmatic Support

Some local governments establish or support programs that facilitate healthy food-related practices. For example, the city of Seattle Department of Neighborhoods runs one of the largest municipal community gardening programs in the country. In existence since the 1970s, the P-Patch program manages community gardens on about two thousand lots on twelve acres of land. The city provides staff, operating, and financial support for the gardens: between 1993 and 2003, twenty-two P-Patch gardens received grants ranging from $2,000 to $15,000 for planning and improvements such as compost bins, trellises, fences, and sculptures. The city supports the program through other policy actions as well. Municipal program support provides access to financial resources for individual projects (such as a single community garden) and facilitates the replication of successful projects.

Regulatory Actions

Local U.S. governments have the authority to regulate how land is developed and used within their jurisdictions. This regulatory authority can support or undermine CFIs. Examples below outline how regulatory tools support food systems:

- Zoning ordinances or bylaws. City governments are modifying zoning ordinances to allow the raising of crops and livestock within city jurisdictions.
- Permits and licenses. City governments are reducing the burden of permits and licensing for healthy food retailers.
- Parking requirements. Some local governments are easing parking requirements for healthy food retailers.
- Density bonuses. Some local governments offer higher-density bonuses to developers that include healthy food retail in their development proposals.

New York City uses many of the above tools through its FRESH program. Store operators seeking to renovate stores or developers seeking to build new stores in underserved neighborhoods receive zoning benefits if they meet particular eligibility requirements, including but not limited to stocking healthy foods (New York City 2009).[5] Operators and developers are eligible to build at higher densities, an attractive proposition for developers in a high-growth market.[6]

Although such regulatory provisions are important, they cannot alone catalyze private investment in CFIs. Recognizing this issue, the city of New York also provides an economic development incentive through its FRESH program (detailed in the next section.)

Reform In Local Government Finance Structure and Priorities

Local governments also have the authority to raise and expend monies for public services and goods. Local government revenue comes from levying taxes (including property, sales, and income tax), fees, and fines within their own jurisdictions and through intergovernmental sources such as state and federal aid. CFIs contribute to these revenues through various mechanisms:

- Sales tax on food products
- Property tax paid by food businesses (growers, processors, distributors, service, retailers)
- Income tax paid by owners and employees of businesses within the CFI
- Licensing fees paid by food businesses

Although CFIs contribute to public revenues, local governments typically do not allocate funds in a systematic or purposeful way for their CFIs. Typically, local public expenditures are dedicated to infrastructure and transportation, education, and public safety services, to name a few. We outline potential ways in which local governments can invest in CFIs, with examples of where this might have occurred in the United States (table 4).

Local government investments may occur through direct operating and capital expenditures. For example, a city's general fund may be dedicated to staff whose jobs explicitly focus on CFIs. Notable examples include Baltimore, Portland, and Madison. Direct expenditures may also occur through local governments' capital budgets. For example, the city of Buffalo's capital budget dedicates funds to maintain Broadway Market, a public market owned and managed by the city.

Foregone public revenues also generate investments, through the reduction or waiver of taxes, fines, and fees, to catalyze growth of CFIs. The most common form of such investment is to levy lower rates of property tax on land used to grow food. Such reduced tax rates were traditionally used to protect rural farmland from development. Strategies for reducing the tax burden on land used to grow food are also underway in urban settings. For example, a new California law permits cities to participate in a statewide program allowing city governments to offer a reduced property tax rate to owners whose parcels are used for urban agriculture (California State Assembly 2013). Some local governments are reducing or waiving the cost of establishing or operating a retail food business. In Kansas City, food vendors in public parks receive a 50 percent discount on their annual park-vending permit if half of their food

Table 4. Plans and feasibility studies by local/regional governments for a particular component of the food system

Date of publication/adoption	Jurisdiction	Goals and scope of plan	Type of government (lead agency)
2011	Dane County, WI	*Southern Wisconsin Food Hub: Feasibility Study* explores the likelihood of increasing agricultural production and economic activity by developing infrastructure to support immediate transactions between growers and wholesale customers.	County (Dane County Planning and Development Department)
2011	Minneapolis, MN	*Urban Agriculture Policy Plan: A Land Use and Development Plan for a Healthy, Sustainable Local Food System* (Amendment to the Minneapolis Plan for Sustainable Growth)	City (City of Minneapolis Community Planning and Economic Development Department)
2013	Baltimore, MD	*Homegrown Baltimore: Grow Local* is an urban agriculture plan resulting from the Baltimore Sustainability Plan, providing a plan to create a local food system. Includes an urban agricultural land assessment.	City (Baltimore City Planning Commission)
2014	Eighteen counties in tri-state region (spanning northwest IL, northeast IA, and southwestern WI)	*Local Food Prospectus for the Tri-State Region: An Analysis of the Wholesale Fruit and Vegetable Industry in Illinois, Iowa, and Wisconsin*	Southwestern Wisconsin Regional Planning Commission (representing five counties)
2014	San Francisco, CA	Movers and Makers Economic Cluster Strategy: Recommendations for San Francisco Food and Beverage Manufacturers and Distributors	City (Planning Department and Office of Economic & Workforce Development)

Source: Adapted from Neuner, Kelly, & Raja (2011, 39).

meets certain nutritional standards. They can also receive greater access to parks and prime vending locations if they increase their healthy food options to 75 percent of the food they offer.

In some cases, local governments offer financial incentives along with regulatory support. The FRESH program in New York City combines regulatory with financial incentives. The financial incentives for eligible store operators and developers include a real-estate tax reduction, sales tax exemption, and mortgage recording tax deferral.

Physical Infrastructure Provision

As noted above, a CFI depends on the availability of physical infrastructure such as land, buildings for food storage and processing, and road networks. Local governments are beginning to identify and fill the gaps in the physical infrastructure. A 2013 national survey by the Wallace Center reports that 4 (out of 107) food hubs are publicly owned. For example, the city of Buffalo owns, operates, and maintains a public market, the Broadway Market, in one of the city's poorest sections. The city is currently exploring ways that the market might play a greater role in linking area farmers with local, underserved residents. As part of implementing a food systems plan for the mid-Ohio region, a collaboration of local governments and private and nonprofit partners, including the Community Economic Development Corporation of Ohio, Mid-Ohio Regional Planning Commission, Ohio State University, city of Columbus, the Godman Guild, and Local Matters, are working to establish a Food Innovation District in the city of Columbus (Food District 2014). Within this district a local food-processing plant will support job training for unemployed residents. Similar efforts are unfolding in other states as the potential of food infrastructure as an economic development activity is recognized.

Human-Resource Investment

Finally, local governments can strengthen CFIs by dedicating staff to serve as the "glue" across disparate food systems stakeholders. Many local governments are adopting this role by identifying staff members who play supportive (or leadership) roles in food policy councils (FPC), which perform various functions in a community, including advising local governments on food policy issues. In Buffalo, New York, city staff (from the Office of Strategic Planning) and county staff (from the Department of Public Health) serve on the city-county FPC. In New York City, staff from both public health and planning agencies developed the FRESH program. A few notable places, such as Baltimore, have staff dedicated to overseeing all public policy related to food systems. Early results from the national Growing Food Connections project suggest that such human resource investment is essential for strengthening CFIs, which are currently the responsibility of no single agency within city governments (Growing Food Connections n.d.).

Cautionary Notes for Planners and Designers Committed to Improving Public Health through Rebuilding CFIs

Distinguish between food-related health behaviors and food-related health outcomes: Food contributes to public health through multiple pathways, including by influencing health behaviors. It is essential to distinguish food-related health behaviors from food-related health outcomes, with regard to the influence of a CFI on public health. Food-related health behaviors are actions by individuals that influence their (or others') health; examples of health-related behaviors include shopping for healthy versus less nutritious foods, eating fresh versus processed food, shopping at a convenience store versus a farmers' market, and so forth. In contrast, food-related health outcomes include rates of obesity, levels of malnutrition, levels of diabetes, cardiovascular disease, and so forth. This distinction between health behaviors and health outcomes is especially important for planners and designers because many planning and design tactics are more logically linked to food-related health behaviors than to disease outcomes. For example, by ensuring the presence of farmers' markets within walking distance of residential neighborhoods, planning and design strategies might more effectively support healthy food purchasing (a behavior), rather than directly combating obesity. To develop effective, evidence-based, and implementable strategies to promote public health, planners must understand the particular pathways by which their specific planning or design strategy might best support community health.

Think beyond regulation, and focus on investment: As noted earlier, local governments most commonly engage in CFIs through regulation (e.g., zoning, ordinances, and licensing). This preoccupation with regulation overlooks the important role of public investment for strengthening and catalyzing CFIs to promote public health.

Engage in whole thinking: As outlined in this essay, a CFI is complex. Attempts to tackle public health concerns (such as low consumption of fruits and vegetables) by using narrow approaches, such as bringing fresh food retail to "food desert" neighborhoods, are unlikely to be successful unless we understand the workings of the larger CFI within which that retail is embedded.

It is important to fully understand the constraints within a CFI and then take purposeful action to overcome them.

Reimagine CFIs as public infrastructure: To be sure, the failure of public policy to attend to CFIs undermines the efficacy of civic groups engaged in food-related practices to rebuild food systems. Yet, there is a more pressing reason for local governments to reimagine CFIs as public infrastructure: Local governments are responsible for the health and well-being of their citizens. Divesting responsibility for rebuilding CFIs to the not-for-profit sector, no matter how exhilarating, exonerates the public sector from its responsibility to ensure public health. Local governments have historically responded to societal problems through restructuring and reform. For example, between 1932 and 1987, the number of special-purpose districts—for fire, parks, and water supply, for example—increased from 14,572 to 29,487 (Ostrom, Bish, and Ostrom 1988), in part due to rapid development and (sub)urbanization. Although this essay is not advocating for the creation of a special food district, local governments must nonetheless respond to growing public health challenges by investing in their CFIs. Investing in CFIs through local government policy and planning is an opportunity to promote public health and economic development.

Notes

We wish to thank Nathan Attard, Donna Banach, and Asleigh Imus for their support.

1. One could rightly argue that rather than focusing at the local government level, food infrastructure needs to be rebuilt at the national scale and that public policy reform at the federal level is essential for this purpose. While we agree that much work must occur at the federal level, planning occurs primarily at the local (and some at the regional) government level. Therefore, this essay focuses exclusively on planning CFIs at the local and regional scales.

2. Many of these programs, such as the Supplemental Nutrition Assistance Program (SNAP) and the Women and Infant Care (WIC) Program, are not funded by local governments, but some local governments are responsible for administering such programs.

3. MAP's genesis dates back to 1992, when a group of residents organized to establish a playground on Buffalo's west side (Raja, Picard, et al. 2014).

4. The steering committee of HKHC comprised representatives from civic organizations, including the Buffalo Niagara Medical Campus, Inc., the Massachusetts Avenue Project, the Wellness Institute, Go Bike Buffalo, and the University at Buffalo, and the State University of New York.

5. Stores must "provide a minimum of 6,000 square feet of retail space for a general line of food and nonfood grocery products intended for home preparation, consumption and utilization; provide at least 50 percent of a general line of food products intended for home preparation, consumption and utilization; provide at least 30 percent of retail space for perishable goods that include dairy, fresh produce, fresh meats, poultry, fish and frozen foods; and provide at least 500 square feet of retail space for fresh produce" (New York City 2009).

6. One additional square foot of residential floor area is available to developers for every square foot provided for a grocery store in a mixed-use building, up to a twenty-thousand square-foot limit.

References

Ahern, M., Brown, C., & Dukas, S. (2011). A national study of the association between food environments and county-level health outcomes. *Journal of Rural Health,* 27(4), 367–79.

Aiello, G., & Gendelman, I. (2008). Seattle's Pike Place Market (de)constructed: An analysis of tourist narrative about a public space. *Journal of Tourism and Cultural Change,* 5(3), 158–85.

American Planning Association. (2014). "What Do Planners Do?" Accessed Dec. 8, 2014. https://www.planning.org/aboutplanning/whatisplanning.htm#2.

Anderson, E. (2004). The Cosmopolitan Canopy. *Annals of the American Academy of Political and Social Science,* 595(14), 14–31.

Arias-Estevez, M., Lopez-Periago, E., Martinez-Carballo, E., Simal-Gandara, J., Mejuto, J. C., & Garcia-Rio, L. (2008). The mobility and degradation of pesticides in soils and the pollution of groundwater resources. *Agriculture, Ecosystems & Environment,* 123(4), 247–60.

Born, B., & Purcell, M. (2006). "Avoiding the local trap: Scale and food systems in planning research. *Journal of Planning Education and Research,* 26(2), 195–207.

California State Assembly. (2013). Urban Agriculture Incentive Zones Act. California AB 551.

Carlson, A., & Frazao, E. (2012). *Are Healthy Foods Really More Expensive? It Depends on How You Measure the Price.* USDA-ERS Economic Information Bulletin no. 96. https://papers.ssrn.com/sol3/papers.cfm?abstract_id=2199553.

Caspi, C., Sorensen, G., Subramanian, S. V., & Kawachi, I. (2012). The local food environment and diet: A systematic review. *Health and Place,* 18(5), 1172–87.

Caton Campbell, M. 2004. Building a common table: The role for planning in community food systems. *Journal of Planning Education and Research,* 23(4), 341–55.

City of Buffalo. (2006). *Queen City in the 21st Century: Buffalo's Comprehensive Plan.* Buffalo, NY: City of Buffalo.

City of Madison, Department of Planning and Development. (2006, updated 2012). *City of Madison Comprehensive Plan.* Madison, WI: City of Madison.

City of Minneapolis. (2011). Urban agriculture policy plan: A land use and development plan for a healthy, sustainable local food system. *Minneapolis Plan for Sustainable Growth.* Minneapolis: City of Minneapolis Community Planning and Economic Development Department.

City of San Francisco. (2014). *Makers and Movers: Economic Cluster Strategy.* San Francisco: City of San Francisco.

City of Seattle, Department of Planning and Development. (2005). *City of Seattle Comprehensive Plan: A Plan for Managing Growth, 2004–2024.* Seattle: City of Seattle.

Dane County, Department of Planning and Development. (2007). *Dane County Comprehensive Plan.* Madison, WI: Department of Planning and Development.

Dane County, Department of Planning and Development. (2011). *Southern Wisconsin Food Hub: Feasibility Study.* Madison, WI: Department of Planning and Development.

Dane County, Local Food Advisory Subcommittee. (2005). *Recipe for Success.* Madison, WI: Local Food Advisory Committee.

Delaware Valley Regional Planning Commission (DVRPC). (2010). *Greater Philadelphia Food System Study.* Philadelphia: Delaware Valley Regional Planning Commission.

Delaware Valley Regional Planning Commission (DVRPC). (2011). *Eating Here: Greater Philadelphia's Food System Plan.* Philadelphia: Delaware Valley Regional Planning Commission.

Food District. (N.d.). Welcome to the Food District. http://thefooddistrict.org/.

Frumkin, H., Lawrence, F., & Jackson, R. (2004). *Urban Sprawl and Public Health: Designing, Planning, and Building for Healthy Communities.* Washington DC: Island Press.

Growing Food Connections. (N.d.). Growing the Next Generation of Food Systems Planners. http://growingfoodconnections.org/.

Halebsky, S. (2010). Chain stores and local economies: A case study of a rural county in New York. *Community Development,* 41(4), 431–52.

Hodgson, K. (2012). *Planning for Food Access and Community-Based Food Systems: A National Scan and Evaluation of Local Comprehensive and Sustainability Plans.* Chicago: American Planning Association.

Kochtitzky, C., Frumkin, H., Rodriquez, R., Dannenberg, A. L., Rayman, J., Rose, K., Gillig, R., & Kanter, T. (2006). Urban planning and public health at CDC. *Morbidity and Mortality Weekly Report,* 55, 34–38.

Lamichhane, A., Mayer-Davis, E., Puett, R., Bottai, M., Porter, D. E., & Liese, A. D. (2012). Associations of built food rnvironment with eietary intake among youth with diabetes. *Journal of Nutrition Education & Behavior,* 44(3), 217–24.

Lockhart, K. M., King, A. M., & Harter, T. (2013). Identifying sources of groundwater nitrate contamination in a large alluvial groundwater basin with highly diversified intensive agricultural production. *Journal of Contaminant Hydrology,* 151, 140–54.

Maloni, M.J., & Brown, M. E.. (2006). Corporate social responsibility in the supply chain: An application in the food industry. *Journal of Business Ethics,* 68(1), 35–52.

Monsivais, P., Aggarwal, A., & Drewnowski, A. (2010). Are socioeconomic disparities in diet quality explained by diet cost? *Journal of Epidemiology & Community Health,* 66(6), 530–35.

Neuner, K., Kelly, S., & Raja, S. (2011). *Planning to Eat? Innovative Local Government Plans and Policies to Build Healthy Food Systems in the United States.* Buffalo: Food Systems and Healthy Communities Lab, University at Buffalo, The State University of New York.

New York City, Department of City Planning. (2009). *Food Retail Expansion to Support Health (FRESH).* New York: Department of City Planning.

Oberholtzer, L., & Grow, S. 2003. *Producer-Only Farmers' Markets in the Mid-Atlantic Region: A Survey of Market Managers.* Arlington, VA: Henry A. Wallace Center for Agricultural and Environmental Policy.

Oleson, J. E., & Bindi, M. (2002). Consequences of climate change for European agricultural productivity, land use, and policy. *European Journal of Agronomy,* 4(16), 239–62.

Ostrom, V., Bish, R., & Ostrom, E. (1988). *Local Government in the United States.* San Francisco: Institute for Contemporary Studies.

Pothukuchi, K., & Kaufman, J. L. (2000). The food system—A stranger to the planning field. *Journal of the American Planning Association,* 66(2), 113–24.

Raj, S., Raja, A., & Dukes, B.-A. (2016). Beneficial but constrained: Role of urban agriculture programs in supporting healthy eating among youth. *Journal of Hunger and Environmental Nutrition,* 12(3), 406–28.

Raja, S., Born, B., & Kozlowski Russell, J. (2008). *A Planner's Guide to Community and Regional Food Planning: Transforming Food Environments, Building Healthy Communities.* Chicago: American Planning Association.

Raja, S., Hall, J., Norton, T., Gooch, P., Raj, S., Hawes, T., & Whittaker, J. (2014). *Growing Together: Ensuring Healthy Food, Viable Farms, and a Properous Buffalo Niagara.* Buffalo, NY: Food Systems Planning and Healthy Communities Lab and University at Buffalo Regional Institute.

Raja, S., Ma, C., & Yadav, P. (2008). Beyond food deserts: Measuring and mapping racial disparities in neighborhood food environments. *Journal of Planning Education and Research* 27(4), 469–82.

Raja, S., Picard, D., Baek, S., & Delgado, C. (2014). Rustbelt radicalism: A decade of food systems planning in Buffalo, New York. *Journal of Agriculture, Food Systems, and Community Development* 4(4).

Schulze, A., Rommelt, H., Ehrenstein, V., van Strien, R., Praml, G., Kuchenhoff, H., Nowak, D., & Radon, K. (2011). Effects on pulmonary health of neighboring residents of concentrated animal feeding operations: Exposure assessed using optimized estimation technique. *Archives of Environmental and Occupational Health* 66(3), 146–54.

Sohi, I., Bell, B., Liu, J., Battersby, S., & Liese, A. (2014). Differences in food environment perceptions and spatial attributes of food shopping between residents of low and high food access areas. *Journal of Nutrition Education and Behavior* 46(4).

Spaargaren, G., Oosterveer, P., & Loeber, A. (2012). *Food Practices in Transition: Changing Food Consumption, Retail, and Production in the Age of Reflexive Modernity.* New York: Routledge.

Tuan, Y.-F. (1974). *Topophilia: A Study of Environmental Perception, Attitudes, and Values.* New York: Columbia University Press.

U.S. Department of Agriculture. (2012).

U.S. Department of Health and Human Services. (2012).

von Blottnitz, H., & Curran, M. A. (2007). A review of assessments conducted on bioethanol as a transportation fuel from a net energy, greenhouse gas, and environmental life cycle perspective. *Journal of Cleaner Production* 15(7), 607–19.

Whittaker, J., Clark, J., & Raja, S. (Forthcoming). Rethinking rural food system governance: The case of Cass County. *Rural Sociology.*

COMMUNITY FOOD INTERVENTIONS FOR HEALING

The Cases of Janus Youth and Lynchburg Grows

TANYA DENCKLA COBB AND CARLA JONES

Rather than thinking of food solely as a necessity of an individual's survival, can one of the purposes of food be community healing? How can the implementation of local community food system interventions be used in the process of rebuilding and strengthening communities? The concept that food and healing are synergistic companions is not novel. The use of agricultural gardens for therapeutic purposes has been documented since antiquity (American Horticultural Therapy Society 2016). Gardens have been shown to be effective therapeutic healing agents in various settings (such as hospitals), for particular illnesses (like Alzheimer's disease), and for certain demographics (an example may be aging populations) (Marcus and Barnes 1999). Additionally, the use of particular foods for healing and self-medicating has a long, evolutionary history (Veerporte 2015). Called *bioprospecting*, these traditions of using plants as food medicine have provided important contributions to health and well-being. Despite this long history of the healing power of food, many countries across the world are now facing a new onset of health challenges as we continue fighting infectious diseases but grapple with the prevalence and persistence of chronic diseases (CDC 2016). Many of these chronic diseases are related to diet and physical activity, which are behavioral risk factors that can be addressed for many individuals through community food system interventions.

Many aspects of the healing properties of specific types of food and the benefits of gardens have been researched and well-documented. What has been emerging since the end of the twentieth century is the idea of planning for food systems at a more localized, community scale (Pothukuchi and Kaufman 2000). Whether developed to address hunger issues, rehabilitate and conserve land, improve local economies, or build social capital, community food system interventions have been contributing to healthy communities in a multitude of ways in communities across the globe.

A food system intervention (FSI) is distinct from horticultural therapy or healing gardens. While horticultural therapy and healing gardens start with the premise and primary purpose of creating an interaction between humans and plants that fosters healing primarily through stress relief, a food system intervention's primary purpose is the creation of greater access to healthy, affordable food. While this may be the fundamental goal, commonly there are other widespread benefits, such as regenerating soil health, improving mental and physical health, educational opportunities, economic development and green job creation, building a sense of community, building job skills, leadership skills, and interpersonal skills, increased awareness of nutrition and food choices and of reduced crime (Dunning, 2011; Jackson 2010).

To explore the healing power of community food system interventions for communities, Tanya Denckla Cobb interviewed community food system pioneers from across the United States. Two of those cases, Janus Youth and Lynchburg Grows, are inspiring examples of the healing potential of community food systems. These cases complement the other essays in the collection by providing insight into two initiatives that demonstrate many of the principles presented in the book.

Janus Youth: A Comprehensive Approach to Healing Through Food

In the Northwest states of Oregon and Washington, Janus Youth offers an instructive story of how a desire to facilitate community healing and empowerment can lead to an unexpected and uncharted journey. The Janus Youth multimillion dollar social services agency serving at-risk and runaway youth, founded in 1972, demonstrates multiple aspects of community healing. This case is a synthesis of interviews conducted with Janus Youth staff by phone over the summer of 2009 and during a site visit in February 2010. Key people interviewed by Tanya Denckla Cobb and Robin Proebsting, then a University of Virginia graduate student, include Tera Couchman Wick, former program director for Village Gardens; Mikael Brust, farm coordinator; three AmeriCorps volunteers (Ryan, Jason, and Asha); Amber Baker, Village Gardens program director; Rosalie Karp, advancement director; and Dennis Morrow, executive director.

A food system intervention can foster healing by marshaling community resources, which in turn can lead to growth, skill building, and transformation and empowerment of individuals to change their lives. In this case the very first community problem was that of at-risk youth, Janus Youth's primary service focus. The first step toward healing occurred in 1996 with something simple: a Janus Youth staff member, Kimberly Cowan, wanted to give youth living in the home for runaway teens, called Harry's Mother, something to do with their time to help ground them in the world. She obtained permission to install a small raised-bed food garden in the parking lot of the home. She conceived this first raised bed as a deliberate therapeutic intervention, a form of horticultural therapy that would help the at-risk youth develop leadership, give them something to tend, and ultimately help them heal.

"Teenagers have a hard time envisioning themselves in the future," explained Wick, who started as a volunteer at Harry's Mother. "Agriculture and gardening give teens a reason to think long-term. Many are often not thinking beyond the moment, or tomorrow. But when they put a seed in the ground, they have to think about being around to water the seed and harvest, and maybe even being around the next year to plant another seed." Wick summarized their goals this way, "We see gardens as a youth development tool, to develop the life skills necessary to become successful adults." While a raised-bed food garden at a home for runaway youth does not rise to the level of a food system intervention, it was enough of a success to inspire further action by Janus Youth.

At the same time it was having some success with this small garden, Janus Youth spoke with Portland's Housing Authority to explore how it could help ease tensions at St. Johns Woods, which, at the time, was one of Portland's most disenfranchised housing projects. St. Johns was described as very diverse, with high crime rates, and with a large number of East African, Laotian, and Hmong residents. People were struggling to feed themselves, and some families had even started food gardens outside their apartments. But because the vulnerable populations had difficulty making rent payments, those doing the gardening were threatened with eviction. An organizer at St. Johns Wood, who had learned of Janus Youth's success with the small horticultural therapy garden, sought their help.

Hunger, which had not been a high-priority issue for the runaway teens, was in St. Johns Woods a pressing priority for survival. So it was only natural that the idea for a community garden for food production arose during the community meetings facilitated by Baker and Janus Youth staff. This garden then became Janus Youth's first real community food system intervention.

While Janus Youth wanted to help address the multiple issues in the St. Johns Woods community, it bears articulating that Janus Youth was strongly grounded in "strength-based" or "asset-based" social theory. The staff were adamant that the key to success for any community intervention was for the community to initiate, own, and implement its own plan. "If we come in with the attitude that 'we're going to help you and give you services,' then this is actually oppressive, and at its core is disrespectful," Wick explained.

While the most obvious need was pressing hunger, the actions of Janus Youth suggests that it understood that the community "wound" ran far deeper and wider than hunger. Residents of St. Johns Woods were shut in by crime, trash, and disenfranchisement. In other words, Janus Youth could have fallen into the trap of applying a bandage, such as providing emergency food assistance to those in hunger or imposing a garden solution on the community. Instead of coming in with their own agenda, staff chose a facilitative approach to support the community discussing and developing their own ideas and vision. The approach was "I am here at *your request,* to help you figure out what *you* want to do. And I can help by bringing in resources as you need them." Wick was clear that her goal was not to accomplish a specific task, but rather to build relationships. This approach conjures up the age-old wisdom that the more you strive to control something, the more it will control you; so "letting it go" in this case means letting a community decide on its own, take ownership, and express self-determination.

The success experienced by the food garden at St. Johns Woods was impressive. The St. Johns Woods community had the highest fifth-grade dropout rate in all of Portland and the highest call rate to the police department. But within only eight months of the community putting in this first community garden, the process of healing began. The Janus Youth staff indicated that the call rate to police dropped dramatically, and residents began picking up garbage, paying their rent on time, and taking community responsibility for what their kids were doing. These results led the Public Housing Authority to request assistance from Janus Youth in the redevelopment of a nearby severely distressed public housing neighborhood into a Hope VI mixed-income, mixed-use neighborhood, to be called New Columbia. The Housing Authority very much wanted Janus Youth to create a community garden in this new, socially engineered community.

If the project had been led by a different organization, a desire for replicating the success of St. Johns Woods might have led the developer to incorporate a community garden into the community design with the goal that "If we build it, they will come." In the hands of Janus Youth, however, its deep grounding in asset-based social theory resulted in an approach that demonstrated the conviction that anything *for* the community must, first and above all, come *from* the community. Using this approach, the Janus Youth staff also believed that leadership should not come from their staff but needed to come from the community itself. What better way to create a leadership program for the now-experienced gardeners from nearby St. Johns Woods than to have them become the mentors for the creation of the new garden in New Columbia. Further, these emerging community leaders from St. Johns Woods would be coached and mentored to understand that the new Hope VI neighborhood would need to decide its own vision, goals, and strategies. If they wanted a food garden, then they should also be the ones to decide how would they manage it, how would they make decisions about allocating garden plots, and what rules would govern their garden.

This leadership model is a clear example of a positive (virtuous) feedback cycle, in which the intervention of a small raised bed garden led to an invitation to help a neighborhood in need, which fostered growth and innovation in that neighborhood, which in turn germinated similar growth and innovation in another neighborhood. Leaders from St. Johns Woods were helping form the foundation for new leadership in New Columbia and fostering growth, empowerment, and the development of new skills. People from St. Johns Woods were developing new skills and transforming their own community, and then by being elevated to leadership positions, became agents of healing in nearby New Columbia. In their new role, they helped that community grow confidence, self-esteem, and its own set of leaders. Communication and connections grew between the two communities, fostering mutual growth, empowerment, and skills. A long-term problem in the city of Portland was finally working toward a solution—all because of a food system intervention that followed a model of marshaling community resources and fostering community leadership, growth, and empowerment.

Additional outcomes resulted from these measures. One outcome of this effort was, as hoped for by the Public Housing Authority, the development of a community garden in the nearby Hope VI New Columbia neighborhood. Managed by leaders in the newly redeveloped neighborhood, this garden was named Seeds of Harmony and boasts a welcome sign that is most unusual. It reads:

Seeds of Harmony Garden
We, the Seeds of Harmony Garden Committee, through the sharing of dreams and ideas, have helped this garden come into being. In the winter and spring of 2006, we the community came together frequently to create and shape a hands-on-hands community garden. We hope this garden will be bountiful, with lots of people sharing their cultures, ideas and love, and that it will bring all the members of this community together. We thank all those who contributed time, energy, and resources to this community project. May 2006

The language of this welcome sign is extraordinary, as it leaves no doubt that, for the founders and leaders of this food garden, the garden is far more than the sum of its parts. Soil combined with seed, water, sun, and labor produces food. In this effort, community discussions moved far beyond the mere planting of seeds and cultivation of foods for community kitchen tables. While the welcome sign does recognize food through its use of the word "bountiful," the overarching purpose of this welcome sign is to invoke a higher-order goal. The community reached for its highest possible outcome and decided their community garden would be a place *of* community, *for* community, a place to *build* community, a place for neighbors to meet neighbors. The sign uses phrases like "sharing of dreams and ideas" and "sharing their cultures, ideas and love" for the ultimate goal of bringing "all the members of this community together." The inclusion of the word "love" is startling and bold and is a declaration that the garden's purpose is beyond growing food, even beyond growing networks and neighbors. The garden's purpose is to heal and build community.

The community garden sign demonstrates that a food system intervention can ultimately catalyze an active form of healing, in which the survivors of a legacy of harm and trauma (hunger and crime) are able to regain identity and spiritual health and able to rebuild the neighborhood to help others regain their identity and spiritual health.

It is worth asking if the aspirations of the founding garden committee were only that: aspirations. But three years after its founding, well into the maturation phase of a community garden, one garden leader, a single white mother with one son, emphasized the neighborhood's enduring commitment. "These people are really serious, meeting every Saturday, and it's important to have that commitment" (Michelle Hanna, personal communication, 2009). She explained that the garden had given all those involved specific job skills—volunteer management, project management, and people skills of working with a broad diversity of people. By working in the garden, she said, she was able to build her résumé and secure a paying job. Another garden leader, a political refugee from the Congo who earned his degree there in social work, underscored the role of the garden in building community. "We would never know each other without the garden." In just the first few years of the garden, hundreds of people in the community met and formed relationships that otherwise would never have been possible (Eca Etabo Wasongolo, personal communication, 2009). Because of the way it had been formed—with, by, and for the community—marshaling community resources and fostering growth and empowerment—the garden had become a generator of social capital in the form of skills, leadership, relationships, and goodwill.

To further demonstrate the power of turning a negative reinforcing loop into a positive reinforcing loop, the effect of Janus Youth's food system intervention did not end with the creation of two community gardens but continued to lead to additional positive programs.

One example of this is Food Works, a program for teen youth, and one of the more remarkable and unexpected outcomes of the garden community building. The idea for Food Works arose from the community itself when the community identified an ongoing challenge with its teen youth. The community wanted to create something that would provide jobs for its teens and would empower them with real skills, confidence, and leadership. With facilitation and support from Janus Youth staff, the idea for a teen-managed garden took shape. In their vision, teens would learn to plan the garden, manage the garden, grow the food, and even market their own produce.

Beginning small, with just a small plot the size of a meeting table, the teens began by growing salad greens, which were easy to grow and easy to market. After selling out within the hour at the farmers' market, the teens decided that a garden was not big enough. They thought big and envisioned managing a real *farm*.

With a few years, Portland's first certified organic farm was up and running on Sauvie Island, seven miles upstream from the New Columbia neighborhood in the Columbia River. Janus Youth had negotiated the purchase of one acre on the historically agricultural island. To this day, the farm is no ordinary farm. Managed entirely by North Portland low-income teen youth aged fourteen to twenty-one, the farm follows a typical model of youth leadership development. Teen farm leaders are empowered in all respects—who to hire (and fire), what to grow, where and how to market their produce, and deciding what portion of their harvest to donate to feed the hungry in their own community.

"Every one of these kids is facing a choice whether to be in a gang or not," said Dennis Morrow, executive director of Janus Youth. "The garden mentors say they can tell when they walk through the community who are garden youth and who's not. The garden youth act respectful. They go out of their way to help." Morrow claims the impact is nothing less than transformative for the youth: involvement with Food Works has led youth to receive college scholarships, excel at sports, and gain recognition in various ways.

By 2016 the empowerment model is still successful, even entrenched. Food Works has tripled in size to three acres, produces over ten thousand pounds of organic vegetables, and builds teen youth skills in marketing and teamwork, retail display, planning, cashiering, and customer service. Currently, the teens donate over half of their produce to their low-income neighbors and market the remaining produce at two farmers' markets, one Portland grocery store, and two groceries within their own community (Janus Youth Programs 2016).

A final example of a successful food system intervention by Janus Youth is the establishment of a corner store in New Columbia. Because of the success of both Village Gardens and Seeds of Harmony Garden, the Public Housing Authority approached the community's garden leadership about establishing a healthy corner store to be run by and for community residents. With the nearest supermarket more than a mile away, by foot or bus, a healthy corner store would bring affordable fruits, vegetables, meats, and spices to the neighborhood. In essence, the community garden had generated local "green jobs" in the form of a corner store that would simultaneously improve neighborhood access to foods that could improve neighborhood health outcomes. Even before the advent of the store, residents were reporting changes in their health—lower blood pressure and cholesterol and better diets. With the corner store, hopes were that health outcomes would further improve. The same single mother spoke of how her son was now eating more vegetables, because vegetables were more *interesting* when they came fresh from the garden.

The Public Housing Authority offered to support the store by sharing the cost of a project coordinator and to lease the building to the community at no cost in perpetuity. Having once stalled the establishment of the first garden at St. Johns Woods because it couldn't meter the water, the Housing Authority was now willing to underwrite all corner store utility costs. Plans for the store included installation of a canning kitchen and flash freezing unit for preserving community garden produce for year-round consumption. The store, in short, was a triple win for the community—local "green" jobs, access to fresh foods, opportunities for better health.

Today, the store sells organic produce and culturally relevant food (and no tobacco, alcohol, or lottery tickets), and it serves as an "information highway" on health and nutrition. Janus Youth writes, the "Village Market is more than a healthy corner store that is community run. It is a central meeting point that brings together a diverse neighborhood where 17 different languages are spoken and 22 countries are represented" (Janus Youth Programs 2016).

Janus Youth exemplifies the power of a food system intervention as community medicine. The identification of hunger as a key issue led to installation of a small food garden at St. Johns Woods, which marshaled community resources and fostered growth and empowerment, which in turn led to at least three other positive effects in the form of a food garden in a neighboring Hope IV mixed-income community, an organic Food Works farm managed by teen youth, and a healthy corner store managed for and by community residents.

Lynchburg Grows Nurtures More Than Just the Cultivation of Food

A second community food project in Lynchburg, Virginia, demonstrates how a food system intervention can catalyze community healing. Tanya Denckla

Cobb and her research team conducted interviews on-site in 2009 to better understand the impacts of this food system intervention. Key people interviewed include Dereck Cunningham, president and cofounder, Michael Van Ness, executive director and cofounder, Scott Lowman, board member and cofounder, John Matheson, board member and father of a child employed at the farm, and Kay Frazier, director of Lynchburg Parks and Recreation. This story begins when a city bulldozer mistakenly flattened a group home's front yard garden. This wasn't just any garden. It was a garden tended daily by Paul Lam, who was living with mental retardation, but because of a speech impediment had been misplaced into a mental institution for the severely disabled for nearly forty years, and who had then transitioned during deinstitutionalization in the 1990s to the group home. The destruction of his garden sparked community outrage: a wrong had been done, and the community wanted to right this wrong. The community set about trying to find a new place for this man's garden. Within months, four men successfully secured a larger garden for Lam, along with tiller, compost, and seeds. But to heal the larger community wound that had been exposed—the marginalization of people with special needs—more would need to be done.

The four men were themselves profoundly changed by their experience. They had come together in the community effort to find a garden space for the man with a speech impediment, and in the process they realized two things: how people with special needs were marginalized in a variety of obvious and subtle ways, and how the act of growing food could be transformative by providing meaning, skill building, and self-esteem. Together, with new awareness of this more profound wound that needed to be addressed, these four men decided they would create a place where people with special needs could sink their hands into the soil and grow food. They didn't know where this would lead, or how their own lives would be changed in the process, but they wanted to help heal this community wound.

The next phase of community healing began when the four men pooled their resources and successfully acquired a former rose nursery with nine historic glass greenhouses to create the community's first urban farm, Lynchburg Grows. Similar to the Janus Youth approach, the Lynchburg Grows leaders knew the community had to be involved from the beginning. Executive director Michael Van Ness explained that a nonprofit's level of success is directly proportional to the degree of community involvement and ownership. The effort wasn't simple, as the former rose nursery was a designated brownfield site, contaminated by the pesticides used to control nursery pests. so the first order of business was to clean up the site so that it could gain organic certification.

In this case, the path for community healing took a slightly different path.

While Janus Youth served as a facilitator and catalyst for growing a more empowered community, from the inside out, using the community's own assets,
the Lynchburg Grows food system intervention galvanized an outside-in approach, where different parts of the community marshaled their resources
to create opportunities for empowering people with special needs. Over 100
student athletes from Randolph Macon College, 250 students from Lynchburg
College, and many students sent many times by the Virginia Episcopal School,
working four days every week for an entire year with Lynchburg Grows staff,
removed the contaminated soil in two greenhouses and then replaced it with
150 tons of new, organic soil. The city began providing about 2,000 tons of
leaves and wood chips annually. A local college provided thousands of pounds
of dining hall waste for the urban farm's composting operation. In just under
five years, thanks to 25,000 volunteer hours donated by students, youth, and
civic groups, and another 8,000 hours donated by five champion volunteers,
Lynchburg Grows was cultivating fresh, organic produce and reaching people
at all income levels through weekly deliveries to a shelter and soup kitchen and
to Lynchburg Daily Bread, a local nonprofit charity, and was offering "scholarship" shares in its weekly Community Supported Agriculture (CSA).

As the farm took shape, numerous community partnerships were formed.
A local high school and community college began to bring special needs youth
to the farm to work as a "Farmer for a Day." Then a local congregation adopted
one of the greenhouses to grow food for the community hungry, extending
the mission beyond people with disabilities and special needs to also assist-
ing people in need. Lynchburg Grows catalyzed community healing by shin-
ing the light on a specific problem and serving as a focal point for the community to gather resources to address the problem.

At the individual level, Van Ness emphasizes that people with disabilities
and special needs often want to contribute to and feel a part of their community. The urban farm addresses and heals this wound by providing jobs
that help give lives meaning while building skills and self-esteem. Individuals
who didn't have a way to contribute to or to be connected to their community
now have a place where they can both contribute and connect. The father of
a young man with Down syndrome explained how his son's life was transformed by coming to Lynchburg Grows first as a volunteer and then as one of
the stipend workers. "[He] just loves it here. It gives him a place to anchor his
life. It's low pressure, but he really feels like he's contributing here. And he'll
eat anything that comes from the greenhouse—even if he doesn't like it" (personal conversation with John Matheson at Lynchburg Grows, 2009).

If one measure of a community is how it takes care of its most disenfranchised members, then the converse may also be true. For each person with special needs that Lynchburg Grows is able to help empower, transform, or heal his or her spirit, there are healing ripple effects out into the community itself. The community identity as a caring and healing community grows. Its willingness to participate and provide recognition and opportunity to the healing effort also grows. The Lynchburg community court, for example, began assigning at-risk youth for job training to work at the farm with people with disabilities. Another job training program was initiated for at-risk youth who have just completed juvenile detention to help them develop business skills through agriculture. And the city Parks and Recreation Department, which manages the city's indoor farmers' market, one of the nation's oldest, obtained a grant to help Lynchburg Grows develop a business plan for becoming the market's anchor and also to provide job training for disabled people to actually run the market.

Today, Lynchburg Grows continues to thrive as it adapts its programs to evolving needs. The urban farm has expanded to feature aquaponics, bees, chickens, and even twelve cultivars of the original heritage roses that had grown rampant in the greenhouses prior to the farm's purchase of the land. In addition to creating curricular programming for elementary schools in nutrition and food systems, they hold classes for children and adults in the greenhouses year-round. The farm's mission has broadened to "help all disadvantaged persons enjoy the healthy benefits of gardening and have access to such spaces." Evidence of this mission is their effort to improve low-income food access in Lynchburg's "food deserts" by setting up a mobile produce stand three days a week in eight different downtown areas where they offer fresh foods at or below cost. Equally important is the vocational training program they offer for disabled and low-income individuals. This, again, is an example of how a food system intervention can activate a shift from disenfranchisement to empowerment and healing.

Shifting Vicious Feedback Loops into Virtuous Feedback Loops

In both Janus Youth and Lynchburg Grows, a food system intervention propelled a major healing shift in the community, in which the survivors of a legacy of harm and trauma are able to regain identity and spiritual health and able to build their strength to help others regain their identity and spiritual health. In other words, borrowing language from systems thinking, a food system intervention that follows this healing progression can cause a shift in direction of a positive feedback loop, from a vicious (downward spiraling) feedback loop into a virtuous (upward spiraling) feedback loop. As noted by Gwendolyn Hallsmith in her seminal work on systems thinking in community planning, *The Key to Sustainable Cities,* something may happen to shift the direction of a negative reinforcing loop into its opposite, a positive reinforcing loop. "For example, if an organization's members perceive it to be doing well, then the goodwill and high morale that comes from that perception can make them perform even better" (Hallsmith 2003, 71). The case of Janus Youth's food system intervention is a clear example of an intervention that shifted the direction of a vicious reinforcing loop—poverty, hunger, disenfranchisement—into a virtuous reinforcing loop of leadership and empowerment. Similarly, in the case of Lynchburg Grows, a food system intervention catalyzed a shift from a vicious feedback loop of marginalization and disenfranchisement of people with disabilities and special needs into a virtuous feedback loop, where the community actively embraced and supported the provision of opportunities to people with special needs in ways that foster their empowerment and healing.

Throughout our country, food system interventions like Janus Youth and Lynchburg Grows are proliferating as "medicine" for community. The power of these food system interventions lies in their ability to change lives by fostering individual and collective contributions and connections and by building skills, opportunities, and choices where there were none. Food system interventions can initiate healing at both individual and community levels. With these interventions, one success can breed more success, and community energy can shift from vicious, downward-spiraling feedback loops into virtuous, upward-spiraling feedback loops that build and focus community energy on healing.

Conclusion

Beyond the many lessons in these cases of the importance of cultivating local leaders, measuring success in creative ways, and forming unexpected partnerships, there are clear implications for community planners, designers, and organizers. A food system intervention can create a powerful healing impact in a way accomplished by few other interventions. The two cases of Janus Youth and Lynchburg Grows were selected to show how two different approaches can achieve the same multidimensional outcomes: increased community and social capital, empowered residents along with neighborhood leadership, empowered youth along with the emergence of youth leaders, development of new jobs, skill building, and community partnerships.

While we cannot know why food gardens in particular demonstrate these impacts, it's nevertheless possible to speculate that food reaches deep into the "reptilian" part of the human "triune brain" that governs basic instinctual needs relating to primitive survival needs and therefore provides greater incentive and reward (MacLean 1989).

Even though there may be an urge to include a food garden in every community because of the healing effects and success of these initiatives and others, these interventions may not be appropriate for all communities. If we examine both the Janus Youth and Lynchburg Grows cases, we come to understand that the conditions for success are not about the gardens, per se, but are about creating a space for the community to have a conversation about its own hopes and dreams and then facilitating pathways for the community to make its dreams real. In Janus Youth, the change agents did this quite literally, facilitating neighborhood conversations only when invited, even calling themselves "invited staff" to distinguish themselves from neighborhood residents who were called "community staff." In Lynchburg Grows, the change agents were careful observers, listening to what mattered to the group home and learning the power of a garden to transform a person's life, and then building on this discovery to manifest a larger, even more powerful version of this healing for people with special needs. Rather than imposing a solution from without, these cases suggest that community change agents may realize greater success through a facilitative approach of listening, observing, empowering residents to make decisions and create their own visions, and then bringing resources to the table.

To further this point, if a community planner had parachuted into Village Gardens with the idea of a food garden "fix-it solution," it likely would have failed. Instead, Janus Youth came in with one intention: it would play a facilitative role. It would not offer solutions but instead would facilitate and elicit community needs, strengths, and approaches. Similarly, once the community identified a desired approach, Janus Youth did *not* proceed to implement the community strategy, a common role for community change agents. Rather, Janus Youth continued to play a facilitative role by helping to marshal resources for the community residents to implement their own strategy.

This facilitative role is a long established core value in the practice of community engagement (International Association for Public Participation 2002). As community engagement becomes an integral expectation for community design, transportation, housing, and other services, more change agents will be assuming this facilitative role. For planners and community designers, the implications are intriguing. How can professional aspirations for creating sustainable and resilient communities be merged with the social theory asset-based, facilitative approach?

While this is not a new idea, and might sound simple, the practice of this approach is challenging. Both of these cases suggest several key pathways for success. First, both Janus Youth and Lynchburg Grows leaders emphasize that an attitude of humility is vital. Humility suggests a willingness to admit that the answer to any given community issue or problem lies in the community itself. An analogy to mediation may be helpful, drawn from transformative mediation theory (Bush and Folger, 2004) and Tanya Denckla Cobb's practice as a facilitative mediator and basic mediation trainer. When teaching basic mediation skills in the facilitative or transformative approach, it is emphasized that disputants have often taken years to get to the point where they were willing to seek mediation. No matter how much information is shared in the mediation session, the mediator, parachuting into this dispute, cannot possibly understand all that went into creating this conflict. Thus, it would be presumptuous for the mediator to propose a particular solution and expect it to work for the parties. The mediator is encouraged to enter the situation with humility, listening carefully, and facilitating the development of a solution that the parties devise for themselves. Mediators are often told to expect to be surprised, as ideas may emerge that never occurred to the mediators. Similarly, applying the same logic to community work, it could be argued that it would be presumptuous for anyone not embedded in a neighborhood to propose a particular solution and expect it to work for the neighborhood.

A second pathway for success is for change agents to focus on developing relationships and viewing those relationships as a clear deliverable, distinct from design, build, or services. In both cases, Janus Youth and Lynchburg Grows leaders emphasize the need to "go slow to go fast," allowing relationships to develop and trust to build. When Lynchburg Grows bought five vacant lots, it hoped to turn them into community gardens. But for the next four years, it just mowed the grass. Neighbors would approach to ask, "What are you planning to do here?" and Lynchburg Grows would respond, "It'll be yours. What do you want to do with it?" When groundbreaking for a neighborhood garden began, the entire neighborhood came out—all ages, all ethnicities, bridging the racial divide. Van Ness attributes this success to valuing relationships, first, and letting relationships then drive results. These lessons are challenging, yet they are key pathways to improving a community's social determinants of health, which, according to the Healthy People 2020 report, means we must create "social and physical environments that promote good health for all" (Healthy People 2020, 2016). They suggest that deep empowerment is a core path to achieving the core social determinant of health principle that "all Americans deserve an equal opportunity to make the choices that lead to good health."

In conclusion, these case studies that continue to expand and succeed illuminate the power of food system interventions to catalyze community healing. Conditions for success include an approach of humility, careful listening and observation, empowering community leaders to create their own vision, and a focus on building relationships and partnerships. As with any new emerging field, food systems interventions can generate great excitement and a desire to replicate that success. When results cannot be replicated, it may be easy to blame selection of the wrong solution for the wrong place. What worked well in one place may or may not work well in another place. What these two case studies suggest is that the approach to the solution—that is, the community building work that leads to the selection of a project, the community marshaling resources, the building of partnerships for implementation, the development of neighborhood leaders—all of this is as important as the solution itself, and perhaps even more important for ultimate success.

References

American Horticultural Therapy Association. (2016). Horticutural Therapy. Accessed March 3, 2016. http://ahta.org/horticultural-therapy.

Bush, B., & Folger, J. (2004). *The Promise of Mediation: The Transformative Approach to Conflict.* 2nd ed. San Francisco: Jossey-Bass.

Centers for Disease Control and Prevention (CRC). (2016). *Chronic Disease Overview.* Accessed March 10, 2016. http://www.cdc.gov/chronicdisease/overview/.

Dunning, R. (2013). Research-Based Support and Extension Outreach for Local Food Systems. Center for Environmental Farming Systems. Accessed March 10, 2016. https://cefs .ncsu.edu/resources/research-based-support-and-extension-outreach-for-local-food -systems-2013/.

Hallsmith, G. (2003). *The Key to Sustainable Cities: Meeting Human Needs, Transforming Community Systems.* Gabriola Island, BC: New Society.

Healthy People 202.0 (2016). Social Determinants of Health. Accessed March 9, 2016. http:// www.healthypeople.gov/2020/topics-objectives/topic/social-determinants-of-health.

International Association for Public Participation. (2002). IAP2 Core Values. https://www .iap2.org/?page=corevalues.

International Association of Facilitators (IAF). (2004). Statement of Values and Code of Ethics. https://www.iaf-world.org/site/pages/statement-values-code-ethics.

Jackson, R. (2010). The role of community gardens in sustaining healthy communities. Designing Healthy Communities, September 29. Accessed March 3, 2016. http://designing healthycommunities.org/role-community-gardens-sustaining-healthy-communities/.

Janus Youth Programs. (2016). Community Food Projects. Accessed March 9, 2016. http:// www.janusyouth.org/programs/VillageGardens.

MacLean, P. D. (1989). *The Triune Brain in Evolution: Role in Paleocerebral Functions.* New York: Plenum Press.

Marcus, C. C., & Barnes, M. (1999). *Healing Gardens: Therapeutic Benefits and Design Recommendations.* New York: John Wiley & Sons.

Pothukuchi, K., & Kaufman, J. L. (2000). The food system. *Journal of the American Planning Association,* 66(2), 113–24.

Verpoorte, R. (2015). Food and medicine: Old traditions, novel opportunities. *Journal of Ethnopharmacology,* 167, 1.

CONCLUSION

The Challenges and Opportunities of Designing Healthy, Flourishing Communities and Spaces

This book has examined from different disciplinary positions, and academic and professional roles, the power of the built environment to influence health and well-being. Together these essays have provided a compelling case for the profound and lasting ways in which the design and planning of cities, neighborhoods, landscapes, and buildings can positively (or too often negatively) impact the lives of their occupants and the possibilities of meaningful and flourishing lives. The essays together show the variety of design considerations that need to be taken into account, the range of opportunities by which to enhance wellness and flourishing—from the architecture of hospitals and healthcare facilities to the ability to walk in one's community to the availability of healthy and nutritious food. These essays together provide a nearly comprehensive agenda of the key dimensions of a healthy community.

Some Future Research Questions to Consider

There is much more research yet to be done, of course. We must continue to develop more systematic knowledge, for instance, of the ways that built environments make us happier and healthier. We know generally that natural elements, such as trees, are associated with lower crime and higher reported health and well-being in urban neighborhoods, but we do not understand the causal dynamics very well. More work is needed in understanding the cumulative health impacts of many smaller natural features and elements of the built environment. We still do not understand well the dose-response relationships for many forms of nature in urban settings (or anywhere, for that matter). What is the minimum daily requirement of nature? It is commonly suggested that a healthy life requires an adequate dose of "Vitamin N" (for nature) or "Vitamin G" (for greenspace), but precisely what amount is needed, and in what duration and intensity, remain unclear. And, of course, this will be a function of location and climate, among other factors, so there is a measure of complexity that future researchers will need to understand and sort through.

Much emphasis has been placed on biophilic design in recent years. This is a positive trend, to be sure, and a necessary antidote to the often unhealthy conditions of modern living. The cubicle office, with minimal daylight, fresh air, or greenery, is a serious health challenge for Americans in their working years. "Sitting is the new smoking," it is often said, and the recent evidence about the amount of time spent sitting is indeed disturbing. We know that actual green elements in the work setting—flowers, plants, trees—will enhance health and well-being, but there remains much research to be done to more systematically understand the impacts of the many biophilic design elements—such as natural shapes and forms, natural materials, and color. Some scholarship and study has been done, but not much, and it is mostly cursory or limited in scope. More research is called for in therapeutic garden design, especially on gardens serving the needs of sufferers of autism and post-traumatic stress disorder. Many evidence-based design studies in the field of architecture need to be replicated to establish their accuracy.

A key challenge moving forward is how we integrate the goals of wellness and flourishing into the evaluative and incentive structures of the design professions that guide design and planning of built environments—homes, offices, and healthcare facilities, but also neighborhoods and urban infrastructures. There was for a while much talk in architecture about performance-based contracts and perhaps the time is right to revisit this discussion. Should not architects and designers be held responsible for (and financially incentivized to think about) the longer-term wellness outcomes of the workers and occupants and patients ultimately using and inhabiting these spaces? Should not post-occupancy evaluations be included in contracts?

Similarly, at the urban level, we now have examples of cities aspiring to be *healthy cities,* which is a good sign, but again we need to find effective ways to encourage and reward the achievement of long-term wellness and flourishing. The emerging example of the city of Birmingham, UK, is instructive here. This city has embarked on a strategy of utilizing its green and blue network (including four hundred miles of streams that run through the city) as the basis for addressing a host of health challenges, from urban heat to hazard mitigation to poverty reduction (Beatley 2017). Other cities are developing similar strategies. How to adequately incentivize and reward these local health-enhancing innovations remains a question.

The Need for a Multiscaled Approach

The various essays and many examples contained in this book make a strong case for the need to advance healthy spaces and environments at multiple geographical scales. While Americans spend much of their time indoors (more than 90 percent by some estimates), it is important to understand that achievement of the more holistic flourishing imagined here will require efforts as well to think beyond the building or structure. The recent events in Flint, Michigan, involving its toxic water supply demonstrate the need to understand the infrastructural elements of place that encourage or work against good health.

Ideally, we must think in terms of spatially interlocking and interconnected strategies. The ability and desire to walk in one's immediate neighborhood will require both trees and sidewalks, of course, but will also depend on proximity to other uses and activities (e.g., nearby shopping, offices), and thus will depend on larger efforts at planning land use and ensuring there are nearby commercial centers. There must be places to walk to and functional reasons for spending time outside. Moreover, investments at the community or city level in bike paths, urban trails, and complete streets will ensure that it is possible to walk, hike, or ride one's bicycle beyond the immediate street or neighborhood. Such public investments are essential foundations for a walking and physically active community. They are also essential conditions for ensuring a city is a coherent social whole, where neighborhoods are not isolated, but are connected and tied together physically, socially, economically. Mindy Fullilove, Columbia psychiatrist, compares a city's streets and pathways to the circulatory system of a body. "People have a pretty easy time accepting the analogy between the body and the city," Fullilove tells the *New York Times Magazine* (Sullivan 2015). It is important to keep those urban arteries open, and Fullilove has been working hard to reopen some of them, such as the High Bridge, now connecting Manhattan and Brooklyn.

We must understand that steps to promote health and flourishing must occur at once at multiple geographical scales—from room to region, or rooftop to region. The design of individual buildings and urban sites will be essential to get right, but these must fit well into a larger healthful landscape and cityscape. This will not be easy, in part because with geographical expansiveness comes jurisdictional complexity. We need effective neighborhood-level organizations pushing for trees and sidewalks and gardens, but we will also need action, political and policy, at the city scale. Advocating for a single park in a single neighborhood will generate important wellness benefits, but we can expand these impacts by orders of magnitude if we adopt city-wide policies (for instance, New York City's vision of every New Yorker residing within a ten-minute walk of a park or greenspace). We also need effective planning and design at the regional level, though this has been more difficult in the U.S. context. The good work of regional planning structures, where they have existed (for instance, Portland Metro and its regional greenspaces vision and plan), is essential to achieving more compact urban forms that set a larger framework for more compact cities, and for the density, mixed uses, and other conditions that ensure that healthful walking, biking, and so on are possible. The work of nongovernmental organizations with a beyond-local perspective, such as the Regional Plan Association (RPA) in New York, is also essential. A regional plan or vision sets a framework for cities, and the planning work of cities in turn provides blueprints for neighborhoods and sites.

There Are Positive Trends to Build On, and Some Good News to Celebrate

While the health challenges facing communities today, in the United States and around the world, are daunting, there is considerable good news to celebrate, and some very positive trends to point to. These include renewed commitments to health among the design and planning community, new collaborations between different design fields, and between designers and doctors, nurses, and public health professionals. There has been over the last decade especially much new research and scholarship focused on this, and new emerging models for designing buildings, urban neighborhoods, and cities with a more holistic, health orientation in mind. Moreover, there are new tools that are helpful in advancing this agenda, from the growing sophistication and use of health impact assessments (as described in Ann Forsyth's essay) to new green building and neighborhood certification systems that are helping to give priority and visibility to healthy design ideas and investments.

While we suggest here that much more must be done to create the conditions for active collaboration between and among the design and planning professions and the medical and public health fields, there are already many positive signs that much of this is already happening, and that these professionals' lenses are broadening and expanding in scope. One optimistic trend has the recent reemergence of health as a central concern in the design and planning professions. In many ways, this book is a direct outcome of this trend.

In the field of architecture, this trend has been most clearly manifested in the design of hospitals and healthcare facilities, a major growth area. Healthcare design has now largely recovered from the 2008 recession, and the size and amount of building suggests continuing opportunities to make innovative strides to healthy hospital and healthcare design. Several of the essays of this book (Tye Farrow, Emily Chmieleski, J. David Hoglund, and Reuben Rainey) have highlighted important new ways in which architecture is expanding, extending, and giving much attention to health and flourishing.

The American Institute of Architects has made health a significant priority in recent years. This has included the establishment, in partnership with the Association of Collegiate Schools of Architecture, of a new Design and Health Research Consortium (with eleven schools of architecture and public health designated as "charter members"). AIA has also been funding research in health design and has been publishing a series of Design and Health Reports. Furthermore, the AIA Academy of Architecture for Health, the AIA Design and Health member group, and the Academy of Neuroscience for Architecture represent important initiatives.

The American Society of Landscape Architecture's Therapeutic Landscapes Research Initiative and its Healthcare and Therapeutic Design Professional Practice Network represent significant efforts, as do other organizations such as the Therapeutic Landscapes Network and the Council of Educators in Landscape Architecture. In the discipline of horticultural therapy in the United States four state universities offer degree programs, and the American Horticultural Therapy Association supports a wide range of educational initiatives at the national level.

In the urban planning profession, there has been even greater attention to health, and in many ways a return to the early days of the field when public health served as its raison d'être (as seen in James Corburn's essay). This shift started more than a decade ago, when much research starting to address and understand the ways in which sprawling, car-dependent land-use patterns have made it difficult to walk, and an association between these patterns and a host of negative health conditions began to emerge in the literature. Much of this research has been supported by the availability of new funding sources, especially from the Robert Wood Johnson Foundation. The Active Living Research Center was formed with Robert Wood Johnson funding in 2001 and has organized an important yearly conference bringing many of the leading researchers and advocates together. There is now a large and growing group of researchers and scholars in the planning community with health, and healthy communities, as a main focus.

The main professional organization of urban planners in the United States, the American Planning Association (APA), has made health a priority issue. It has created, for instance, a Planning and Community Health Center, which does many things, from webinars to reports, to elevate health among planning professionals. Evidence of new commitments in the planning world, and new collaborations within and between the design professions around health, can be found in several new initiatives. The APA and the American Public Health Association (APHA), for instance, began a collaboration called Plan4Health Coalitions, which aims to "build local capacity to address population health goals and promote the inclusion of health in non-traditional sectors." (APA n.d.).

The essays in this book demonstrate well that creating healthy communities requires a breadth of perspective and comprehensive approach to community planning and design. Health can and must be advanced through our investments in mobility (and especially walking, as Andrew Mondschein's essay shows), in access to healthy food (as the essays by Samina Raja and Jennifer Whittaker and by Tanya Denckla Cobb and Carla Jones show), and in the provision of adequate public spaces (as Ellen Bassett shows). There will be special design challenges for healthy aging (as Chmielewski and Hoglund demonstrate in their essay), but also ways in which innovations in design and planning will benefit all age groups. Increasingly we recognize that truly healthy communities will need to be intergenerational communities.

There is a robust and growing community of architects and design professionals exploring and testing new design ideas intended to enhance the experience and healthfulness of these places. Hospitals are increasingly understood as requiring a much more comprehensive and holistic approach to design. Furthermore, new institutions have emerged to facilitate these needed collaborations and to promote and advance collaborative research. The School of Architecture at the University of Virginia formed the Center for Design and Health in 2010. Other similar efforts have been underway for some time in other places, and at other universities, such as Texas A & M University, Clemson University, the University of Nebraska, the University of Illinois, the University of Minnesota, and Texas Christian University.

And there are new certification tools and organizations that have helped raise the visibility about the ways buildings and built environments impact the environment and also offer incentives and help in creating new building products that are at once more sustainable and healthier. Green building certification systems have grown in importance, and the numbers of certified buildings have grown significantly. In the United States, the work of the U.S. Green Building Council and LEED certification is especially important; it has done much to expand and deepen interest in green building and has been helpful in making the case for the economics and value of investing in green building. Many of the design measures encouraged through certification systems such as LEED certainly are helpful from a health and wellness point of view (e.g., natural daylight, ventilation, less toxic building materials). And newer more ambitious certification systems, notably the Living Building Challenge, are pushing the envelope even further. One of the main "petals" that building design must address in this system, for instance, is biophilia (an idea explored thoroughly in Judith H. Heerwagen's essay). And the last several years have seen the development of health-specific building certification systems, such as WELL-certified buildings, and now even a program for WELL-certified neighborhoods.

While the green building story is not a perfect one, with certified and highly trumpeted buildings sometime not living up to their energy and environmental claims, it is nevertheless a helpful and positive trend. And it has also helped to show that many important design and planning ideas must now be expanded and applied to larger scales. There is now a LEED-ND certification and other efforts aimed at promoting green and sustainable neighborhoods— for instance, the work of Eco-Districts, which is sponsoring pilot eco-districts in a number of cities and organizes a large annual conference.

In addition, there is now much greater awareness of the problems associated with communities and built environments that preclude or discourage active, outdoor, nature-connected lives. There has been increasing special awareness about the impacts on children. Thanks to the work and writing of people like Richard Louv there is more attention to the needs of children relative to nature (Louv 2008). Louv speaks passionately of the "New Nature Movement," a recognition of the need to combat what he calls Nature Deficit Disorder. Louv and others have formed the Children and Nature Network, for example, and have been instrumental in efforts around the country to "leave no child inside."

Many in the medical community have been listening to Louv (as he is a frequent speaker at medical and health conferences), and there has been a renewed interest in getting children outside. For instance, the initiative DC Parks Rx has been developed by a physician there and is a GIS-database that allows residents to type in their zip code and find the nearest park (Sellers 2015). These are also positive trends.

Future Directions in Practice

The essays in this book provide many impressive examples of buildings, sites, neighborhoods, and cities that more centrally place health and flourishing at the center. There is already much new practice to celebrate—new and emerging building exemplars, new policies, new collaborative initiatives—but there is more to be done. And we can and must be bolder in rethinking design and planning assumptions and pushing for new, innovative models. We must normalize many of the wellness-related design ideas that are working, but we must also promote innovation and experimentation moving forward. Changing circumstances (environmental, demographic, economic) will suggest new ways to experiment.

We need to (continue to) imagine, or reimagine, different kinds of hospitals and health facilities, for instance. Here we are reminded of the story of the Khoo Teck Puat Hospital (KTPH) in Singapore. The CEO of this remarkable facility issued an unusual charge to its designers: We want a hospital where the heart rates and blood pressures of patients checking in go down, rather than up. And by the way, we also want to the facility to serve as a biological ark, providing important new habitats for birds and butterflies! The city of Singapore has taken this to a larger level in aspiring to a future vision for the entire city as a garden or rain forest, so that nature is all around and immersive. From the beginning this hospital has been thought of as a place to heal humans, but also to heal the planet, and as a place for understanding the central and important ways these two agendas must work together.

KTPH is a different sort of hospital for other reasons also. It is not isolated, walled off from the surrounding community, but rather doubles as a community center. Children come to the hospital, with its benches and tables set among the verdant background, to do their homework. Why don't we see hospitals as community spaces where multiple generations come to celebrate life and living, not just places we go to at times of stress or impending death? We are also now in a time when we are rethinking what a place of healing includes and must include. Views of nature, to be sure, but much actual nature. Can we continue the shift from small spaces that patients visit to the notion of a hospital in a garden? From Garden in the Hospital to Hospital in a Garden?

The essays in this book also provide a number of positive design examples and models of what is possible, and offer more cause for optimism. Tye Farrow's Credit Valley Hospital includes a spectacular lobby with tree-like shapes offering shelter, for instance, and David Kamp's Joel Schnaper Garden reduces the stress of HIV/AIDs patients by adapting to changing medical protocols and providing a safe restorative environment. Reuben Rainey and Christina Mullen, in their essay, similarly show the power of the graphic and performing arts in the healing mission of hospitals, and they describe a number of emerging exemplars of medical facilities implementing some form of "arts in medicine."

There remain many questions about design and planning for flourishing. Where do we go from here? Do we need to push the design and planning envelope, and in what ways? Are there especially creative design or planning or development ideas that address health and thriving that we want to build on? Do we need more experimentation in design and planning, more testing of models from which to choose?

There are also new and emerging models of a healthier office setting and work spaces, where most of us spend much of our adult lives. The Bullitt

Center in Seattle represents one such emerging model, a building designed to function literally like a Douglas Fir Forest. The HOK offices in London might represent another, where offices are awash in natural daylight and where it is possible to spread a blanket out in the center of the office and have a picnic. Of course, partly we must design new offices that seek to propel us outside, and that also help us overcome the inside-outside barriers so common in design. One such building that does the latter is the new 300 Lafayette, underway in the SoHo neighborhood of New York. Designed by CookFox, it includes lushly planted green terraces that at once support nature (and views of nature) for the neighborhood but also pull the outside natural world into the heart of the interior of the structure. Again, we must begin to understand and emphasize the ways in which these disparate buildings and environments can be stitched together to form healthy neighborhoods and cities, and much new work here is happening as well. From New York City's Active Design Guidelines to new efforts in many cities to ensure adequate opportunities to buy (and grow) healthy food, there are reasons to believe that flourishing at a neighborhood, city, and regional level are also possible. We have daunting challenges in designing and planning in new ways, but there are exciting new and emerging models, which are cause for much optimism.

The Need for a New Paradigm of Education

The diverse and far-ranging initiatives charted in this volume, if they are to succeed in the future, must rely in part on a dynamic and sophisticated system of education. This should include all levels, K through 12, college, graduate school, and continuing adult education. Curricula will, of course, vary depending on age and audience, but it is important to begin early. The state of the art of digital technology will also have an important role to play in these curricula by creating engaging interactive presentations and updated access to resource materials. However, whatever the level of discourse and curricula, certain fundamental themes should pervade them all:

1. Health is not simply the absence of disease. It includes psychological and social well-being as well as physical.
2. The environment we live in and the way we design and plan that environment has a profound influence on our health.
3. We have an ethical duty to ourselves, the worldwide human community, and all living creatures to take responsibility for maintaining and enhancing our individual health and the health of others and of our planet as a whole. This is the full meaning of "sustainability."

These three themes combining an ethical imperative and scientific knowledge are the solid foundation for the building of various educational efforts. Its implications are wide-ranging and powerful. This foundation would make it absolutely clear that no society whose members suffer from poverty, unemployment, prejudice, injustice, lack of safety, and exposure to toxic substances can claim to be "healthy." It would highlight the importance of a more holistic medicine, taking into account the importance of social and psychological well-being—a medicine including an emphasis on compassion and palliative care and one highlighting personal responsibility for one's health as a key form of preventive medicine. This would transform our present health system from a disease-care system to a true healthcare system. Also, calling attention to the effects of the designed environment on health could lead to more salutogenic design of cities, neighborhoods, individual buildings, and green spaces, design that would actually create health rather than just prevent disease. Essays by Timothy Beatley and Tye Farrow have stressed the importance of this approach.

Furthermore, our understanding of "sustainability" or "resilience," often focused mostly on conserving natural resources and protecting ecosystems, would be expanded to include human health and well-being as a major component, adding depth to our understanding of the interconnected web of all living things and the initiatives required to preserve and enhance it.

Some of these basic insights are being taught at various levels in our present educational system in the United States, and some are not. The prevailing emphasis at the K through 12 levels on personal hygiene, sex education, nutrition, and environmental science is valuable, but not sufficient. Especially lacking is emphasis on the health effects of the designed environment. This lack, of course, is not confined to elementary and high school education. Despite promising recent developments, it exists at the college and graduate levels, especially in universities preparing professionals in architecture and related design disciplines. This must change.

Thus a paradigm shift along many educational fronts is needed. This should be fueled, not so much by a scenario of doomsday avoidance, but by a vision of an enriched, vibrant well-being on a global scale, not only for humans, but for all living things, a vision shared and hoped for by the authors of this book. This vision of healthy, flourishing communities is gaining ground, we believe, and as the essays in this book convey, it is already manifesting in many new and creative ways: in new designs for buildings, in healing gardens and spaces, and in neighborhood and city planning that takes a more holistic view and understands that flourishing will require social contact and vibrant public spaces, restored and restorative natural environments, opportunities for walking and for enjoying healthy food, among many other elements. The health challenges faced by communities today are daunting, and with climate change and rapid global population growth and urbanization, they are even more challenging to solve. We are optimistic, however, and if we begin to better harness the health-enhancing aspects of built environments, if we more clearly and intelligently design and plan, the vision and goal of flourishing places are within reach.

References

American Planning Association (APA). (N.d.). Plan4Health. https://www.planning.org/nationalcenters/health/psecoalitions/.

Beatley, Timothy. (2017). *Handbook of Biophilic City Planning and Design.* Washington, DC: Island Press.

Louv, R. (2008). *Last Child in the Woods: Saving Our Children from Nature Deficit Disorder.* Chapel Hill, NC: Algonquin Books.

Sellers, F. S. (2015). D.C. doctor's Rx: A stroll in the park instead of a trip to the pharmacy. *Washington Post,* May 28. https://www.washingtonpost.com/national/health-science/why-one-dc-doctor-is-prescribing-walks-in-the-park-instead-of-pills/2015/05/28/03a54004-fb45-11e4-9ef4-1bb7ce3b3fb7_story.html?utm_term=.8906ec145f9c.

Sullivan, R. (2015). The town shrink: Trained as a psychiatrist, Mindy Thompson Fullilove now puts entire cities on the couch. *New York Times Magazine,* June 23. https://www.nytimes.com/2015/06/28/magazine/the-town-shrink.html.

AFTERWORD

HOWARD FRUMKIN

Imagine you're a zookeeper. You're sitting in your zoo office one day when you get a call that a shipment of butterflies, or frogs, or otters, is about to arrive. What's the first thing you think about?

There's no doubt. You want to be sure you have the right habitat for the animals: the right combination of temperature, humidity, and light; the right vegetation; adequate provision of hiding places; the right food; clean water. You'll set about designing and maintaining their habitat according to these mandates. And you'll evaluate your success according to one fundamental metric: are the animals thriving?

Importantly, you'll set a high standard for that thriving: *all* the animals need to thrive. If only a subset of the animals thrived—say, those of a particular size, shape, or color—that would not count as success.

Moreover, you'll plan ahead. You might create a great habitat, but if you burn through all the zoo's resources in maintaining it, the animals' future is uncertain. Success means not only that today's animals thrive, but that their offspring, and their offspring's offspring, also thrive. The habitat needs to be sustainable.

These ideas are neither complicated nor controversial. They are pure common sense for any zookeeper. What's remarkable, though, is how rarely we apply these ideas to human habitat. Those who design the spaces we occupy— from interior designers and architects at the small scale to urban planners, landscape architects, and transportation planners at the large scale—often seem to aim for different outcomes than human thriving. Perhaps they're designing something splashy and edgy; success would mean an architectural award or a cover story on a design magazine. Perhaps they're designing with economics in mind; success would mean a tidy profit for the client. Perhaps they're constrained by regulations; success would mean compliance with relevant laws and codes. There's nothing unreasonable about these goals, but if they eclipse the central importance of human thriving, then design can go astray.

In recent years, we've seen a growing recognition that places can and should be built to support health and well-being. This is a very positive development. Both in the United States and globally, despite some welcome health trends (such as declining infant mortality rates globally, and declining coronary heart disease mortality rates in the United States), we continue to face daunting health challenges. In fact, some trends are moving in precisely the wrong direction. Obesity and associated conditions such as diabetes are rising. Asthma is rising. Allergies and autoimmune diseases are rising. Attention-deficit/hyperactivity disorder has increased precipitously. Anxiety disorders and depression are disturbingly common and may be rising.

Not only are some health trends worrisome, but some of the upstream factors that determine health also give cause for concern. Sedentary lifestyles are far too common, as are unhealthy diets. Studies show that Americans carry substantial body burdens of large numbers of chemicals—and not just adults, but even newborns. In an increasingly urban world, many people have little or no access to the natural world and forfeit the benefits that such contact offers. Climate change is unfolding faster than had been predicted, both posing health risks and requiring mitigation and adaptation strategies.

The built environment certainly can't account for all these health trends or risk factor profiles, nor do all the solutions lie in the built environment. But it has an important role to play. Research in recent years has blossomed at a remarkable rate (Jackson, Dannenberg, and Frumkin 2013). Investigators have carefully studied the effects of building design, neighborhood configurations, transportation strategies, nature contact, and many other features of the human habitat. This research has been facilitated by emerging technologies: geospatial data systems, devices that measure everything from people's activity levels to energy flows in buildings, satellites that quantify land-use patterns, big data analytics. Investigators have examined not only direct effects on health and well-being, such as indoor air quality in buildings, but also indirect pathways, such as effects mediated through social capital. The links between health and the built environment are increasingly prominent on the agendas of professional conferences in diverse fields. There are listservs, websites, textbooks, university courses, and joint degree programs. Importantly, consumer preferences are shifting, and markets are delivering innovative products (although in some cases these are rediscovered time-tested designs more than actual innovations): green, healthy buildings; walkable neighborhoods; healing gardens in hospitals. Research findings are increasingly being translated into action.

Based on the growing evidence base, and on experience with progress in the built environment over recent years, we can identify several themes. First, we should aim to promote health and well-being, and not simply to treat (or even to prevent) illness. Second, we should design for the populations of tomorrow, not for populations of yesterday. Third, social equity is fundamental. Fourth, since "everything is connected to everything else," design needs to be grounded in broad systems thinking—and to embrace concurrent challenges such as climate change. Fifth, we should do what works, and stop doing what doesn't work; we need to collect, respect, and utilize evidence. Finally, when conventional practice doesn't work, let's innovate. The following paragraphs explore each of these themes.

Let's Promote Health and Well-Being, Not Just Treat Illness

In 1948, the World Health Organization constitution defined *health* broadly, establishing a framework that remains highly relevant today: "a state of complete physical, mental and social well-being and not merely the absence of disease or infirmity." Like the zookeeper who began these pages, we aim to create habitats in which people thrive. So while the technical aspects of architecture and urban planning are certainly important—buildings stand or fall based on uncompromising physical principles—these fields might better be conceived as domains of social science.

If placemaking is a social undertaking, as much grounded in cultural anthropology and environmental psychology as in engineering—what considerations are relevant? Certainly, we need to consider ways to avoid unhealthy exposures such as contaminated indoor air or trip-and-fall hazards. Just as certainly, we need to understand the design of health-promoting places, such as places that encourage walking and cycling (Saelens, Sallis, and Frank 2003; Van Dyck et al. 2012). But we need to focus on the fundamental ways in which people relate to their environments—on the determinants of comfort, legibility, even inspiration (Alexander et al. 1977). We need to understand the sense of place (Lippard 1997; Tuan 1977) and the phenomenon of place attachment (Altman and Low 1992; Manzo, Devine-Wright, and Manzo 2014), especially as these evolve in an increasingly rootless and online society. We need to probe mental health in relation to place (Evans 2003). We need to understand the allure of secret spaces of childhood (Goodenough 2003), what makes sacred spaces sacred (Sheldrake 2001), what kinds of places make people happy (de Botton 2006; Montgomery 2013; Wernick 2008). This broad vision of healthy habitat extends well beyond the medical model, to take in many dimensions of human relations to their environments.

Let's Design for the Populations of Tomorrow, Not for Populations of Yesterday

Populations are shifting in important ways. Worldwide, people are moving from rural areas to cities (United Nations 2015). In the United States, millennials are eschewing car ownership for walking and transit (National Association of Realtors and Portland State University 2015), and avoiding large homes for more compact ones. The average household size has been shrinking for years with changing family dynamics (although this trend paused following the Great Recession, as millennials returned to live with their parents [Fry 2015]). The U.S. population is becoming increasingly diverse (Frey 2014), and in the United States, as in much of the world, the population is aging rapidly (United Nations 2013; Ortman et al. 2014).

Speaking in broad strokes, then, the populations of tomorrow will be more urban, more diverse, and more likely to live in small households than those of yesterday. The proportion of the population that is elderly will be far larger. With more people coming, but without much more land available, cities will be denser, and the people who live there will desire urban amenities such as vibrant commercial centers, ample sidewalks, reliable transit services, and nearby parks. We need to be designing places that satisfy these needs.

Social Equity Is Fundamental

Another trend is rising inequality (Piketty 2014). Gaping inequalities across a society violate the precepts of most ethical systems, corrode social capital, impede economic growth and prosperity (Cingano 2014), and undermine health and well-being (Pickett and Wilkinson 2014). For those concerned with healthy environments, there are at least two important conclusions.

First, it is essential to direct creative energy, resources, and collaboration to the most vulnerable—a core precept of public health. Poor people are disproportionately likely to live in substandard housing—undermining their dignity and security (Dupuis and Thorns 1998) as well as their health (Adamkiewicz et al. 2013). Improving housing in low-income settings offers enormous potential to improve people's lives (Haines et al. 2013). Equally compelling is providing housing to those who are homeless—a direct and effective way to improve their health and well-being (Ellen and O'Flaherty 2010; Fitzpatrick-Lewis et al. 2011). Similarly, schools in low-income settings are disproportionately likely to be in poor condition (Alexander and Lewis 2014), threatening children's health and learning. And deprived neighborhoods are disproportionately likely to confront residents with dispiriting, even squalid conditions, with unhealthy food choices (Walker et al. 2010), and with inadequate access to amenities such as greenspace (Wolch, Byrne, and Newell 2014) and transit (Bullard and Johnson 1997). Such neighborhoods are unhealthy (Diez Roux and Mair 2010; Jokela 2015); features of the built environment compound such challenges as poverty, pollutants, and violence, cumulatively undermining health and well-being (Morello-Frosch et al. 2011). From housing to schools to neighborhoods, the built environment is very much a part of achieving health equity (Frumkin 2005).

Second, healthy habitats may do more than function as an element of health equity; they may actually help mitigate the effects of poverty. Studies from the Centre for Research on Environment Society and Health (CRESH) in Scotland suggest that nearby greenspace not only improves health and well-being but also offers greater benefits to poor people than to wealthy people—attenuating socioeconomic gradients in health (Mitchell and Popham 2008; Mitchell et al. 2015). As these authors noted, "If societies cannot, or will not, narrow socioeconomic inequality, research should explore the so-called equigenic environments—those that can disrupt the usual conversion of socioeconomic inequality to health inequality" (Mitchell et al. 2015, 80). Healthy built environments, with features such as greenspace, may be a key such strategy.

Everything Is Connected to Everything Else; We Need to Think Broadly

Human habitats need to do more than just promote human health and well-being. Our buildings, our cities, our means of travel, have far-reaching implications for the physical world—for energy use, for land cover, for air and water quality, for biodiversity. At a time when planetary boundaries are increasingly breached (Rockström et al. 2009), and when global changes such as climate change threaten calamity (IPCC 2014), we need to consider the environmental consequences of placemaking choices. Thus, a strategy that has few direct human health benefits, but that helps reduce deforestation or manage storm water, should be integrated with healthy placemaking.

A paradigm for this approach is the concept of co-benefits, which has emerged prominently in the climate change literature. Co-benefits are the benefits that flow when an action taken for one purpose yields benefits in additional ways. For instance, a shift away from automobile travel toward walking, cycling, and transit use is a climate change mitigation strategy, reducing the use of fossil fuels in transportation. But such a shift offers a range of collateral benefits: more physical activity, improved air quality, reduced motor vehicle fatalities, reduced traffic congestion, enhanced social capital (Woodcock et al. 2009; Grabow et al. 2012; Shaw et al. 2014). Such mutual benefits have been well described for other built environment strategies, ranging from energy generation to green building to urban forest canopy (Younger et al. 2008; Smith and Haigler 2008; Preval et al. 2010; Jack and Kinney 2010; Milner and Wilkinson 2012; Smith and Woodward 2014). Clearly, when considering placemaking, we need to think broadly, appreciate the many ramifications of our decisions, and optimize as many goals—human, environmental, economic, and others—as possible.

Supporting this broad systems thinking is life cycle assessment (LCA), which enables full accounting of the costs, impacts, and benefits of alternatives. For instance, a building may be made of wood, steel, or concrete. Each material has a life history. Wood comes from a forest that may or may not be sustainably harvested, is cut and processed by workers who may or may not work under safe conditions at fair wages, and may be transported short or long distances to the construction site. A certain amount of waste occurs during the production and construction phases. Once constructed, the wood structure will have a certain lifespan, after which the wood may either be reused or disposed of. A similar sequence exists for steel and concrete. So a complete assessment of the environmental, social, and economic costs of a building (or any other built environment project) requires this comprehensive "cradle to grave" analysis (Thomas and Graedel 2003; U.S. EPA 2006; Finnveden et al. 2009). (As a reminder of the importance of reuse and recycling, some authors have reformulated this concept as "cradle to cradle" [McDonough and Braungart 2002; Marshall-Baker and Tucker 2012].)

A related approach—ideally, a component of life cycle assessment—is health impact assessment (HIA), which is defined as a systematic process for assessing the human health implications of a policy, program, or project. Suppose, for example, that a state is considering whether to expand a highway, and if so whether to include bicycle lanes in the project. A HIA might consider the impacts on air quality of the increased traffic flow and the resulting impacts on health of nearby communities; the impact on physical activity and safety of installing the bicycle lanes; the noise that would result from the increased traffic; and other factors. Recommendations from the HIA would ideally be integrated into decision making about the project. HIA is becoming more widely used in public works projects (NRC 2011; Bourcier et al. 2015).

Let's Do What Works, and Stop Doing What Doesn't Work

One of the most far-reaching paradigm shifts in modern health sciences has been the advent of evidence-based medicine, defined as "the conscientious, explicit and judicious use of current best evidence in making decisions about the care of individual patients" (Sackett et al. 1996). This framework demands that medical interventions—both those that prevent and those that treat—be supported by evidence demonstrating both efficacy and safety (and often cost-effectiveness) (Katz 2001; Sackett 2005). Entire fields, such as comparative effectiveness research, interrogate clinical practices for their evidence base (Ashton and Wray 2013). The expectation of such evidence is now woven into the very fabric of health care, and no specialties or practices are exempt.

Not so for the built environment. There are, of course, important exceptions, such as the growing appreciation of evidence-based design in healthcare architecture (Ulrich et al. 2008; Cama 2009). But for the most part, design professionals have not grounded their work in evidence that the places they create enhance the health, well-being, comfort, and delight of the people in them. Artistic sensibilities, aesthetic preferences, and intuition are fine, but they are insufficient to guide design and construction. In health care, "efficacy" connotes that a medication successfully improves patients' health. In the built environment, we need a corresponding concept of efficacy—one equally grounded in evidence (Frumkin 2003). This calls for an expanded culture of research in schools of architecture, landscape architecture, and planning, in design firms, and in agencies. It calls for cross-training that combines design and public health, in the curricula of both sets of professions—a trend that, happily, is growing (Botchwey and Trowbridge 2011; Dyjack, Botchwey, and Marziale 2013). It calls for the normalization of post-occupancy evaluation; just as physicians follows their patients' progress after initiating a treatment (and not to do so would be negligent), design professionals should routinely look into the human impacts of the buildings, neighborhoods, and transportation systems they create (NRC 2002). Conclusions then need to be looped back into the design process so they can inform future design. This process of iterative, data-based, continuous improvement will help assure healthy human habitats.

When Conventional Practice Doesn't Work, Let's Innovate

Finally, we need to be open to innovation, as conventional practice often falls short of the mark. The preceding paragraphs mention some of the marvelous innovations now available: new technologies such as sensors; big data analytics; new assessment procedures that integrate health and sustainability into building; new cross-disciplinary training pathways in graduate schools of architecture, urban planning, and public health. We also need new legal arrangements, such as reformed land-use, zoning, and building codes and regulations (Feldstein 2011). And we need innovative economic arrangements, such as the landmark agreement between Seattle City Light, the Bullitt Foundation, and the city of Seattle, under which the utility purchases energy savings—"negawatts"—produced by the deep green Bullitt Center, making radical energy savings a win-win proposition (Barringer 2013). Cultural innovations such as the sharing economy (Heinrichs 2013) should be harnessed in the service of health, sustainability, equity, and efficiency. While some elements of healthy habitat, such as walkable communities, are age-old, others can be greatly facilitated by creative innovations.

The essays in this book wonderfully address these (and other) themes. They extend from healing those who are ill to promoting health and well-being in a broad sense. They are forward-looking. They consistently weave social equity into their narratives. Individually and as a whole, they take a systems approach, extending beyond a biomedical approach to planetary health, beyond human health to sustainability, beyond individual places to the global commons. These essays rely heavily on solid evidence, and they offer a range of innovative ideas. After reading this book, I hope you share my reaction: captivated, inspired, and hopeful, about the potential for healthy, equitable, and sustainable habitats for all people.

References

Adamkiewicz, G., Spengler, J. D., Harley, A. E., Stoddard, A., Yang, M., Alvarez-Reeves, M., & Sorensen, G. (2013). Environmental conditions in low-income urban housing: Clustering and associations with self-reported health. *American Journal of Public Health,* 104(9), 1650–56.

Alexander, C., Ishikawa, S., Silverstein, M., Jacobson, M., Fiksdahl-King, I., & Angel, S. (1977). *A Pattern Language: Towns, Buildings, Construction.* New York: Oxford University Press.

Alexander, D., & Lewis, L. (2014). *Condition of America's Public School Facilities: 2012–2013.* NCES 2014–022. Washington, DC: U.S. Department of Education, National Center for Education Statistics. https://nces.ed.gov/pubsearch/pubsinfo.asp?pubid=2014022.

Altman, I., & Low, S. M. (1992). *Place Attachment.* New York: Plenum Press.

Ashton, C. M., & Wray, N. P. (2013). *Comparative Effectiveness Research: Evidence, Medicine, and Policy.* Oxford: Oxford University Press.

Barringer, F. (2013). Making energy efficiency attractive for owners of older Seattle buildings. *New York Times,* June 18, p B8. http://www.nytimes.com/2013/06/19/real estate/commercial/making-energy-efficiency-attractive-for-owners-of-older-seattle-buildings.html?_r=0.

Botchwey, N. D., & Trowbridge, M. J. (2011). Training the next generation to promote healthy places. In: Dannenberg, A. L., Frumkin, H., & Jackson, R. (2011), *Making Healthy Places: Designing and Building for Health, Well-Being, and Sustainability.* Washington, DC: Island Press.

Bourcier, E., Charbonneau, D., Cahill, C., & Dannenberg, A. L. (2015). An evaluation of health impact assessments in the United States, 2011–2014. *Preventing Chronic Disease,* 12, E23.

Bullard, R., & Johnson, G. (1997). *Just Transportation: Dismantling Race & Class Barriers to Mobility.* Gabriola Island, BC: New Society.

Cama, R. (2009). *Evidence-Based Healthcare Design.* Hoboken, NJ: Wiley.

Cingano, F. (2014). Trends in Income Inequality and Its Impact on Economic Growth. *OECD Social, Employment and Migration Working Papers,* no. 163, OECD. *http://dx.doi .org/10.1787/5jxrjncwxv6j-en.*

de Botton, A. (2006). *The Architecture of Happiness.* New York: Pantheon.

Diez Roux, A.V., & Mair, C. (2010). Neighborhoods and health. *Annals of the New York Academy of Sciences,* 1186, 125–45.

Dupuis, A., and Thorns, D. C. (1998). Home, home ownership and the search for ontological security. *Sociological Review,* 46, 24–47.

Dyjack, D. T., Botchwey, N., & Marziale, E. (2013). Cross-sectoral workforce development: Examining the intersection of public health and community design. *Journal of Public Health Management and Practice,* 19(1), 97–99.

Ellen, I. G., & O'Flaherty, B. (Eds.). (2010). *How to House the Homeless.* New York: Russell Sage Foundation.

Evans, G. W. (2003). The built environment and mental health. *Journal of Urban Health,* 80(4), 536–55.

Feldstein, L. M. (2011). Policy and legislation for healthy places. In: Dannenberg, A. L., Frumkin, H., & Jackson, R. (2011), *Making Healthy Places: Designing and Building for Health, Well-Being, and Sustainability.* Washington, DC: Island Press.

Finnveden, G., Hauschild, M. Z., Ekvall, T., Guinée, J., Heijungs, R., Hellweg, S., et al. (2009). Recent developments in Life Cycle Assessment. *Journal of Environmental Management,* 91(1), 1–21.

Fitzpatrick-Lewis, D., Ganann, R., Krishnaratne, S., Ciliska, D., Kouyoumdjian, F., & Hwang, S. W. (2011). Effectiveness of interventions to improve the health and housing status of homeless people: A rapid systematic review. *BMC Public Health,* 11, 638.

Frey, W. H. (2014). *Diversity Explosion: How New Racial Demographics Are Remaking America.* Washington, DC: Brookings Institution Press.

Frumkin, H. (2003). Healthy places: Exploring the evidence. *American Journal of Public Health,* 93(9), 1451–56.

Frumkin, H. (2005). Health, equity, and the built environment. *Environmental Health Perspectives,* 113(5), A290–A291.

Fry, R. (2015). More millennials living with family despite improved job market. Pew Research Center, Social & Demographic Trends, July 29. http://www.pewsocialtrends.org /2015/07/29/more-millennials-living-with-family-despite-improved-job-market/.

Goodenough, E. (2003). *Secret Spaces of Childhood.* Ann Arbor: University of Michigan Press.

Grabow, M. L., Spak, S. N., Holloway, T., Stone, B., Mednick, A. C., & Patz, J. A. (2012). Air quality and exercise-related health benefits from reduced car travel in the midwestern United States. *Environmental Health Perspectives,* 120(1), 68–76.

Haines, A., Bruce, N., Cairncross, S., Davies, M., Greenland, K., Hiscox, A., et al. (2013). Promoting health and advancing development through improved housing in low-income settings. *Journal of Urban Health,* 90(5), 810–31.

Heinrichs, H. (2013). Sharing economy: A potential new pathway to sustainability. *Gaia,* 22(4), 228–31.

IPCC (2014). *Climate Change 2014: Impacts, Adaptation, and Vulnerability. Part A: Global and Sectoral Aspects. Contribution of Working Group II to the Fifth Assessment Report of the Intergovernmental Panel on Climate Change* [Field, C. B., Barros, V. R., Dokken,

D. J., Mach, K. J., Mastrandrea, M. D., Bilir, T. E., Chatterjee, M., Ebi, K. L., Estrada, Y. O., Genova, R. C., Girma, B., Kissel, E. S., Levy, A. N., MacCracken, S., Mastrandrea, P. R., & White, L. L. (Eds.)]. Cambridge: Cambridge University Press.

Jack, D. W., & Kinney, P. L. (2010). Health co-benefits of climate mitigation in urban areas. *Current Opinion in Environmental Sustainability,* 2, 172–77.

Jackson, R. J., Dannenberg, A. L., & Frumkin, H. (2013). Health and the built environment: 10 years after. *American Journal of Public Health,* 103(9), 1542–44.

Jokela, M. (2015). Does neighbourhood deprivation cause poor health? Within-individual analysis of movers in a prospective cohort study. *Journal of Epidemiology and Community Health,* 69(9), 899–904.

Katz, D. L. (2001). *Clinical Epidemiology and Evidence-Based Medicine: Fundamental Principles of Clinical Reasoning & Research.* Thousand Oaks, CA: Sage.

Lippard, L. R. (1997). *The Lure of the Local: Senses of Place in a Multicentered Society.* New York: New Press.

Manzo, L., Devine-Wright, P., & Manzo, L. C. (Eds.). (2014). *Place Attachment: Advances in Theory, Methods, and Applications.* London: Routledge.

Marshall-Baker, A., & Tucker, L. M. (2012). *Cradle to Cradle Home Design: Process and Experience.* New York: Fairchild Books.

McDonough, W., & Braungart, M. (2002). *Cradle to Cradle: Remaking the Way We Make Things.* New York: North Point Press.

Milner, J., Davies, M., & Wilkinson, P. (2012). Urban energy, carbon management (low carbon cities) and co-benefits for human health. *Current Opinion in Environmental Sustainability,* 4(4), 398–404.

Mitchell, R., & Popham, F. (2008). Effect of exposure to natural environment on health inequalities: An observational population study. *Lancet,* 372, 1655–60.

Mitchell, R. J., Richardson, E. A., Shortt, N. K., & Pearce, J. R. (2015). Neighborhood environments and socioeconomic inequalities in mental well-being. *American Journal of Preventive Medicine,* 49(1), 80–84.

Montgomery, C. (2013). *Happy City: Transforming Our Lives through Urban Design.* New York: Farrar, Straus and Giroux.

Morello-Frosch, R., Zuk, M., Jerrett, M., Shamasunder, B., & Kyle, A. D. (2011). Understanding the cumulative impacts of inequalities in environmental health: Implications for policy. *Health Affairs (Millwood),* 30(5), 879–87.

National Association of Realtors and Portland State University (2015). 2015 Community and Transportation Preferences Survey. http://www.realtor.org/reports/nar-2015 -community-preference-survey.

National Research Council (NRC), Committee on Health Impact Assessment (2011). *Improving Health in the United States: The Role of Health Impact Assessment.* Washington, DC: National Academies Press.

National Research Council (NRC), Federal Facilities Council (2002). *Learning from Our Buildings: A State-of-the-Practice Summary of Post-Occupancy Evaluation.* Washington, DC: National Academies Press.

Ortman, J. M., Velkoff, V.A., & Hogan, H. (2014). *An Aging Nation: The Older Population in the United States.* Current Population Reports P25–1140. Washington, DC: U.S. Census Bureau. http://www.census.gov/library/publications/2014/demo/p25-1140.html.

Pickett, K. E., & Wilkinson, R. G. (2015). Income inequality and health: A causal review. *Social Science & Medicine,* 128, 316–26.

Piketty, T. (2014). *Capital in the Twenty-First Century.* Cambridge, MA: Belknap Press of Harvard University Press.

Preval, N., Chapman, R., Pierse, N., & Howden-Chapman, P. (2010). Evaluating energy, health and carbon co-benefits from improved domestic space heating: A randomised community trial. *Energy Policy,* 38(8), 3965–72.

Rockström, J., Steffen, W., Noone, K., Persson, Å., Chapin, F. S., III, Lambin, E., et al. (2009). Planetary boundaries: Exploring the safe operating space for humanity. *Ecology and Society,* 14(2):32.

Sackett, D. L. (2005). Evidence-based medicine. In: Armitage, P., & Colton, T. (Eds.), *Encyclopedia of Biostatistics,* 2nd ed. Hoboken, NJ: John Wiley & Sons.

Sackett, D. L., Rosenberg, W. M. C., Gray, J. A. M., Haynes, R. B., & Richardson, W. S. (1996). Evidence-based medicine: What it is and what it isn't. *British Medical Journal,* 312, 71–72.

Saelens, B. E., Sallis, J. F., & Frank, L. D. (2003). Environmental correlates of walking and cycling: Findings from the transportation, urban design, and planning literatures. *Annals of Behavioral Medicine,* 25(2), 80–91.

Shaw, C., Hales, S., Howden-Chapman, P., & Edwards, R. (2014). Health co-benefits of climate change mitigation policies in the transport sector. *Nature Climate Change,* 4(6), 427–33.

Sheldrake, P. (2001). *Spaces for the Sacred: Place, Memory, and Identity.* Baltimore: Johns Hopkins University Press.

Smith, K. R., & Haigler, E. (2008). Co-benefits of climate mitigation and health protection in energy systems: Scoping methods. *Annual Review of Public Health,* 29(1), 11–25.

Smith, K. R., & Woodward, A. (2014). Human health: Impacts, adaptation, and co-benefits. Chapter 11 in: IPCC (2014). *Climate Change 2014: Impacts, Adaptation, and Vulnerability. Part A: Global and Sectoral Aspects. Contribution of Working Group II to the Fifth Assessment Report of the Intergovernmental Panel on Climate Change* [Field, C. B., V. R. Barros, D. J. Dokken, K. J. Mach, M. D. Mastrandrea, T. E. Bilir, M. Chatterjee, K. L. Ebi, Y.O . Estrada, R. C. Genova, B. Girma, E. S. Kissel, A. N. Levy, S. MacCracken, P. R. Mastrandrea, and L. L. White (Eds.)]. Cambridge: Cambridge University Press.

Thomas, V. M., & Graedel, T. E. (2003). Research issues in sustainable consumption: Toward an analytical framework for materials and the environment. *Environmental Science & Technology,* 37(23), 5383–88.

Tuan, Y.-F. (1977). *Space and Place: The Perspective of Experience.* Minneapolis: University of Minnesota Press.

Ulrich, R. S., Zimring, C., Zhu, X., DuBose, J., Seo, H. B., Choi, Y. S., et al. (2008). A review of the research literature on evidence-based healthcare design. *Health Environments Research & Design,* 1(3), 61–125.

United Nations, Department of Economic and Social Affairs, Population Division (2013). *World Population Ageing 2013.* ST/ESA/SER.A/348. New York: United Nations.

United Nations, Department of Economic and Social Affairs, Population Division (2015). *World Urbanization Prospects: The 2014 Revision* (ST/ESA/SER.A/366). New York: United Nations.

U.S. Environmental Protection Agency (EPA) (2006). *Life Cycle Assessment: Principles and Practice. EPA/600/060.* http://nepis.epa.gov/Exe/ZyPURL.cgi?Dockey=P1000L86.txt.

Van Dyck, D., Cerin, E., Conway, T. L., De Bourdeaudhuij, I., Owen, N., Kerr, J., et al. (2012). Perceived neighborhood environmental attributes associated with adults' transport-related walking and cycling: Findings from the USA, Australia and Belgium. *International Journal of Behavioral Nutrition and Physical Activity, 9,* 70.

Walker, R. E., Keane, C. R., & Burke, J. G. (2010). Disparities and access to healthy food in the United States: A review of food deserts literature. *Health & Place, 16*(5), 876–84.

Wernick, J. (Ed.). (2008). *Building Happiness: Architecture to Make You Smile.* London: Black Dog.

Wolch, J. R., Byrne, J., & Newell, J. P. (2014). Urban green space, public health, and environmental justice: The challenge of making cities "just green enough." *Landscape and Urban Planning, 125*(0), 234–44.

Woodcock, J., Edwards, P., Tonne, C., Armstrong, B. G., Ashiru, O., Banister, D., et al. (2009). Public health benefits of strategies to reduce greenhouse-gas emissions: Urban land transport. *Lancet, 374*(9705), 1930–43.

Younger, M., Morrow-Almeida, H. R., Vindigni, S. M., & Dannenberg, A. L. (2008). The built environment, climate change, and health: Opportunities for co-benefits. *American Journal of Preventive Medicine, 35*(5), 517–26.

CONTRIBUTORS

ELLEN M. BASSETT is an Associate Professor in the Department of Urban and Environmental Planning at the University of Virginia. Her areas of research interest and expertise are land use planning and law, climate change planning, health and the built environment, and international development. She is particularly interested in community decision making around land and natural resources, including understanding how different societies and cultures create institutions (like property rights systems or policies) for their management. Bassett came to UVA from Portland State University in Portland, Oregon, where she taught for five years at in an urban studies program. Prior to that, she taught at Michigan State University's School of Planning, Design, and Construction. Bassett's professional experience is in international development; she worked from 1989 to 2001 as a technical adviser in East Africa (Kenya and Uganda) with bilateral aid agencies and international NGOs. Her current research projects are heavily focused on climate change and its impact upon urban areas and vulnerable populations such as slum dwellers.

TIMOTHY BEATLEY is the Teresa Heinz Professor of Sustainable Communities in the Department of Urban and Environmental Planning, School of Architecture, at the University of Virginia, where he has taught for the last thirty years. Much of Beatley's work focuses on the subject of sustainable communities and creative strategies by which cities and towns can fundamentally reduce their ecological footprints, while at the same time becoming more livable and equitable places. Beatley believes that sustainable and resilient cities represent our best hope for addressing today's environmental challenges. Beatley is the author or coauthor of more than fifteen books on these subjects, including *Green Urbanism: Learning from European Cities* (recently translated into Chinese); *Habitat Conservation Planning: Endangered Species and Urban Growth; Native to Nowhere: Sustaining Home and Community in a Global Age;* and *Planning for Coastal Resilience.* He has coauthored two books with Australian planner Peter Newman: *Resilient Cities: Responding to Peak Oil and Climate Change* and *Green Urbanism Down Under: Learning from Sustainable Communities in Australia.* Beatley's book *Ethical Land Use* was declared, by the American Planning Association, as one of the "100 Essential Books in Planning." His most recent book is *Biophilic Cities: Integrating Nature into Urban Design and Planning,* which argues that cities can and must be designed to permit daily contact with the natural world. It identifies a variety of means for doing this, from green walls and green rooftops to urban forests and sidewalk gardens. Beatley recently collaborated on a documentary film about green cities and urban nature, entitled *The Nature of Cities,* which has been shown on PBS stations all over the United States. He also writes a regular column for *Planning Magazine,* called Ever Green, about environmental and sustainability matters. His research has been funded by a variety of agencies and organizations including the National

Science Foundation, Virginia Sea Grant, and the National Oceanic and Atmospheric Administration, among others. Beatley holds a PhD in city and regional planning from the University of North Carolina at Chapel Hill, an MA in political science from UNC, a masters of urban planning from the University of Oregon, and a bachelors of city planning from UVA.

EMILY CHMIELEWSKI is a founding member of Perkins Eastman Research, an industry forerunner of practice-based environment-behavior research. She is an advocate for research in practice and assists clients and designers in creating better-built environments by pushing the boundaries of professional knowledge and improving environmental design. In addition to conducting in-house research, she offers a valuable service that has resulted in multiple client-funded and grant-sponsored studies. Her current research areas of focus are senior living, health care, and K-12 educational environments. Chmielewski's experience ranges from concise environmental audits that gather major lessons learned to more in-depth research studies that evaluate multiple aspects of a facility's physical environment and building occupants' satisfaction and use patterns. She has also established a standard procedure for post-occupancy evaluation as part of Perkins Eastman's project completion process. She is an Evidence-Based Design Accreditation and Certification (EDAC) certified professional and has a master of science in applied research in human-environment relations from Cornell University and a bachelor of science in architecture from The University of Michigan.

JASON CORBURN is Professor of City Planning and Public Health and directs the Institute of Urban and Regional Development (IURD) and the Center for Global Healthy Cities at the University of California, Berkeley. He also coordinates the joint master of city planning (MCP) and master of public health (MPH) degree program at UC Berkeley. His research focuses on the links between environmental health and social justice in cities, notions of expertise in science-based policy making, and the role of local knowledge in addressing environmental and public health problems. Corburn leads research projects in Richmond, California, Nairobi, Kenya, and Medellin, Colombia, all focused on integrating community-based expertise into planning and public health interventions that improve environmental and human health for the least well-off populations and places. He sits on the advisory boards of the International Society for Urban Health and the International Council for Science, Program on Urban Health and Wellbeing. Corburn has published five books on the subject of planning, equity, and human health, including *Slum Health: From the Cell to the Street* (2016); *Healthy Cities: Critical Concepts in Built Environment* (2016); *Healthy City Planning: From Neighbourhood to National Health Equity* (2013); *Toward the Healthy City: People, Places, and the Politics of Urban Planning* (2009); and *Street Science: Community Knowledge and Environmental Health Justice* (2005). His book *Street Science* won the 2007 Paul Davidoff best book award from the Association of Collegiate Schools of Planning (ACSP), and the book *Slum Health* was highly commended in 2017 by the British Medical Association.

TANYA DENCKLA COBB, Director of the Institute for Environmental Negotiation (IEN), is a seasoned mediator and facilitator in environmental public policy, author, and teacher. At IEN since 1997, she is passionate about bringing people together to discover common ground and create solutions for mutual gain, and she works on a broad range of environmental, agricultural, and community issues. In recent years at IEN, she has worked on issues of sea level rise in coastal Virginia, tobacco harm reduction, community food systems, and Virginia food heritage. At the state level, she spearheaded and facilitated the 1st Virginia Food Security Summit in 2007, then facilitated the founding of the Virginia Food System Council and again in 2011 facilitated the 2nd Food Security Summit to launch Virginia's first statewide strategic food plan. She has authored numerous articles as well as two books: *The Gardener's A to Z Guide to Growing Organic Food* and *Reclaiming Our Food: How the Grassroots Food Movement Is Changing the Way We Eat*—which was named by Booklist as "one of the top ten books on the environment in 2012" and also won the Nautilus 2012 Gold Green Living Award for books that "promote spiritual growth, conscious living, positive social change, stimulate the imagination, and offer new possibilities for a better life and a better world."

TYE FARROW is a senior partner at Farrow Partnership Architects, a global architecture, master planning, and urban design firm based in Toronto. He is recognized internationally for creating places where people can thrive—economically, culturally, and physically. The Stockholm-based World Congress on Design and Health identified him as a global leader who is making "a significant contribution to health and humanity through the medium of architecture and design." His firm's portfolio of work includes multiple international awards for designing some of the most technically advanced facilities in the world. Farrow has initiated a global "Cause Health" movement aimed at raising public expectations for design. He sees unlimited opportunities to rethink public and private sector places for their potential to optimize health and well-being rather than cope with disease. His projects across North America, the Caribbean, Asia, Africa, and the Middle East demonstrate leadership in this visionary quest. He holds a bachelor of architecture degree from the University of Toronto and a master of architecture in urban design from Harvard University.

ANN FORSYTH, trained in planning and architecture, is a Professor of Urban Planning at the Harvard Graduate School of Design. Her work focuses on the social aspects of physical planning and urban development, particularly how to make cities more sustainable and healthy. To do this she has investigated large-scale model communities (e.g., new towns) and also examined specific topics that prove to be the most challenging to deal with in such models. These include overall suburban design (aesthetics, sense of place), walkability and other aspects of healthy places, social diversity, and environmental issues. In doing this work she has created a number of new tools and methods in planning. Her publications include three books—*Constructing Suburbs* (1999), *Reforming Suburbia* (2005), and *Designing Small Parks* (2005, with Laura Musacchio). In addition she has written over 160 articles, reviews, and chapters in planning, geography, health, and design and has won over 50 awards, honors, and fellowships for professional and research work. Currently she is working on a new Health and Places Initiative (HAPI) that is investigating connections between environments and health globally. This draws on her earlier award-winning project, Design for Health.

HOWARD FRUMKIN is Professor of Environmental and Occupational Health Sciences at the University of Washington School of Public Health, where he served as Dean from 2010 to 2016. He is an internist, environmental and occupational medicine specialist, and epidemiologist. Previously he directed the National Center for Environmental Health and Agency for Toxic Substances and Disease Registry (NCEH/ATSDR) at the U.S. Centers for Disease Control and Prevention (2005–2010) and was Professor and Chair of Environmental and Occupational Health at Emory University's Rollins School of Public Health (1990–2005). His research interests include public health aspects of the built environment, climate change, energy policy, and nature contact. He is author or coauthor of over 200 scientific journal articles and chapters, and his books include *Urban Sprawl and Public Health* (2004), *Safe and Healthy School Environments* (2006), *Green Healthcare Institutions: Health, Environment, Economics* (2007), *Making Healthy Places: Designing and Building for Health, Well-Being, and Sustainability* (2011), and *Environmental Health: From Global to Local* (3rd ed., 2016). Frumkin was educated at Brown (A.B.), Penn (M.D.), and Harvard (M.P.H. and Dr.P.H.).

JUDITH H. HEERWAGEN is a psychologist whose work focuses on human health, well-being, and occupant experience in buildings linked to indoor environmental quality. She is currently serving as a program expert with the U.S. General Services Administration Office of Federal High Performance Green Buildings. She is also an affiliate faculty member in architecture at the University of Washington and has her own consulting business. She has conducted post-occupancy evaluations of more than a dozen sustainable buildings and has served as a consultant to design projects including courthouses, schools, and office buildings. She has published widely in both scholarly and professional journals and has delivered invited talks and keynotes at national and international conferences. She is coeditor of the award-winning book *Biophilic Design: The Theory, Science and Practice of Bringing Buildings to Life* (2008).

J. DAVID HOGLUND is a principal and executive director of Perkins Eastman and an international leader in senior care design. He brings extensive knowledge and skills in programming, planning, and design for older adults. He is a frequent contributor to industry publications and presents on issues of changing demographics, facility repositioning, culture change and trends impacting design, continuing care retirement communities, assisted living, long-term care, and memory support environments. He is the author of *Housing for the Elderly: Privacy and Independence in Environments for the Aging* and coauthor of *Building Type Basics for Senior Living Design* (2013, 2nd edition). He teaches the course Planning and Design for a New Generation of Seniors at the University of Southern California, School of Architecture, Graduate Design Studio. He is recognized as a Fellow of the American Institute of Architects and is an active member of LeadingAge, IAHSA, and numerous state organizations dedicated to senior care.

CARLA JONES, PhD student at the Rollins School of Public Health at Emory University, researches the intersection of human health and the built and natural environments—specifically, the relationship between mental health and the availability, accessibility, and quality of nature in dense, urban environments. Prior to beginning the PhD program, she was a Lecturer and Program Director at the University of Virginia, where she taught small seminars and large lecture courses, such as Healthy Communities, Community Food Systems, and Global Sustainability. She also directed programs within the Center for Design and Health that focused on cross-disciplinary research to aid the design and planning of effective environments for human health and well-being. Within the Center for Design and Health's scope of work, she has offered research assistance to the Biophilic Cities Project since 2012. In addition to her academic experience, she has provided technical assistance to local governments across Maryland and Virginia. Through her position with a public health institute, she worked with these municipalities to craft policies that promote healthy eating and active living environments. Jones holds a master of urban and environmental planning, master of public health, and bachelor of urban and environmental planning from the University of Virginia.

ANDREW MONDSCHEIN is Assistant Professor of Urban and Environmental Planning, University of Virginia. He focuses on transportation and how transportation systems facilitate broad urban planning goals such as access to opportunities, sustainability, community building, and economic development. Recent research includes topics such as how people cope with congestion, the role of information technologies and automated vehicles in future cities, and how people experience cities through everyday transportation. His research is founded on the premise that cities function best when individuals are able to make use of a wide range of transportation options, and the appropriate balance of transportation modes will vary from person to person and place to place. His teaching links transportation to land use, urban design, and the environment from both practical and theoretical perspectives. His courses include Transportation Planning and Policy, Transportation and Land Use, and Planning Methods. He draws on his experience working as a professional transportation planner at Gruen Associates to demonstrate how planners deal with issues including transit corridor planning, the "complete streets" concept, and providing a wide range of transportation options whether in cities, the suburbs, or beyond. Mondschein holds two urban planning degrees, an MA and PhD, from the University of California, Los Angeles. He also has a BA in architecture from Yale University.

TINA MULLEN is an artist living in Gainesville, Florida. She is also the Director of Shands Arts in Medicine—a program that brings the arts to patients and families struggling with serious illness. She has been a drawing instructor at Santa Fe Community College and the University of Florida, as well as Interim Director of the University Galleries at UF. She is also a working artist who has exhibited her work throughout the United States. She has received numerous awards including the Individual Artist Fellowship from the Florida Department of Cultural Affairs. She has been a visiting artist at Penland School of Crafts in North Carolina, the Ringling School of Art in Sarasota, Florida, and the Ucross Foundation in Wyoming. Mullen has a BA from Fort Lewis College in Durango, Colorado. She studied abroad at the Cleveland Institute of Art Program (now SCAD) in Lacoste, France, and has an MFA from the University of Florida.

REUBEN RAINEY, William Stone Weedon Emeritus Professor of Landscape Architecture, has taught in the University of Virginia School of Architecture for forty years and is a former chair of the Department of Landscape Architecture. His present courses focus on the design of various types of healthcare facilities. As Co-Director of the School of Architecture's Center for Design and Health, he is also engaged in a number of research projects centering on the design of patient-centered medical facilities and healthy neighborhoods and cities. A former professor of religious studies at Columbia University and Middlebury College, he entered the field of landscape architecture in midcareer. His publications cover a wide range of topics, including Italian Renaissance gardens, nineteenth- and twentieth-century urban parks, and the work of twentieth-century American landscape architects. His coauthored book on the garden of the Harlem Renaissance poet Anne Spencer received an honor award from the American Society of Landscape Architects. A documentary filmmaker as well, he coproduced the PBS series *GardenStory*, depicting the way gardens improve the lives of individuals and their communities. He is also a member of the Council of Fellows of the American Society of Landscape Architects. His most recent book is *Architecture as Medicine: The UF Health Shands Cancer Hospital, A Case Study*, coauthored with Alana Schrader.

SAMINA RAJA, Professor of Urban and Regional Planning, is the Principal Investigator of the Food Systems Planning and Healthy Communities Lab in the Department of Urban and Regional Planning at the University at Buffalo, The State University of New York. Her research program, which focuses on the role of planning and policy in building sustainable, healthy, and equitable food systems and communities, is funded by local and national sponsors including the National Institute of Food and Agriculture, Robert Wood Johnson Foundation, and others. Her research is published in leading planning and health journals. She is the lead author of the *Planners Guide to Community and Regional Food Planning: Transforming Food Environments, Building Healthy Communities*, one of the earliest guidance reports on food systems planning published by the American Planning Association. She directs Growing Food Connections, a national research initiative that aims to build the capacity of local governments to use planning and policy to strengthen food systems.

JENNIFER WHITTAKER is a doctoral student in Urban and Regional Planning at the University of Pennsylvania and a clinical research coordinator at PolicyLab at Children's Hospital of Philadelphia (CHOP). She received her master's in Urban and Regional Planning from the University at Buffalo, State University of New York, where she also worked as a research associate in the Food Systems Planning and Healthy Communities Lab. Her research and professional interests include addressing health equity, rural development and health, and community-based participatory action research. She is dedicated to working at the intersection of planning and public health to create communities that allow people to live full and healthy lives.

INDEX